THEOLOGY OF COMMUNITY

Tribal Theology in the Making (Revised and Enlarged)

K. Thanzauva

Christian World Imprints

Published in 2022 by

Christian World Imprints
Christian Publishing & Books from India
A-71 Group, Wazirpur Industrial Area
Delhi-110052
cwidelhi2017@gmail.com
www.ChristianWorldImprints.com
Phone: +91 11 41526079

ISBN: 978-93-95457-02-6

This is a revised & enlarged edition of the work published in 2021, done with the written permission of the copyright holder. We believe this work is culturally important and is useful for the theological students.

Printed in India.

Cordially Dedicated
to
My Parents
CHALHLEIA AND NISUNGI

Acknowledgements

I would like to acknowledge with sincere gratitude the contribution of the Society for the Promoting Christian Knowledge-Australia (SPCKA) towards the publication of this book. I would like to record my heartfelt gratitude to Mr. Bill Walker who encouraged me to publish this book and contacted SPCKA on my behalf. I am deeply grateful to my wife Prof. R.L. Hnuni who helped in the arrangement and reading the manuscripts.

Since this book is the outcome of my thesis, I would like to acknowledge the contribution of my supervisor, Prof. Dr. Frank Rees who gave me new insights and shaped my thoughts during my study at the Melbourne College of Divinity. I am also deeply grateful to the Box Hill Baptist Church for providing me with family scholarship and accomodation. My family would never forget the warm welcome, fellowship and constant support of the Box Hill Baptist Church, Melbourne. I am indebted to the Whitley College for granting me Worboys Scholarship. I would like to express my sincere gratitude to the Baptist Missionary Society (London) for travel scholarship, to the Baptist Church of Mizoram and the Eastern Theological College for granting me study leave, to Prof. N.P. Moritzen and Prof. F. Hüber for their help. I am grateful to my children John, Judith and Mapuia for bearing with me.

Date 18.11.1997 K. Thanzauva

FOREWORD

To have meaning and relevance, theology must be contextual. Whether acknowledged or not, this has always been the case. Recognising this fact, many dynamic contemporary theologies begin with an analysis of the context in which they seek to make meaningful God's word to humankind. Because there are many contexts there are similarly many theologies. Some of the more familiar include *liberation theology, minjung theology, dalit theology, black theology*.

During the past decade there has begun to emerge in North East India a group of theologians seeking to develop a theology that is rooted in their context. Pre-eminent among them is Professor K. Thanzauva. The rapidly growing Christian community in the region is predominantly tribal. The work of developing a theology in this context is complicated by the fact that there are a large number of tribes, each with its own language and culture. It would be difficult and, indeed, undesirable to promote theologies for each of these. That would only tend to enhance the exclusive elements in tribalism that have been so disruptive in the region. In the past Christianity served as a powerful instrument for developing harmonious relationships within and between tribes by affirming universal values. Unfortunately, if often did this by offering European contextual theology as the "universal" Gospel. The lack of theological relevance in North East India today is due in no small measure to the effort to superimpose the theology developed in the European context on the quite different historical and cultural context of this region. For this reason the inherited theology is unable to address the political, social and religious problems of the present time. If Christianity is to be part of the solution to today's problems instead of part of the problem, it must develop a theology that is both rooted in the north eastern context and affirms the universality of Gospel.

It is possible to do this by defining the context in socio-economic terms. After all, the social and economic problems faced by all the tribes of the Seven Sisters of North East India are similar. Even though the author's primary concern is with social transformation, he believes that a theology that is based simply on the analysis of contemporary social and economic problems is not likely to bring about significant change. It must be rooted. Rooting involves taking seriously both the received biblical and theological traditions developed by Christians over nearly two thousand years and the cultural traditions of the people. Professor K. Thanzauva takes both sources as necessary, but here concentrates on the second. His primary concern is to root Christian theology in tribal culture without contributing to the exclusiveness that often characterised those cultures. In order to do this he searches for that which is both distinctive and common to those cultures.

This, he suggests, is the communitarian nature of those cultures. Though his illustrative material and application is largely taken from his own Mizo culture, he rightly believes that all tribal cultures place emphasis on community as distinct from individualistic values. He demonstrates how tribal communitarianism can be used as a foundation for social ethics, ecclesiology, eco-theology (including an understanding of the human relationship to land) and a vision for a new egalitarian tribal society (with special attention to the question of gender relationships). In the process the author addresses important methodological issues. Of special interest is his demonstration of the importance of song as a method of doing theology. His analysis of the historical roots of the contemporary reality of North East India is also valuable, both for those who belong to the region and those who do not.

Though the author sees this book only the beginning, in it he has made significant progress towards the realisation of his own stated goals :

A theological approach to social problems should be goal-oriented. It should work towards the realisation of the Kingdom of God. For this reason, a theological reorientation of the people to invoke their faith and deepen their commitment to the cause of social transformation as a valid manifestation of the kingdom values will be our primary concern.

Frederick S. Downs
Eastern Theological College,
Jorhat, Assam, India
December 1997

Table of Contents

CHAPTER I
MEANING OF THE TERM "TRIBAL"

CHAPTER II
TRIBAL SITUATION IN NORTH EAST INDIA

CHAPTER III
METHODOLOGICAL ISSUES IN TRIBAL THEOLOGY

CHAPTER IV
TRIBAL HERMENEUTICS

CHAPTER V
TRIBAL CONCEPT OF HUMANITY

CHAPTER VI
TRIBAL SOCIAL ETHICS

CHAPTER VII
TRIBAL ECLESSIOLOGY

CHAPTER VIII
THE COMMUNITY OF GOD-HUMAN-WORLD

CHAPTER IX
COMMUNITY LAND

CHAPTER X
COMMUNITY OF MEN AND WOMEN

CHAPTER XI
SINGING THEOLOGY

CHAPTER XII
THEOLOGY OF DEVELOPMENT

CHAPTER I

MEANING OF THE TERM "TRIBAL" : Is "Tribal" a Redeemable Term?

The term "tribe" or "tribal" does not originate with those people who are identified as tribals. It is a term used by anthropologists to denote "a group of poeple speaking a common language, observing uniform rules of social organization, and working together for some common purposes such as trade, agriculture, or warfare. Other typical characteristics include a common name, a contiguous territory, a relatively unifrom culture of way of life, and a tradition of common descent."[1] The terms are also popularly used in India to denote who live a relatively isolated life and are technologically backward. In the popular sense it is sometimes a pejorative term, and for that reason many among those identified as tribals in North East India are questioning the appropriateness of the term.

A. Original Meaning

The English word "tribe" derived from the Latin tribus (tri = three, bhuour or bu = to be) literally means "to be three." It was used to identify the three basic divisions of the Roman people - the Tintienses, Ramnenses and Luceres.[2] It was used primarily for the division of Roman citizens without a derogatory connotation. All Roman citizens, both provincial communities (civitates) and individuals who were granted Roman citizenship under the empire (after 27 BC) were enrolled in one or other of the tribes. This division was used for the purpose of taxation, military conscription and census taking.[3] Using it in the ancient Roman sense, I.M. Lewis argues that the term 'tribe' need not be discarded.[4]

Nineteenth century anthropologists made a distinction between "tribal" societies and "modern" societies based upon their legal and political institutions. Morgan, for instance, describes tribal societies as having social but not political organization. For him the basis of tribal

---

1 "Tribe," in *Encyclopedia Britannica,* Micropaedia, Vol. X, (1979, p. 115)

2 "Roman Tribe," in *Ibid.*

3 *Ibid*, p. 116

4 "Tribal Society," *International Encyclopedia of the Social Sciences*, Vol 15, (1968), p. 146

society is kinship, not political system of geogaphic boundaries.[5] Further research made it clear that tribal societies did have forms of political organization and a sense of geographic territory or boundary. Therefore twentieth century anthropologists no longer accept the earlier ideas of what constitutes the difference between modern and tribal societies. Now they defined tribal societies as consisting of a relatively small number of members, restricted in the spatial and temporal range of their social, legal and political relations, and possessing a morality, religion and world view of corresponding dimensions.[6] However, tribal society was still constrasted with modern society as a pre-industrial, pre-literate folk society.

B. The Indian Usage

To the general public in India the word tribe has a pejorative sense. It suggests primitive people living in the hills and forests, the original but not highly developed inhabitants. Some of the names used for them are Vanjajati (forest caste), Vanvasi (inhabitants of the forest), Pahari (hill dwellers), Adimjati (primitive people), Janjati (folk people), Anusuchit Janjati (scheduled tribes) which is the constitutional term, and Adivasi (first settlers).[7]

Though the term "Scheduled Tribe" is extensively used in the Constitution of India, no definitive explanation of its meaning is given there. It simply declares in Article 342 that which the President may specify by public notification.[8] The power exercised by the President under Articles 341 and 342 to identify castes and tribes as Scheduled Castes and Scheduled Tribes cannot be extended either to include or exclude any caste or tribe from the list of SCs ad STs by him. Therefore only the parliament vied Article 341(2) and Article (2) may by law include or exclude from the list of these castes and tribes issued by the President.

The criteria used for determining which groups constitute Scheduled Tribes are religious identity on the one hand and social and

---

[5] L.H. Morgan, *Ancient Society*, edited by Lesli A. White (originally published in 1877, reprinted in 1962), p. 55

[6] L.M. Lewis, *Op cit.*, p. 147

[7] L.P. Vidyarthi and B.K. Rai, *The Tribal Culture of India*, (New Delhi: Concept Publishing Company, 1985), p. 25

[8] S.K. Ghosh, *Law of Enforcement in Tribal Areas*, p. 5

economic status on the other. In other words, they must first of all be a homogeneous community which belongs neither to the Hindu or the Muslim communities and, at the same time, must be economically poor and socially marginalized. Using this criteria it is very difficult, in the present Indian context, to decide who are tribals and who are not. Though more and more communities have been declared tribals, many more that should rightly be so designated have not for certain historical and other reasons.[9] Thus, for instance, the tribal labourers in the tea gardens of Assam have not been given tribal status though they are in fact tribals. For they are not officially recognized, they are not entitled to the benefits and opportunities granted to Scheduled Tribes. Why has this happened? It is a complex issue that must be approached from a historical perspective if it is to be fully understood.

According to a commonly accpted theory, the stratification of Indian society can be traced back to the Aryan invasion. When the Aryan invaders entered the sub-continent, they called the non-Aryans residents *Dasyus*.[10] In the encounter that followed, some of them were absorbed into Hindu society at the lowest level (now known as Scheduled Castes) while others were forced into the forest and hills and now called tribes. The tribes are neither specifically Hindu nor Muslim. They are today called tribes because they are believed to be descended from those original inhabitants and do not belong to one of the two major religious communities - not necessarily because they continue to live in isolated or marginalized conditions.[11]

Attempts were made before Indian Independence to distinguish tribals from their Hindu and Muslim neighbours. But the Superintendents of the census of 1901 and 1931 frequently expressed practical problems in differentiating some tribal groups from Hindus. M.G. Lacey, the Superintendent of Census for Bihar and Orissa described the complex situation thus :

---

9 The Rajbongshi tribe in Assam was recently recognized as a scheduled tribe while the Garden labourers have not been scheduled as tribe, but they are tribals.

10 L.P. Vidyarthi and B.K. Rai, *Op cit*, p. 26

11 *A Social and Economic Atlas of India*, (Delhi: Oxford University Press), 1987, p. 26

> An aboriginal (tribal) will adopt certain Hindu customs, he will join in certain Hindu processions, he may even make offering to certain Hindu deities, and at the same time he may adhere in the main to his old tribal beliefs and practices. It is often quite impossible to say when he crosses the line to Hinduism. Again, he will often call himself a Hindu for no better reason than that he believes he will thereby improve his social status. In most cases these communities (tribal communities) have, as a result of a more complete absorbtion in Hinduism, lost their aboriginal characteristics to a greater extent, and comparatively few of them have remained faithful to the gods of their fathers.[12]

In spite of the problems cited above, the first serious effort to classify tribes was made in the 1931 census. As a result, the British parliament in 1932 took the decision to prepare a separate electorate for the depressed classes, including the tribes. However, prior to 1935 the term "Scheduled Caste" and "Scheduled Tribe" were not used. The present classification was developed as a result of Mahatma Gandhi's objection to the proposal to establish a separate electorate for the depressed classes on the basis of their social condition and their historical response to Hinduism.[13] Though earlier efforts had been made to classify tribes, the first official reference to them was made in the Government of India Act, 1935, where they were referred to as the "Backward Tribes". According to the thirteen schedule of the Government of India (Provincial Legislative Assembly) Order, 1936, certain tribes were specified as backward in some provinces.[14] After the Constitution came into force, a comprehensive classification of scheduled tribes was made. The list of Scheduled Castes and Scheduled Tribes contained in the schedules were appended in the Constitution (Scheduled Caste/Scheduled

---

[12] M.G. Lacey, *Census Report*, 1931

[13] Gail Omvedt, "Gandhi and Ambedkar," a review article on *The Moral and Political Writings of Mahatma Gandhi*, Vol. I, in the *Economic and Political Weekly*, Vol. XIX, (May 4, 1991); and B.T. Rajshekar, *Mahatma Gandhi and Babasaheb Ambekar*, (Bangalore: Dalit Sahitya Academy, 1989), pp. 19 & 20; M.E. Prabhakar, "The Search of A Dalit Theology," *Towards a Dalit Theology*, (New Delhi: ISPCK, 1988), p. 43

[14] C. Parvathamme, *Scheduled Castes and Tribes*, (New Delhi: Ashish Publishing House).

Tribe) Order, 1950, and in subsequent orders. According to the census of 1981, excluding Assam where the census could not be held, there were 51,628,538 people belonging to the category "Scheduled Tribes". They constituted 7.74% of the total population, as compared with 6.82% in the 1971 census. In the 1991 census, 67,758,000 persons were counted as belonging to Schedule Tribes constituting 8.08% of the total population, (excluding Jammu and Kashmir where 1991 census was not taken).[15]

As mentioned above, the primary factors used to determine which groups should be classified as tribes in India are basically two: (1) They do not belong to either the Hindu or Muslim communities, and (2) they are backward - which implies that they are poor, illiterate, simple people. The backward communities within the Hindu fold are called scheduled castes; the non-Hindus are known as tribes.

However, there is a great difference between the tribes of North East India and those in other parts of the country. Dr. Ambedkar recognized this when the Constitution was being framed. He noted that while the tribes in other parts of India were more or less Hinduised and assimilated into the culture of the people among whom they lived, this was not true of the tribes in North East. They were still rooted in their own cultures, with their own laws of inheritance and marriage, and their own customs which were very different from those of their neighbours.[16] Accepting the recommendation of a sub-committee of the Constituent Assembly, the Sixth Schedule was promulgated in the constitution to deal with the administration of the hill tribes in North East India. The Fifth Schedule deals with tribes elsewhere.

Apart from the provisions of the Fifth and Sixth Schedules, certain specific provisions dealing with tribes were made in the Constitution. Article 330, 332 and 334 provide for the reservation of seats for the Scheduled Tribes in the Lok Sabha and state legislative assemblies. Article 335 provides for the reservation of jobs in the services. Article 275 provides for financial assistance to the states for implementing these

---

[15] S.K. Ghost, *Op cit.*, p.8 and *Census Report of 1991* (Scheduled Castes and Tribes), p. 11

[16] *Constituent Assembly Debates*, Vol. IX, p. 1025; and R.N. Prasad, *Government and Politics in Mizoram*, (New Delhi: Northern Book Centre, 1987), p. 98

constitutional provisions. In recent years several accords have been made with tribal insurgent groups in the North East. These include the Six Point Agreement with the Naga's People Convention 1960, the Shillong Accord 1975, the Mizoram Accord (Memorandum of Settlement) 1986, the Accord with the Tribal National Volunteers (TNV) in Tripura, and the Bodoland Accord 1993. These created new provisions for the legal protection of the cultural identity and the development of the tribes concerned.

C. Is "Tribal" A Redeemable Term?

Though the original scholarly and even official usage of "tribe" did not connote contempt, the way it has come to be used in history has made it unacceptable. It is unfortunate that in the history of India particular groups have been discriminated against and reduced to the status of slaves. Though history cannot be reversed, it can be redeemed. All the provisions mentioned above were created for the purpose of redeeming history.

1. An Unredeemable Term : One view is that history may be redeemed, but the term "tribe" has accumulated so many pejorative meanings that it cannot be. The reasons for this are as follows :

(a) An Imposed Term : None of the groups of people called tribes in India have traditionally called themselves "tribes". It was originally introduced by anthropologists, and was in due course imposed by the Indian government. For a long time it has been popularly used in a derogatory sense. Educated persons among the communities concerned in the North East India find it increasingly difficult to accept "tribe" as a part of their essential identity. They prefer to be identified by the name of their respective communities, e.g. Naga, Mizo, Khasi. Using a term that the people themselves have rejected is unacceptable. "Tribal" or "tribe" has never been accepted by the people concerned as a generic term applicable to them, but the question of special provision has to be answered. What does rejection of the term would mean in the context of India? Whether rejection of the term would imply deprivation of constitutional provisions intended for them or those provisions will be retained not because they remain as tribals but because they are poor and in need of development and protection.

Behind this is a much debated issue. The Marxists, for instance, have been suggesting that poverty alone should be used as the criteria for making special protective and developmental provisions, not the caste and the tribe. Classification of society for the Marxists, supported by a large number of privileged Muslims and the high caste Hindus, should be based solely on the economic condition of a person, not on the ethnic-religious identity. Of course, the elite tribals who reject their identity as "tribal" should be aware of the implications of shifting from "ethnic" to "economic" criteria that they would be the first to be deprived of the provisions that they have been enjoying on the basis of their ethnic rather than economic identity.

(b) The Psychological Problem : The term "tribal" does not elicit pride. The associated notion of backwardness tends to make people dependent and passive. It destroys self-esteem and confidence. In contrast, names like Mizo, Naga or Khasi are positive identities in which those concerned take pride. When they encountered their enemies in situations of conflict, the Mizo men used to shout "Mizo tlangval" (Mizo youngman) in order to encourage themselves and exert their power. Such self-esteem is completely lost when such traditional identifies are replaced by a tribal identity. The loss of self-esteem and confidence after many centuries of subjugation has become a serious problem for some plain tribals. I am aware that ethnic pride can create problems of its own (e.g. tribalism), but its loss is an even more serious problem. Considering all these factors, there are many who believe that the term "tribal" must be rejected as unredeemable, even the term "Negro" has been rejected by African Americans.

2. A Redeemable Term : Over against those who take the position just described, are those who hold the view that the term "tribal" cannot be compared to the term "Negro" as it was used in America. "Negro" was a name used by the masters for their slaves; "Tribal" is a name that includes all human beings, because at one time all without exception were tribals. Every society has gone through certain stages of evolution, from tribal to modern. There is nothing to be shame of about the name. Those who are called tribals today will not remain so. In fact, some of the tribes of the North East are progressing at a more rapid rate than their non-tribal neighbours.

(a) Re-Affirmation of History : By using the term "tribe" we are reaffirming that we are primal people who are not spoiled by modern scientific technology and its philosophy of individualism. We are thus closer to God's intended society as expressed in the Bible. We should take pride in being tribal, of being beautiful and original. The people whom God chose as his instruments were tribals, the people of the twelve tribes of Israel.

The term "tribal" also is an affirmation of our history of suffering from exploitation and discrimination. When we examine the history of tribals, we understand that it is a history of alienation. With pride the Israelites affirmed the history of their wandering Arameans ancestors who were once enslaved by the Egyptians but were delivered from bondage by the mighty hand of God. Their historical experience of enslavement and liberation became the foundation of their faith in Yahweh. The use of the term "tribal" similarly reminds us of our own history of suffering and alienation - and of the way God has liberated us from that situation. We were driven out of our own land by invaders, we were once wandering tribes in search of food and shelter - but God has brought us to this place and made us a strong people. Our historical experience must become the ground of our faith in God.

(b) Not the Term, but the Attitude of Deminant Group : The term "tribal" also reflects the attitude of the dominant groups towards minority communities who are vulnerable. The problem is not the term as such, but the attitude of the dominant groups. We have noted that there is nothing wrong with the original meaning of the term. It was the definitions of it given by the dominant groups in India that made it unacceptable. Therefore what has to be changed is not the term, but those attitudes. It is unlikely that by chinging the term, the attitude of the dominant groups will be changed. What really matters is the transformation of the actual living conditions of tribals.

(c) A Search for Common Identity : In a place like North East India, where society is segmented into numerous tribes and sub-tribes, the search for a common identity is important. Right now the term "tribal" serves this function. It is the only term in used that embraces all people belonging to the different tribes. Since it has been used in the Constitution, it is extensively used by scholars as well as the common people. It is difficult to find a suitable alternative term. Some time ago I suggested "Notheasterners" as an alternative, but that is too vague again. It includes all the people in North East India, both tribals and non-tribals. I do hope that the time will come when we can use "Northeasterners" as a common name for the people in the region, but now it is more appropriate to use "tribe" or "tribal" as the common name.

Clubbing together all the people of North East India under the one name, "Northeasterners" implies ignoring their differences in culture, economic condition and historical experience. Only in recent years the attention been given to the problems of tribals. Due to historical deprivation and alienation, the tribal people need special protection and provisions in order to catch up others. As long as this need exists, it is appropriate to retain the term "tribal".

In short, having considered the pros and cons of the use of the term "tribal", I conclude that it should be retained for some time. It is good that some are critical about the term. That in itself is a sign of progress. The best way of doing away with the term is not to simply reject its use, but improve the living conditions of the people. In the meantime we should be proud of the positive contributions that tribal societies, with their social and cultural treasures, have to share with the whole humanity.

CHAPTER II

TRIBAL SITUATION IN NORTH EAST INDIA

An analysis of a particular social situation, for which a theological construction is going to be made, is an essential methodological implication of any theology that seeks transformation of society. Theologians, committed to the cause of liberation, are convinced that the only way to change the present evil condition of human society is to diagnose the cause of the problems without being afraid of those findings. In this chapter, the tribal situation of North East India will be analysed in general. The purpose of this analysis is to identify a theological agenda for this book. In response to the findings, a theological construction will be made in the following chapters. The analysis offered here is made in terms of a *pastoral* interpretation of the contemporary scenario of the tribal society in the North East India, rather than a scientific-technical analysis. There can be other ways of understanding the data and situation examined, some of which might claim to be 'scientific', 'value free', or without ideological conjectures. This analysis makes no such claims. The analysis is done from a Christian perspective with a specific intention and purpose.

The tribal situation in the hill regions of North East India cannot be properly understood except by viewing it in its historical and sociological context. Therefore, a 'historico-social analysis' seems to be the most appropriate analytical method to identify a theological agenda for this situation. In some cases, special reference is made to Mizo society. The issues identified in the analysis, however, are common challenges for the churches in North East India generally.

A. Tribals : The Alienated People

The largest concentration of tribal people anywhere in the world, except Africa, is in India. Basing on the 1991 census, by now there should be about 100 million tribals in India. The total number of tribal communities in India as identified by the Anthropological Survey of India (here in after reffered to as (ASI) is 461, of which about 172 are segments.[1] However, the ASI itself admits that this is not a complete

---

[1] K.S. Singh, *The Scheduled Tribes: People of India, National Series*, Vol. III, (Delhi: Anthropological Survey of India, 1994), p. 1. In 2020, it is estimated that there are 705 ethnic groups, 104 million, they comprise 8.6%

list of tribal communities in India. The schedule tribes are primarily derived from four major racial stocks, the Negrito (the Great Andamaneses, the Onges and the Jatawas), Proto-Austroloid (the Munda, the Oraon and the God), the Mongoloid (tribes of North East India) and the Causasoid (the Toda, the Rabari and the Gujar). These 461 communities are labelled as tribes not necessarily because they are tribal in the sense of backward, but because their origins are tribal and profess none of the major religions of this sub-continent.[2] K.S. Singh suggests that "tribe" in India should be perceived as an administrative and political concept. Thus, the scheduled tribes are determined by the public notification of the President on the basis of the finding of a commission appointed by the President of India.

They are the most exploited and impoverished people in most parts of the world. The history of tribals is a history of suffering from genocide, exploitation, discrimination, displacement and alienation. In some places, for all practical purposes to do with law and civil rights, their existence was ignored by the dominant groups.[3] The tribals in India are so diverse in culture, language and origin, their only commonality being the poverty, exploitation and alienation they suffered from time immemorial. They have suffered from the hands of Aryan invaders, the Muslim rulers, the British administrators and the privileged people of India today. The tragedy is that after 70 years of the Constitution being operative, the scheduled castes and tribes remain at the bottom of the Indian social structure. They are culturally alienated, socially stigmatised, economically exploited, poor and politically powerless.

B. Tribal Situation in North East India

As it was pointed out in the first chapter, the great difference between the tribals in North East India and in the rest of India was

---

2 *A Social and Economic ATLAST of INDIA*, (Delhi: Oxford University Press, 1987), p. 26

3 This is quite evident in the case of the tribals in Africa, North America particularly with the Amerindian tribes Australian aborigines and in most of the Asian countries, John Hookey, "Settlement and Sovereignty," *Aborigines and the Law, Essays in Memory of Elizabeth Eggleston*, edited by Peter Hanks and Bryan Keon Cohen, (Sydney: George Allen & Unwin, 1984), p. 1

recognised by Dr. Ambedkar when the Constitution was being framed. He said that the tribes in other parts of India were more or less Hinduised and assimilated with the culture and civilisation of the people with whom they lived. But this was not the case in regard to the tribes in North East India. They had roots in their own culture and civilisation. They had their own laws of inheritance and marriage and their own customs which were very different from those of their neighbours.[4] Accepting the recommendation of the Sub-Committee of the Constituent Assembly, the Sixth Schedule was promulgated in the Constitution of India for the administration of the hill tribes in North East India. The 5th scheduled of the constitution is meant for the rest of the Scheduled Tribes in India.

The tribals in North East India today can be broadly divided in two categories on the basis of geographical location as the Hill Tribes and the Plain Tribes. The hill tribes are various groups of the Mizo-Kuki-Chin family living in Mizoram, Manipur and Tripura; the Nagas in Nagaland and Manipur; the Arunachalis in Arunachal Pradesh, the Khasi in Meghalaya and the Garo in Meghalaya and Assam. They are mostly Christianised except for the Arunachalis who have been isolated and protected from the Christian missionaries for many years. The first census took place in Arunachal Pradesh only in 1961. Though there is some influence of Buddhism and Hinduism on their religious belief, in the main the Arunachalis practise the primal religion. Whatever change has been taking place, it is mostly due to the efforts of Government. Most of the hill tribes except Khasis were late comers who arrived in their present habitat in the 17th and 18th centuries.[5]

The plain tribes, on the other hand, are indigenous people who have been living in the Brahmaputra Valley of Assam, Barak Valley of Cachar District and in the plain are of Tripura. Once they were the

---

4 *Constituent Assembly Debates*, Vol. IX, p. 1025 and R.N. Prasad, *Government and Politics in Mizoram*, (New Delhi, Northern Book Centre, 1987), p. 98

5 The origin of "Khasi" is obscure, as some of the Khasi scholars like Mr. R.T. Rymbai and others, basing on their myths, claimed that they were the original and autonomous people of Khasi Hills. It is quite probable that they also belonged to the Mongoloid stock but adopted the language of Mon-Khmer in the course of migration. Like other hill tribes they also came from the East.

owners of land with their own kingdoms, but today they are reduced to colonial state.[6] Their problems are different from those of the hill tribes. They have been suffering from alienation of land and culture, from displacement, from illiteracy and from indeptedness. The Ahoms in Assam and the Meiteis in the plain area of Manipur, the most *sanskritized* (Hinduised) tribals who claimed themselves as non-tribals, are today not counted as tribals.

Another tribal group is the labourers commonly known as *Adivasis* in the tea gardens of Assam, who were originally brought by the British tea planters or who migrated into Assam in search of work during the years 1840-1961 from Orissa, Bihar and Andhra Pradesh. There are no reliable statistics about this population, though it is estimated to be 1.5 million labourers[7] and scattered around the 800 tea gardens which produced over 300 million KG of tea annually. At present the descendants of garden labourers are distributed throughout the Brahmaputra valley and have became a major labour force of Assam. The dominant group does not want the *Adivasi* identity to emerge as a distinct ethnic identity, so no accurate figures of the population are made available. Though they originally belonged to either scheduled caste or tribe, the Government of Assam does not recognise them as such. They have been unjustly deprived of the benefits provided by the Constitution.

For various reasons the response of tribal people to Christianity has been good. The ASI has analysed the trends in tribal region and observed that there has been a remarkable spread of Christianity among the tribes in North East India, namely Manipur (94.55% among the tribals), Nagaland (94.55% among the Nagas), Andaman and Nicobarese

---

6 G.K. Ghosh, *Tribals and their Culture: Assam, Meghalaya; and Mizoram*, Vol. I, (New Delhi: Ashish Publishing House, 1992), pp. 13-61. The Bodo population in Assam in 1971 census was 6,10,459 which was more than the total population of Nagaland and almost double of the Mizoram population. They were believed to be ruling India with Dravidians during pre-Aryan era and were eventually pushed to North East India.

7 Sebastin Karotempel (ed), *Tea Garden Labourers of North India:* (Shillong, Vendrame Institute, 1990), p. vii, 35 and K. Thanzauva, "A Study on the Problems of Garden Labourers in Assam", unpublished paper presented in the Consultation on the Problems of Garden Labourers conducted by UCM, Jorhat Unit, (1985).

(92.60% particularly among the Nicoberese), Mizoram (88.46% among the tribals including the Chakmas), Arunachal Pradesh (4.25%), today, 2021 it is estimated 65% belong to ST. Tripura (3.95), Bihar (11.87), Kerala (5.62%).[8] In 1981 the Scheduled Tribes, mainly from North East India, formed about 20% of the total Christian population of India; the Scheduled Castes formed 45%.[9] About 75% of the Christian population of India is derived from the people of tribal origin.

1. Tribal Policy in North East India : In this discussion, the tribal policy is not necessarily confined to the Government's policy towards tribals in North East India. It is rather an investigation of the fundamental principles and ethos responsible for what has been done to the tribals in North East India throughout history. This is clearly necessary because the tribal problems of today are the products of the attitude and policy of the dominant groups towards tribal people.

(a) Suppression : In the plains of Assam and Tripura, the tribals in their interaction with Ahoms, Aryans, Muslims and British administrators suffered discrimination, exploitation and alienation. They have been alienated from their land and culture. Their rights of land and right to live as human beings in freedom were not recognised by the invaders. The tragedy today is that this attitude has not disappeared. This is the fundamental reason that the concern for development and legal protection of the tribals has become a crucial issue for the Government. S.K. Chaterjee has rightly observed that the basic problem with the tribal development today lies not in the constitution but in the social ethos of the dominant group. His argument is that the socio-economic and cultural backgrounds of the sections propagating the Gandhian or the Communist or the Socialist ideology were rooted in the same dominant ethos, their ideologies vied with each other in objectifying and mystifying the real issues of the tribals and the dalits'.[10] The *Tribal Voice* published from Guwahati has expressed the tribal condition as follows :

---

[8] S.K. Singh, *Op cit*, p. 11

[9] M.E. Sargunam (ed), *Mission Mandate: A Compendium on the Perspective of Mission in India*, (Madras: Mission in India 2000, 1992); p. 11

[10] S.K. Chatterji, "Why Dalit Theology?" *Towards A Dalit Theology*, (New Delhi: ISPCK, 1988), p. 23

> Many unfortunate tribes have already taken farewell from the world. Civilisation has squeezed them out of this world. The rest are facing a serious threat of extinction or a life of slavery. Our big brothers want us to be their coolies; when we refuse, they plan to finish us. Ruthless exploitation, deprivation from human rights, alienation from land, suppression of our ethnic identity and derogation of our culture and traditions have been almost paralysing us.[11]

This is the feeling of most of the tribals in India today. It is evident from the tribal living conditions and increasing atrocities against them that the policy of suppression continues and event rampant.

(b) Assimilation : The assimilation of tribals in India is cultural, religious and physical. Though the tribal cultures and religions in ancient India provided the raw materials to build Hinduism, in the process of integration, the tribals were later on mostly absorbed into the low caste Hindus. The process of assimilation into Hindu society may be best expressed by the idea of "sanskritization", propounded by M.N. Srinavas, and defined as a process of social, cultural and religious change whereby low status people in India adopt the Sanskrit terminology and ritual procedures embodied with Brahmanism. This process tends to weaken tribal religion until it is finally absorbed in Hinduism.[12] Anthropologists and sociologists studied the conversion of tribal people to Christian faith and wrote extensively blaming missionaries for converting simple tribals. Comparatively very little effort has been made to investigate how the tribal people have been converted and absorbed into Hinduism.

Sanskritization in North East India at one point in time was vigorous and successful. At some time in history, the various tribes of the Bodo group of Tibeto Burman family, Mechs, Mishings, Tipperas (Tripuris), Garo, Kochs, Hajongs, Dalus, Rabbas and others in the plain of Assam, all spoke their own dialects, and maintained their own independent cultural and territorial identity. They practised tribal religions which are vaguely

---

11 R.J. Kr. Kootoom, "Tribal Voice is Your Voice," *Tribal Voice of the Persecuted Tribals*, 15 Nov. Premier Issue, p. 1

12 H.K. Bhat, "Hinduization of Tribes: Critique and Perspective," *Tribal Thought and Culture*, edited by Baidyanath Saraswati. (New Delhi: Concept Publishing House, 1991), p. 223

and perhaps superficially called animism. Today the sanskritized tribals in the plain area have, in some cases forgotten their own cultures and languages. The process of sanskritization was carried out in Assam, Manipur and Tripura under royal patronage. Later on, in the plain of Assam, it was mostly done by Hindu priests and immigrants.[13]

The actual process of sanskritization could be varied from place to place, tribe to tribe. In some cases its reason was economic as suggested by N.K. Bose, but in the main, as suggested by Srinavas and many others, it was for socio-political and religious reasons that the tribals were assimilated by the dominant groups. The procedure usually started with a simple claim of the group as being members of Hindu society by creating myths.[14] This is the reason that J.H. Thumra blamed E.G. Gait for converting tribals in Manipur by fiction.[15] The conversion of Meiteis and Tripuris to Hinduism was *en masse* that did not reduced all of them to the status of low caste but introduced a certain form of caste system.

The fundamental problem of sanskritization among the tribals in North East India was the segregation of a tribal community into different castes and the subsequent subjugation of the tribals most of whom were adopted into the low-caste. On the one hand, conversion to Hinduism for most of the tribals meant not only loss of identity but becoming a servile class of Hindu society. On the other hand, it is clear that within the sanskritized tribal groups, there were those who regarded themselves as having climed the social ladder higher than their fellow tribals who were not sanskritized. Today, the yardstick of religious affiliation is, however, being replaced by the educational and economic achievements of individuals to determine their social status.

With regard to physical assimilation, the hill tribes remained free. The victims were mostly the plain tribes in Assam and Tripura. The

---

[13] D.N. Majumdar, "A Study of Tribe-Caste Continuum and the Process of Sanskritization among the Bodo Speaking Tribes of the Garo Hills," in *Tribal Situation in India, Op cit*, p. 267ff

[14] S.T. Das narrated how the Brahmin priests created myths to relate the tribals with the mythical heroes in Hinduism. S.T. Das, *Tribal Life of North Eastern India*m (New Delhi, Gian Publishing House, 1986), p. 3

[15] J.H. Thumra, "An Implication of Sanskritization," *The Assam Tribune*, (December 11, 1989). He held E.A. Gait responsible for this method.

Tribals in these two states were the first settlers. The origin of assimilation may be traced back to the coming of Ahoms in about the years A.D. 1226. It was they who later on in the 1650s accepted Hindu religion through their king Chatumla. Significantly he himself eventually adopted a Hindu name called Jaiyadhaja Singh.[16] The Ahom kingdom in Assam was a tribal kingdom. The Ahoms themselves were originally of the Shan tribe in Burma. The Burmese invasion of the Ahom kingdom in Assam in the 19th century led to British intervention and annexation of Assam into British territory, ratified by the Treaty of Yandaboo, on 24th Feb. 1826.

When the British occupied the erstwhile Assam, they brought Bengalis to assist them in the running of administration, and the tea planters brought labourers from Bihar, Orissa and Andhra Pradesh into Assam. This was followed by a constant influx of immigration from East Bengal (now Bangladesh) and other parts of India. Though assimilation of tribals in Tripura was a long process, a sudden increase of this influx happened during Indias independence, dramatically changing the demography of Tripura. The confrontation between Hindus and Muslims in Bengal pushed thousands of Hindus from East Bengal (Bangladesh) into Tripura. The tribals, who formed the majority and ruled Tripura with their own kings before Indian independence, are today reduced to a minority. The population increase in these two states between 1901-1951 was: 137.80% in Assam and 273.41% in Tripura respectively, against 51.50% all India average in the same period.[17] The policy of national integration in India today sounds to many tribals as a modern version of the old assimilation policy.

A similar attitude towards tribal assimilation was expressed by Rohini Kumar Choudhury in the Constituent Assembly debate that, "We want to assimilate tribal people (hill tribes). If you want to educate the tribal people in the art of self-government, why not introduce the

---

16 M.L. Bose, *Social History of Assam*, New Delhi, Concept Publishing Company, 1989,

p. 38. The Ahoms were originally a Shan tribe who wandered into Brahmaputra valley from Burma (Myanmar).

17 A.K. Agarwal, *Economics Problems and Planning in North East India*, (New Delhi: Starling Publishers, 1987), p. 25, Table 2.1

Municipal Act? If you want to keep them separate, they will combine with Tibet, they will combine with Burma, they will never combine with the rest of India.[18] The problems of assimilation are mainly alienation of tribal culture and land, which eventually cause tribal unrest and revolt. The fundamental problem with Sanskritization lies in the fact that the tribals are usually absorbed either in low and out castes. This could well be the reason that Ambedkar blamed Hinduism for the stratification of Indian society. To him, Hinduism and social union were incompatible.[19]

(c) Isolation : The policy of the British Government in India towards tribals in general was 'isolation', which was supposedly intended to protect tribals from the interference of non-tribals in their affairs. The first important legislation for the protection of tribals in India was the Regulation XII of 1833 which declared Chotanagpur as non-regulated area. In 1870, the British Parliament passed an act empowering the Government of India to regulate affairs in tribal areas. With the enactment of the Government of India Act of 1870, a few tracts were specified as "scheduled tracts", viz. in the Himalayan region - the former Assam, Darjeeling, Kumaon and Garhwal, the former Pargans, Jaunsar-Bawar Lahual and Spiti; in middle India - Chotanagpur and Santal Pargana, Angul Mahal, Chanda, Chhatisgarh, Chhindwara, Manpure (Indore), Jhansi, Mirzzapur, Ganjam; in Western India - Panch Mahals, Mewasi (Khandesh); in south India - Vizagapatam (Visakhapatnam), Godavari, and Lakshadweep. The Inner Line Regulation of 1873, framed by the Lt. Governor of West Bengal, was approved when a uniform law, the Scheduled District Act, was promulgated in 1874 by the Government of India to embrace all the tribal concentrated areas throughout the country.[20] A number of other regulations of this nature were brought into force during this one hundred year period.

---

18 *Constituent Assembly Debate*, 4, Nov. 1948, Vol. 11, Appendix p. 102

19 Dhannanjay Keer, *Dr. Ambedkar: Life and Mission:* (Bombay, Popular Prakhasa, 1962), p. 302

20 R.R. Prasad, "Tribal Development in India: Strategies and Programmes," *Journal of Rural Development*, Vol. 7, No. 1, Jan. 1988, p. 84. In the Bengal Eastern Frontier Regulation (1) of 1873, the Inner Line for Cachar district affecting Northern Lushai Hills was laid down. Similarly an Inner Line for Chittagong Hill tracts, effecting Southern Lushai Hills, was also laid down by the Government of Bengal on 20th June 1879. The Regulation (V) of Bengal Eastern Frontier Regulation was extended to the Lushai Hills district under the Scheduled District Act 1874.

The Assam Frontier Tracts Regulation (Regulation II) of 1880 was issued 'to provide for the removal of certain frontier tracts in Assam - those inhabited or frequented by barbarous or semi-civilised tribes from the operation of enactments in force therein'. On November 8, 1882, the Dibrugarh Frontier Tract was established. The Assam Frontier Tract Regulation 1880, was applied in 1894 to the Naga Hill District and the North Cachar Hills, Garo Hills and Khasi and Jaintia Hills, and to Mikir Hills.[21]

In 1890, J.W. Quinton, Chief Commissioner of Assam, proposed the taking over of the North Lushai Hills. In the meantime, the Chin-Lushai Conference in 1892 recommended that a large number of Chin-Lushai people belonging to Tibeto-Burman families should be grouped together to create the Chin-Lushai land.[22] The recommendation was discussed by the Governor General in Council, who recommended that the North and South Lushai Hills with a portion of Arakan Hill Tracts should be placed under the Assam administration. But Alexander Mackenzie, Chief Commissioner of Burma, opposed the proposal. The Governor General in Council altered their decisions which they had arrived at after the Chin-Lushai conference. As proposed by Alexander Mackenzie, the Chin Hills remained with Burma. Only the amalgamation of the North which was under Assam and the South Lushai Hills under Bengal took place.[23]

The Chin Hills Regulation (Regulation V) of 1896, passed to protect the people from outsiders, had also authorised the Superintendent or the Deputy Commissioner to order an 'undesirable outsider' to leave the areas as well as to tax the residents - permanent or temporary -

---

21 S. Chube, *Hill Politics in North East India*, pp. 16 & 17

ESTIMATED NUMBER		CENSUS 1901
Tibetan	43,024	2,35,229
Himalayan	1,94,234	1,90,585
North Assam	36,910	41,731
Bodo	6,17,909	3,96,411
Naga	2,92,799	2,47,780
Kachin	1,920	1,23,775
Kuki-Chin (Mizo)	3,64,091	6,24,149

22 The Tibeto Burman Family as in 1901 Census

23 S. Chatterjee, *Mizoram Under the British Rule*, *Op cit.*, pp. 122-26

houses, clans and villages. In October 1911, the Regulation was extended to the Khasi and Jaintia Hills (excluding the Shillong municipal and cantonment areas where only the provision for taxation would apply), to the Naga Hills and to the Mikir Hills.[24]

The Government of India Act of 1919 did not change the policy of isolation, but tried to define and determine the limits and extent of isolation. From this Act arose what were called "Wholly Excluded Areas" and "Areas of Modified Exclusion". On November 8, 1927, Simon's Commission was set up to examine the problem of further constitutional reform. The recommendations of Simon's Commission were embodied in sections 91 and 92 of the Government of India Act of 1935, which declared areas as "Excluded Areas" and "Partially Excluded Areas". The list of the areas was embodied in the Government of India (Excluded and Partially Excluded Areas) Order, 1936.[25] The Superintendent of Lushai Hills, N.E. Parry had suggested to the Simon's Commission, along the line of the recommendation of Chin-Lushai Conference in 1892, that all the hill areas inhabited by tribals should be clubbed together and be kept under one administration. But that was again rejected. Thus, some of the tribes particularly the Garo, the Mizo and the Naga, became people divided by international boundaries. The worst effected is the Mizo tribe. Half of its population remains outside of Mizoram.

---

24 S. Chube, *Hill Politics in North East India, Op cit.*, pp. 17 & 18

25 "Excluded Area" means an area which was kept beyond the preview of federal and provincial legislatures. The administration of this area was vested exclusively in the Governor. The Lushai Hills, the Naga Hills, and the North Cachar Hills in North East India were "Excluded Areas". There were "Partially Excluded Areas" which came under the administration of the Minister of Provincial Government. The Minister of Provincial Government acted under the supervision and control of the Governor to administer the area. The Khasi Hills and the Garo Hills came under this category. In reality, the colonial government was not especially interested to set up administrative machinery in the hill tribal areas which would simply incur huge amounts of expenditure without profit. For security reasons they annexed the hill areas. Garo Hills was annexed in 1816, Manipur Hills 1820, North Cachar Hills 1829, Jaintia Hills 1835, Mikir Hills 1866, Naga Hills 1889 and Lushai Hills 1889. The British administrators neither set up effective government structures nor did they make efforts for development.

The time of Indian independence was ac crucial period of transition for the hill tribes in North East India. Among the tribal leaders the political consciousness was beginning to develop that was suppressed by the administrators. The common people were not aware of what was going on except a few leaders who, unfortunately, had different opinion about the future course of politics which the tribal people might have taken. While some leaders preferred to remain under Indian union with certain conditions and special provisions, some wanted to be under the British crown as a colony for ten more years, and some opted for political independence from India. Jawaharlal Nehru, the first Prime Minister, expressed how he considered the hill areas of North East India might be best treated: "Owing to their inaccessibility and their importance to India in its defence strategy, their retention as a British possession is most unlikely. One view is that with the end of sovereignty in India, the new government of India will enter into the same relation with tribal areas as the Governor General maintains now, unless the people of these areas choose to seek integration with India.[26]

There was a proposal from the British administrators, but not openly, to keep the hill areas under the British crown colony for some time. Revealing the proposal, S.R. Thosen expressed his displeasure about it and said, "The British government, it is said, had a plan of getting a 'crown colony' formed comprising all the excluded areas and partially excluded areas, the Chittagong Hill Tracts and the North East Frontier Agency."[27] G. Bordoloi, the then Chief Minister of Assam, admitted this when he explained to the Constituent Assembly the background of the Sixth Schedule.

> It is not unknown to you that the rule of the British Government and the activities of foreign missionaries always went together. During the war (Second World War), the then rulers and officers developed in the minds of these tribal people a sense of separation and isolation and gave them assurances that at the end of the war they will be

---

[26] Cited in the Memorandum of MNF, V.L. Hluna, *Church and Political Upheavals in Mizoram*, 1987, Appendix vi; V.K. Nuh, *Nagaland and Church and Politics*, (Kohima; V.K. Nuh and Bro. 1986), p. 123

[27] S.R. Thausen, "Why the Hills and Plain Do Not Unite," *A Common Perspective for North East India*, (Calcutta, 1967), p. 176

> independent states, managing their own affairs in their own way. They were made to believe that the entire hill would be constituted into a province and put under some irresponsible government (crown colony). You might possibly have read in the papers, that plans were hatched in England in which the ex-Governor of Assam evidently took part to create a sort of kingdom over there.[28]

The Interim Government of India realised the critical situation in North East India and formed a sub-committee of the Constituent Assembly, with the late Gopinath Bardoloi, Chief Minister of Assam, as its chairman, to study on the spot the hopes, interests and aspirations of the poeple. The Sixth Schedule was framed on the basis of the recommendations made by the sub-committee for the administration of the hill areas in North East India.

The Sixth Schedule was enforced after the independent of India. It provided for an autonomous council to be formed to look after the affairs of the hill regions. Accordingly, autonomous district councils were formed in all the hill regions except in Nagaland. From the very beginning the Nagas did not want to participate in the formation and implementation of the Sixth Schedule. They demanded separation from Assam.[29] Soon after the Sixth Schedule came into operation, the hill tribes began to feel that the powers vested in the District Council were extremely inadequate for the protection and development of their society. A.P. Sinha rightly observed that no responsibility and powers were given to the district councils for development, planning and administration of their respective areas. It was more a measure to provide protection than provide

---

28 *Constituent Assembly Debate*, (4th November, 1948), Vol. II, Appendix, p. 1011

29 The Sixth Schedule [under Article 214(2) and 275 (1)] provides for the administration of tribal areas in North East India. It is a lengthy schedule which goes into the detail of the administration in the tribal areas concerned. It has provision to form District Councils to look after the affairs of tribals by the people themselves. Only five district councils were formed in 1952, the Garo District Hills District Council, the United Khasi and Jaintia Hills District Council, the North Cachar Hills District Council, Mikir Hills Council, and the Mizo District Council. This schedule can be amended by simple majority of the Indian Parliament.

opportunity for experimentation in development. It was in effect not different from that of the earlier British policy of isolation and preservation rather than assimilation and change. In fact, the British legacy was being maintained.[30]

While the hill tribes, like any other weaker section of society in the world, were certainly in need of protection and preservation of their culture, this was not sufficient to enable them to live an authentic human life. The discontentment and frustration of the people eventually erupted in armed struggle for independence from India in Nagaland and Mizoram. This was followed by the uprising of tribals in Assam, Manipur and Tripura, demanding autonomy within the union of India.[31]

Above all, legal protection does not guarantee the actual protection of their cultural identity and rights in their existential situations. The Protection of Civil Rights Act of 1955 and the Scheduled Caste and Scheduled Tribe (prevention of atrocities) Act of 1989 did not stop atrocities against scheduled tribes. The protection of tribals does not simply lie in the promulgation of laws, but in their socio-economic development. The National Commission for Scheduled Castes and Scheduled Tribes for 1986-87 rightly identified economic vulnerability as one of the basic reasons for increasing atrocities against Scheduled Castes and Scheduled Tribes.[32] The best way to protect the tribals is to strengthen their economic and political power.

(d) Modernisation : Here we will briefly deal with the contribution of the British administration and the Government of India to the process of modernisation and detribalisation. The contribution of

---

30 A.P. Sinha, "Politics and Economic Development in the Hill District of Assam," *Tribal Situation in India, Op cit*., p. 341

31 The National Socialist Council of Nagaland (NSCN) in fighting for a sovereign and independence for Nagaland, the Mizo National Front (MNF) for Mizoram, Tribal National Volunteer (TNV) for tribal communities in Tripura, the All Tripura Tribal Force (ATTF) is also demanding independence from India, while the Assam Bodo Students Union (ABSU) and the Bodo Security Forces (BSF) are fighting for Bodo land within Assam, the Karbi Students Union for Karbi state, the Kukis in Manipur are fighting for Kuki Homeland.

32 *Reports of the National Commission for Scheduled Castes and Scheduled Tribes for 1986-87, No. 1-10; The Week*, (August 25, 1991).

Christianity, while it is inter-connected with this broad process, will be considered separately.

(i) *British Administration and Modernization :* The contributions of British administration in the hill regions towards the process of modernisation were mainly limited to the restoration of peace and tranquillity, introduction of a unified political system and administrative structure, maintenance of law and order, construction of link roads and a few buildings for their administration, introduction of a monetary system and along with it the introduction of taxation to subsidise their expenditure for administration. The British occupation finally opened the way for missionaries to come into hill areas. The coming of the British which brought about radical social change to the region is certainly one of the primary factors responsible for modernization and detribalization. F.S. Downs remarked,

> The most important political event was the coming of the British who, during the course of one hundred years, brought the entire region under their control. Not only was the whole region brought within a single political system for the first time in its history, but it was brought within an administrative structure that had its centres of power outside of its own boundaries. Not only was the historical isolation of the North East brought to an end, but numerous outsiders, British and Indian, came to hold considerable administrative and economic power.[33]

Despite their policy of no interference into the internal affairs of the people, the British occupation brought radical change which was the first stepping stone toward modernisation and detribalisation.

(ii) *Christianization and Modernization :* The contributions of Christian missionary societies operating in North East India towards moderniation were mainly in the field of education, literature, health and social reform.

---

[33] F.S. Downs, *Christianity in North East India*, 1992, p. 12. The Burmese occupation prior to British administration was also controlled from outside of the region, but the Burmese neither controlled the whole region nor set up an elaborate administrative system.

(iii) *Development and Modernization :* Here we will deal with the development efforts after Indian independence and its consequences. Development has been the fundamental instrument for modernization of the tribes in India as it has been globally. Though, from the tribal perspective, substantial progress in education and health was achieved through the missionaries' efforts, the tribals are still at a very low level of subsistence and development. Since the time of independence, development has been the fundamental theme in the efforts to deal with the tribal problems.

The primary objective of the Government of India's policy towards tribal people, enshrined in the Constitution, is "protection and development" - an objective drawn from Nehru's vision for tribal society.

> The problem of Tribal areas is to make the people feel that they have perfect freedom to live their own lives and to develop according to their own wishes and genius. India to them signifies not only a protection force but a liberating one. Any concept that India is ruling them and that they are ruled, or that customs and habits with which they are unfamiliar are going to be imposed on them, will alienate them.[34]

The protection of tribal culture, social customs and traditional accupations, along with protection from exploitation, are seen as integral to tribal development. The National Committee on the Development of Backward Areas expressed its concern that, "a quickening of the pace of development in the hill areas of this region (North East India) carried with it the risk of the tribals being exploited. Protective and promotional measures to avoid this must be an integral part of the development strategy for this region."[35]

The concern for tribal development is expressed in the Constitution Articles 275, 330, 332, 334, 335 and 339. Article 275 made provision for financial assistance to the States from central consolidated funds for promoting the welfare of Scheduled Tribes or raising the level

---

34 Cited by S.T. Das, *The Tribal Life of North East India, Op cit.*, p. 27

35 Report on *Development of North Easter Region: National Committee on the Development of Backward Areas*, Planning Commission, Government of India, (New Delhi: November, 1981).

of administration in the scheduled areas. Articles 330, 332 and 334 provide for reservation of seats for the Scheduled Tribes in the House of People and the State Legislatures for a certain period. Article 335 provides for reservation of jobs in the government services. Article 339 authorised the President to appoint a Commission at the end of every ten years from its commencement to report on the situation of scheduled areas.

Under the Ministry of Community Development, multipurpose tribal blocks were initiated during the second Five Year Paln and Rs. 2.7 million was provided.[36] The purpose of these blocks was to bring about rapid improvement in the economic and social condition of the Scheduled Tribes.[37] Based on the recommendation of Varrier Elwin's committee in 1959, Tribal Development Blocks (TDB) were introduced. These were slightly different from Community Development Blocks.[38] During the 3rd Five Year Plan, 480 Tribal Development Blocks were opened in the country and by the end of the 4th Five Year Plan 504 TDB were established, 89 of which were found in North East India.

In 1969, a study team headed by Shilu Ao pointed out the failure of tribal development programs and recognised distinctive problems being faced by various tribal groups in the country. The committee suggested an intensive and specific study of the tribal problems in order to make concrete recommendations for future tribal development efforts. Thus, the tribal development scene was critically reviewed on the eve of the 5th Five Year Plan. The 5th Planning Commission defined its tasks for tribal development as "elimination of exploitation in all forms, speeding

---

36 A Tribal Development Block was introduced in the second Five Year Plan for the areas with a predominantly tribal population.

37 R.R. Prasad, "Tribal Development in India-Strategies and Programmes," *Journal of Rural Development*, Vol. 7, No. I, (Jan. 1988), p. 86

38 The idea of Tribal Development Blocks derived from the recommendation of the Elwin Committee which investigated the problem of tribal development. The Committee pointed out the deficiency of Community Development which failed to meet the need of tribal people and suggested that development activities must be carried out in accordance with the tribal culture. *Report of the Committee on Special Multipurpose Tribal Blocks*, (Delhi: Manager of Publication, 1960)

up the process of socio-economic development, building the inner strength of people and improving their organisational capability."[39] Having the tribal concentrated areas as the target of development, the "Tribal Sub-Plan" was introduced for intensive implementation in 18 States in North East India, Assam, Manipur and Tripura came under this scheme.

Under this approach, however, a number of tribal majority States and Union Territories, namely Arunachal Pradesh, Meghalaya, Mizoram, Nagaland, Lakshadweep and Darra and Nagar Haveli were not included. For these states, it was intended that development should be planned by the tribal themselves for their own people. The planning of these States was to be directed and approved by the Central Government and funded from the central consolidated fund as per the Constitutional provision found in Article 275. Both the plan as well as the non-plan expenditures in these States were financed by the Central Government. The funds allocated for these States have increased rapidly in recent decades as indicated below:

Unit in Crores of Rupees

	Fourth Plan **1969-74**	Fifth Plan **1974-79**	Sixth Plan **1980-85**	Seventh Plan **1985-90**
Meghalaya	36	99	260	440
Mizoram	5	46	128	364
Nagaland	39	97	230	400

As a result of the Government's effort and increasing financial assistance, in comparison with previous conditions, significant improvements in the infrastructure, employment and per capita income have been achieved. But the tragedy is that the living conditions of the majority either remain the same or worse than before, raising serious questions about the validity of the policy, philosophy, strategy and especially implementation of development. Our task is to critical evaluate the policy and strategy.

2. Tribal Struggle as the Basis of Assessing the Credibility of Tribal Policy : Scholars and policy makers are interested to know why the whole of North East India has been in turmoil. A number of explanations have been proposed :

[39] Cited by Prasad, *Op cit.*, p. 90

(a) Irruption of the tribal traditional practice of head hunting.

(b) A defence mechanism inbuilt in the tribal minority groups, common in other minority groups as well.

(c) Rapid social change.

(d) Christian missionaries were held responsible for conscientizing and instigating trouble among the simple tribals.

(e) The long negligence and indifferent attitude of Government towards the hill tribes in North East India.

(f) The integrity and capability of North East Indian tribals, unlike other tribals in the plains, to fight for their liberation.

While it is not possible here to discuss at length the causes of crisis in North India, it seems reasonable to conclude from the preceding outline that the main cause of the tribal revolt in North East India lies in the policy of the dominant groups throughout the history. The process of sanskritization often placed the tribals at the bottom of society, and inevitably created suspicion about the credibility of the Government. The British policy of isolation and the geographical location itself kept the hill tribes intact and capable of fighting for their rights. The missionary education indirectly made them aware of their social realities and helped them to be concerned for their future. All these contributed to the tribal revolt which inflamed the whole region.

Indeed, the turmoil has vibrated throughout the North East. The armed struggle for political self-determination started with the Naga National Council (NNC) in the 1950s and was followed by the Mizo National Front (MNF) revolt in the 1960s. The National Socialist Council of Nagaland, both the factional groups of the NSCN (Isaac-Muivah) and the NSCN (Khaplang), continues to fight for political self-determination. The struggle of the All Assam Student Union for the protection of Assamese identity against the influx of foreigners to Assam in 1970s was changed to a struggle for political self determination, under a new organisation called *United Liberation Front of Assam* (ULFA). The tribals in Assam, the Bodos and the Karbis, are fighting for separation from Assam for their own autonomy and politial identity. The People's Liberation Army (PLA) and the People's Liberation Army of Kanglai Pak (PLAKP) took up arms to achieve their goal of social justice and self-determination in Manipur. The Tribal National Volunteers (TNV), Tripura National Liberation Front (TNLF), All Tripura Tribal Force (ATTF) and Tripura National Army (TNA) have been fighting for tribal autonomy in their home land. The Khasi Student Union (KSU) started an anti-foreigner movement, demanding the introduction of inner-line regulation in Khasi Hills, as practised in other hill States of North East India and cancellation of trade liceses issued to the non-tribals.[40] The Arunachal Pradesh, the only abode of peace in the whole region, is now demanding repatriation of the Chakma refugees.

Whatever may be the causes of the crisis, this turbulent situation is a clear indication of the failure of the tribal policy in North East India. The tribal development envisaged in the Constitution based on Nehru's ideal was not translated into reality. The dominant policy in North East India has been national integration which is for many tribals a modern version of assimilation, entirely different from the vision of the Indian Constitution. R.N. Haldipur observed that integration is the keynote of the administrative policy in North East India.[41] All nations in the world are concerned for national integration, but the prejudice that has been created in the tribal mind in North East India is that national integration for them means assimilation into Hindu culture at the expense of their own cultural identity. This attitude had developed among the tribals not from the study of what scholars had written about the policy of national integration but from their daily encounter with their neighbouring plain people. In their encounters with plain people in the markets and some other places, they have been the victims of cheating and exploitation. They also saw the miscarble conditions of their fellow tribals who were assimilated ad exploited by the plain people. These experiences contributed to the development of negative attitude towards plain people which eventually erupted into violent struggle

40 Some of the many book dealing with the chaotic situation in North East India are: VIK. Sarin, *Indian's North East in Flame*, 1980, B.B. Goswami, *The Mizo Unrest*, 1979; Sanjayya, *Assam, A Crisis of Identity*, 1980; N. Hasker and Luigam Lultul, *Nagaland File*, 1984, B.P. Shukla, *What Ails India's North East?* 1980; Adiss Arnold (ed), *Crisis in North East India*, 1981; Vijay Kumar Dewan, *Assam Issue: The Beginning - the End and the Beginning*, 1985, Phanjoubam Tarapot, *Insurgency Movement in North Eastern India*. (New Delhi: Vikas Publishing House, 1993).

41 R.N. Haldipur, *Tribal Situation in India*. (Introduction), p. xviii

Ever since 1959, seven years after the implementation of the provisions of Sixth Schedule, many commissions and committees, such as Vaghaiwalla Committee, Tarlok Singh Study Team, Pataskar Commission, Durbar Commission, Elwin Commission, etc. were constituted to look into the problems of tribal development in North East India. Each of these made certain concrete recommendations about financial administration and departmental coordination to ensure speedy execution of development plans concerning the hill district. A.P. Singha was surprised that those recommendations were neither implemented by the Government nor taken seriously by the tribals themselves.[42] The fact is that Tribals leaders were convinced that unless they were given political rights and freedom to decide and plan for their own development, there would be no true development whatsoever. Thus, they have stuck to their demands and struggled for political self-determination. This struggle had led to the disintegration of the erstwhile Assam into seven different states.

3. Dialectic-Historical Model as the Tribal Approach to Social Change : It is quite evident from the sociological point of view that the tribal approach to social change in North East India implies a conflictive model, perhaps to be described as a dialectical-hitorical approach. It is interesting to note that the tribal Christians in this region - the overwhelming majority of the population - are mostly evangelical conservatives who strongly reject Marxism and never have taken interest in reding Karl Marx. Their violent struggle for liberation in no way was inspired by Marxism. It was their tragic experience of alienation, neglect and exploitation that compelled them to take up arms. The formation of the National Socialist Council of Nagaland (NSCN) in 1980 was not the result of conviction in communist ideology; rather a strategy to make the movement more powerful.[43] In fact, "Nagaland for Christ" is the slogan of the NSCN.

---

[42] A.P. Singha, "Political and Economic Development in the Hill District of Assam," *Tribal Situation, Op cit.*, pp. 348 & 349

[43] S. Chube, *Hill Politics in North East India*, (Bombay, Orient Longman, 1973), p. 156 When the volunteers returned from China (February, 1968), Rev. Longri Ao denounced the action of the rebels as not authorized by the Naga people.

It is difficult to arrive at a conclusive and commonly accepted statement whether violence is a legitimat means to bring about social transformation, or whether it contradicts the most fundamental Christian principles. From the practical experience in the region itself, one may put forward an argument against the use of a conflictive model. Neithr Meghalaya nor Arunachal Pradesh used violent means or demanded secession from India but peacefully obtained statehood of their own. On the other hand, those who were involved in the violent struggle particularly the Nagas and the Mizos would certainly claim that in addition to their own achievement of statehood, the Assam Re-organisation Bill and the subsequent North Eastern Reorgnisation Act 1971, which provides for the establishement of the State of Manipur, Tripura, Meghalaya and of the Arunachal Pradesh, were the indirect result of their struggle. The Chinese aggression in 1962 was another impetus to the Government to consider more seriously the tribal problems in North East India. The threat for the Government of India was that if the tribal problems in North East India was not immediately addressed, they may support the Chinese expansionism. Niharanjan Ray, in his introductory address to a seminar on the Tribal Situation in India in 1969 said,

> Ever since the Chinese aggression in 1962, the tribal disturbances along our North Eastern Frontiers and in Bastar in Madhya Pradesh, the rumblings of growing discontent and unrest in a number of other tribal areas of this vast country, Indian intellectuals in general and anthropologists, administrators and leaders of public opinion and makers of policy in particular, have been alerted to the vital significance of the extensive northern and North-Eastern tribal border regions as much as the 'tribal' peoples of other areas of the country.[44]

Since violent struggle in North East India evolved not from ideological conviction but from the situation, it should not be endorsed as the ultimate approach of the tribals for all times. While we may condemn violence against the fundamental principle of Christian belief,

---

[44] Niharanjan Ray, 'Introductory Address,' A Seminar on Tribal situation in India held in 1969, under the auspices of the Indian Institute of Advanced Study and the Advanced Study in Sociology of Delhi University, *Tribal Situation in India*, p. 3

it is important to have a comprehensive understanding of violence and recognise also the violence of the structures and system which dehumanises people. Today among the hill tribes, though some insurgent groups are struggling for political self determination, the struggle has shifted from armed struggle to transformational struggle as some tribes have obtained, to a certain extent, autonomy and political identity of their own. Thus, social transformation is the core issue for both the Churches and the State government alike.

C. FROM ARMED STRUGGLE TO TRANSFORMATION STRUGGLE

While some tribal groups, the Bodos and Karbis in Assam and the Tribals in Tripura, are still desperately struggling for their political identity, the hill tribes have obtained political identity of their own. In their struggle they have reached agreement and made accords with the Central Government. The quest for on-going transformation is not an easy task for the tribals who had been isolated in a very wretched condition for many years.

In the present struggle for transformation of the tribal society, development has occupied the central place. Since the concern in this book is construction of a theological basis for social transformation in the context of the present struggle of the hill tribes, the present, dominant ideology of development along with major social issues must be critically examined with a view to identifying the root causes of the problems for further transformation. The findings will provide the theological agenda which will determine the actual theological construction.

1. Beginning of a New Era for Development : Some of the hill tribes in Meghalaya, Nagaland, Mizoram and Arunachal Pradesh are responsible for the planning and implementation of the development programmes of their respective States. The dawn of a new era, an era of development, has opened the opportunity for the people to struggle for their own socio-economic transformation. The allotment of fund for development, as shown in the Five Year Plan expenditure between 1969-90, has been increased significantly. As a result, people are experiencing significant increase in the per capita income and the subsequent improvement of living conditions. In this era of development, the writer contends, it is important to see that the society is transformed towards the values of the Kingdom of God. As a first step, it will be important to examine and evaluate critically the ideologies and policies of development, as seen in the experience of other developing societies, so that mistakes of the past are not repeated in the hill areas of North East India.

2. Critical Analysis of Development Ideology and its Impact : The common experience of development in the Third World Countries is that it discriminates the poor giving them false hope but blesses the rich. This experience has made the Third World Liberation theologians critical about development. They regard liberation as a pre-requisite for development. However, genuine development in the sense of "a multi-dimensional development process involving the reorganisation and reorientation of an entire economic and social system" is not different from liberation.[45] Since development activities have been, to a great extent, determined by the Government's policy, it is important to analyse and evaluate the policy of Government in North East India. M.N. Karna rightly pointed out that evaluation of development efforts requires not only a thorough analysis of the programs and schemes but also an appraisal of their guiding principles.[46]

The literature on economic development over the past 40 years has been dominated by basically four major theories: (a) linear stages of growth model, (b) theories and patterns of structural change, (c) the international dependence revolution and (d) the neoclassical, free market counter-revolution.[47] The thinking of the 1950s and early 1960s focussed mainly on the concept of stages of economic growth in which the process of development was viewed as a series of successive stages through which all countries must pass. This was replaced in the 1970s by the theories and patterns of structural change on the one hand, and by the theory of international dependence on the other. Now a new classical counter - revolutionary theory has appeared which emphasises the beneficial role of free markets with government intervention only in

45 Michael P. Todrado, *Economic Development in the Third World*, (Fourth Edition), (New York ad London: Longman, 1989), p. 62

46 M.N. Karna, "Aspects of Tribal Development in North East India," *Tribal Demography and Development in North East India*, edited by Ashish Bose et. al, (Delhi: B.R. Publishing Corporation, 1990), p. 7

47 Michael P. Todrado, *Op cit.*, p. 62 ff

areas of heavy economic cost.[48] It is not our purpose in this thesis to examine the details, nor the relative merits, of these theories. Rather, drawing upon a range of theoretical perspectives, some of the problems with tribal development in India will be discussed.

(a) Cultural imperialism in tribal development policy : No nation follows a particular theory of development rigidly. With regard to the tribal development, the idea of "catch up" has been the dominant ideology from the very beginning. R.R. Prasad said that the strategies and programs launched to fulfil the Constitutional obligation in free India is to make tribals catch up with non-tribals in the race for social, political and economic prosperity - the kernel of planned action in different Five-Year Plan periods - could not be fully appreciated if the special situation of the tribals and tribal areas during British rule is not taken into account.[49] The idea of "catch up" obviously originated from Rostows' idea of stages of growth which has to a certain extent become obsolete.[50] This ideology, together with evolutionary theory of social change, is rooted to the uni-linear concept of history, according to which certain societies are far more advanced than the tribal societies and become the goal for backward people. In this ideology, cultural imperialism is deeply imbued.

The basic problem with this particular ideology is that there is no room to be different in the development policy and effort. It is a development model which does not regard other cultures and technologies as capable of solving their own problems. It expects others to follow the exact footsteps of the developed countries.

Indian intellectuals and policy makers maintained double standards in applying "catch up" policy to tribals. This ideology of development has been severely criticised and rejected by Third World intellectuals when used in the international relations between the Third World and

---

[48] *Ibid*, p. 63

[49] R.R. Prasad, *Op cit.*, p. 83

[50] Rostow, in the opening chapter of his *Stages of Economic Growth*, identified the traditional society, the pre-condition stage for take off, the stage of self-sustaining growth, the stage of drive towards maturity, and the stage of high mass consumption as stages to be followed by all societies. *The Stages of Economic Growth: the Non-Communist Manifesto*. (London: Cambridge University Press, 1960), pp. 1-4

the First World, the North and the South, but the same is applied to the weaker sections in their own countries. Thus, in the spiral of oppression, the tribals are at the bottom bearing all the burden and become the victims of double alienation.

(b) Dependency in tribal development : The question of economic dependency is one of the most crucial questions addressed at the international, national and regional levels. The fundamental issue in hte international debate on economic dependency is that the coexistence of the rich and poor nations in the international system, dominated by such an unequal power relationship between the centre (developed countries) and the periphery (Third World countries), hindering attempts by the poor nations to be selfreliant and independent in their development efforts. This unhealthy relationship makes such efforts difficult and sometimes even impossible.[51]

The concern in this thesis is the tribal dependency in the micro level within their own country, particularly in the hill regions of North East India. The tribal States in North East India are practically run by the Central Government which has made the people dependent, powerless and in some ways irresponsible. The question why and how the tribal people have become dependent is an important issue which concerns all the tribes.

Lt. Colonel J.Shakespeare, who came to Mizoram as invader and later on became the first superintendent of Mizoram from 1897-1905, said that the Mizos had everything necessary for their day-to-day

---

[51] The idea of dependency was developed from Marxist analysis. Theotonio Dos Santos said, "Dependency is a conditioning situation in which the economies of one group of countries are conditioned by the development and expansion of others." On the other hand, the neo classical counter revolution holds the view that the Third World is under developed not because of the predatory activities of the First World and the international agencies that it controls, but rather because of the heavy hands of the State and the corruption, inefficiency, and lack of economic incentives that permeate the economies of developing nations. However, international dependence theories alert us to the importance of the structures and workings of hte world economy and the many ways in which decisions taken in the developed world can effect the lives of millions of people in the developing world. (M.P. Todaro, *Op cit.*, p. 78ff)

living.[52] Of course, Shakespeare talks about the primitive economy as self-sufficient.Until recently the tribal people were self sufficient in their own way unless catastrophies or natural calamities caused severe scarcity of food. The major factors which have contributed to the development of economic dependency among tribals are basically three: the failure of the traditional agricultural system (*jhum* cultivation); rapid social change; and the system of development itself. Each of thes will be examined.

(i) *Failure of jhuming :* The failure of the traditional agriculture system to meet the increasing requirement of food stuff is one of the primary factors of dependency. Since agriculture, particularly paddy cultivation (*jhuming*),[53] has been the backbone of the tribal economy throughout their history, their stories, songs and dance, time and religion were related to their *jhum*. As integral part of their social life, it is not easy for them to give it up. And the rice cultivation, despite repeated low yields, has been traditionally practised for many years for it can withstand water during monsoon season.

The problem is that 75% of the total workers in the tribal communities in NEI are still engaged in jhum cultivation which makes

---

[52] Lt. Colonel J. Shakespeare, *The Lushai Kuki Clans*, (Aizawl: Tribal Research Institute, 1988), p. 14

[53] *Jhum* cultivation is a shifting cultivation practised by most of the tribals living in the hill areas all over the world. The process of *jhum* cultivation in hills of North East India is as follows: A section of hill is set aside each year for the whole village by the village chief in consultation with his elders or the village council in some cases. Each family selects a plot of land, slashes the jungle in the month of January and February and exposes it in the sun for some days to dry the slashes. It is usually burnt in the month of March which is followed by dibbling and sowing the seeds, weeding, watching protection of their crops. Then come harvesting, threshing and transporting to home, culminating in the harvest festival. The common characteristics of *jhum* cultivation may be summarized as: (a) Rotation of field rather than crops, (b) Use of human labour as chief input instead of employing other power such as animal and machinery, (c) Nomadic life is required when the duration of cycle of land becomes shorter and less fertile, (d) Land is usually owned by community and (e) Crops are generally grown mixed, with a variety of crops in the field.

no effective contribution to the improvement of the State economy. While the population and consumption have greatly increased, the means of production remain the same. Thus, the central thrust of Five Year Plan is self-sufficiency in food grain, rather than making a serious attempt to find out an alternative means of living and production. The planning committee often identifies *Jhum* cultivation as one of the primary hindrances to achieve self-sufficiency in food grain. But no serious analysis of the system of 'development' which is clearly failing, nor any suggestion of alternative approaches, is made.[54] It is quite evident that if government continues along the same line, it will experience the same failure.

(ii) *Rapid social change :* The social change that has occured in the tribal society is rapid and radical. A society which had no alphabets at the beginning of this century is exposed to modern world where they have to compete with others and learn new technologies. This rapid social change compels them to depend on others. For example, the change in building technology has compelled them to depend not only on imported raw materials but als on the non-tribal skilled labours coming from neighbouring States. The tribals who used to built their houses mainly with bamboos and timbers are now constructing their houses with rods and cement. This is certainly an integral part of the shift from nomadic life to settled life; but the problem with this change is that they have not learned the technology of building a concrete building with iron rod and cement. In this situation dependence on others is unavoidable.

In the economic sector, the tribal economy was fundamentally subsistence economy. Production has been perceived in terms of a family requirement. It is therefore a difficult process for tribals to switch over to market economy as they have to compete with those who have been living with market economy for more than a century. This is the reason why business in the tribal areas is controlled by the business people from the plains. As those business people live in plains and do their business in the hills, the resources in the hills are drained out causing serious economic problems to hill tribes.

The present educational system is the continuation of basic education introduced by missionaries in the beginning of this century

---

[54] Government of Mizoram, *Annual Plan 1991-1992*, p. ix

Since it was meant for learning how to read and write with the aim of character building, it does not contribute much for the economic development. Moreover, the prolifiration of science and technical education. This has placed the tribal children in a very difficult situation to go for science and technical education. In brief, education in the hill areas has not been oriented to produce technically competent persons for economic development.

(iii) *The system of development* : In the existing system, as mentioned above, the development effort in the hill States of NEI is financed by the Central Government. The way it is financed seems without rationale, the planning is frequently impracticable and the execution is poorly administered. People become objects or recipients, not the subject of development. They have no part in the process itself. As long as people are not made responsible for their own development, they will remain dependent. Suffice is to say that the present system does not have room for people participation. It needs to be thoroughly studied and improved, if there is to be a significant future for the development of North East India.[55]

Dependency is not confined to the economic sector alone. The hill States in North East India are heavily depending on outside labour force for construction of road and building.

Tribals in the hills are interested in education, but education is another area in which a trend towards dependency is seen. As a result of economic improvement, the number of students who do their studies outside of North East India were rapidly increased. Many students undertake their study outside of North East India. Most of the students interviewed by the writer indicated the inadequacy of education in NEI to get a job, to find admission in the medical and technical institutions or to compete in all-India competitive exams of any kind. It is inevitable for the hill States in NEI to send some students for technical education, but spending a huge amount of money every year outside of NEI for general education is a serious economic drain.

(c) Planning in Tribal Development : "Five Year Plan" has become a common expression in India, and the concept of national

[55] The failure of the system is quite evident from my field research, and was also admitted by several development officers interviewed by the writer.

planning has become more and more accepted all over the world as necessary for economic development. The basic idea of economic planning is that the state should take an active, initiative and indeed the *decisive* role, in the economy by its own acts of enterprise and investments. By its various controls, inducements and restrictions over the private sectors, the government should initiate, spur and steer economic development for the common good of the people. These public policy measures should be rationally coordinated and the co-ordination be made explicit in an overall plan for a specific number of years ahead.[56] The ideology of state initiative and control for the common good of all citizens undergirds the economic development of the country and applies to all sections of the people with no exception to be made of the tribals. While planning is inevitably necessary for India, the problem, as C.T. Kurien expressed it, is that the means are often regarded as the end itself.[57] That is, government initiatives and plans for development do not guarantee the well-being of the people. It is necessary to go beyond planning and into implementation, to ensure that the outcome is in fact for the common good.

The simple tribals neither participate in the planning nor have knowledge about those plans. The planning has been the imposition of an alien idea, not the result of field investigation as far as the hill States of North East India is concerned. The Planning Commission formed a National Committee of the Development of Backward Areas for the 6th Five Year Plan. This Committee confessed,

> However, in the case of North East the committee has not been able to do this (field research) because of the disturbed condition in the area. Field level investigation by the committee members was not possible. The seminar on development problems of the North East was scheduled but could not be held, once again, because of disturbed conditions in the area.[58]

---

56 Gunnar Myrdal, *Asian Drama: An Inquiry into the Poverty of Nations*, (Abridged by Seth S. King), (London: Penguin, 1972), p. 108

57 C.T. Kurien, *Our Five Year Plan*, (Bangalore: CISRS, 1966), p. 33

58 Planning Commission, *Government of India, Report on Development of North Eastern Region*, (New Delhi: 1981), p. 1

Against this the writer argues that there was no serious problem in those days which should prevent the Committee from coming into North East India. Rather the above quotation reveals the extent to which the planners in both national and state levels are not serious in their task of planning. The planning has often been made from the perspective and interest of the planners, without serious engagement with the needs of the situation. The bureaucrats and politicians take advantage of the ignorance of the people and misuse their poewr to monopolise the whole development process through the planning itself. This is made possible by the economic system in which the State is responsible for initiating and controlling the development process. This is one of the basic reasons why corruption is rampant. For those who are ignorant about the practices of corruption, it will be hard to explain the discrepancy between the figures for development outlay and the actually observed building-up of individual or social "productive assets". This results in a new social stratification, increasing the gap between the rich and the poor, encouraging mutual distrust between the people and their leaders, and precipitating the emergence of a class system in the tribal egalitarian society.

It was also observed in the writer's field research that the notion of accountability plays an important role in the practice of corruption. For exampla, the churches are accountable to the people and to God, while the State Government with all its servants perceives their accountability as to the Central Government of India. While the churches, are comparatively free from corruption, each and every department of the State Government is penetrated by corruption.

It is also noted that the way Central Financial asistance has been given to hill States in NEI is irrational. It was the political change that brought huge amounts of funds from the Centre. Such a handsome amount of development funding came as a result of their political struggle. It is no wonder that today the development activities in NEI are highly politicised and much of the funding for incentive, e.g. assistance, loans, is used for political purposes. That has not only crippled development work, it has become a source of corruption. It is said that a society which did not use locks and keys thirty years ago is now facing a serious problem of corruption. Moreover, Meghalaya, Mizoram and Nagaland are the only states where Christians formed a majority in a country where 97% of the population belong to Hindu and Muslim communities. The folklore of corruption has tarnished the image of their leaders, creating mutual distrust and frustration. This is a challenge to tribal Christianity.

(d) Identity Crisis : F.S. Downs has used "identity" as an integrated principle for understanding the Christian movement in Manipur, Meghalaya, Mizoram and Nagaland. This view is supported by sociologists who also regard "identity crisis" as a key factor of the whole tribal movement in North East India.[59] "The tribal movement in North East India is a manifestation of the fight for identity although based on ethnic considerations."[60] A search for identity is inevitable because the social context is dynamic and shifting, not static. The way people perceive and understand themselves is continually changing. As a consequence, in a rapidly changing context, the tribal people have experienced in acute sense of identity crisis. There are two reconisable phases in this crisis, first the impact of British Administration and with it the conversion to Christianity, then the recent social upheavals.

The spread of British administration and their conversion to Christian faith led the tribal people to a new consciousness of their identity. That consciousness was the beginning of their search for identity. Several tribes such as Ao, Angami, Sema, Lotha, Chakesang, Konyak, Phom, Zeliang, Tangkhul and others began to accept "Naga" as their common identity.[61] A new Naga consciousness emerged, and yet a search for identity is still going on. Likewise, the Lushais and many other sub-tribes in Mizoram accepted "Mizo" for their new common ethnic identity. Some tribes have replaced the names of their tribes (mostly given by others) with their original names. The Mikirs adopted *Karbis*. Lakher was replaced by *Mara*, the Pawis in Mizoram adopted

59 F.S. Downs, "Identity: The Integrative Principle," *Journal of Social Sciences and Humanities*, (North Eastern Hill University), Vol. 9, No. 3, (July Sept, 1991), p. 7ff; B. Datta Ray, *Tribal Identity and Tension in North East India*, (New Delhi. Omson Publication 1989), pp. viff, 28ff. Various papers presented in the seminar on Questions of Nationalities, Ethnicity and Cultural Identity in the Context of North East India, organised by NEICSSR, Shillong, 1986.

60 Datta Ray, *Tribal Identity and Tension in North East India*, p. vii

61 M. Horam, *Naga Polity*, (New Delhi: B.R. Publishing Corporation, 1975), pp. 25, 61

Lai; some of the Kukis adopted *Thado*, Arunachalis no longer accepted *Bhutia*, *Daflas* was changed to *Bangri*, while the *Tuikuks* in Mizoram adopted *Riangs* for their new identity, the *Lothas* of Nagaland become *Kyongs*, the *Semas* become *Sumi* and so on. S.C. Chube has rightly observed,

> A close examination of the tribal situation would suggest that new tribal identities are still in the process of evolution. As new identities emerge, old ones are obliterated. In the process, old tribal names are discarded and new ones adopted (derogatory names given by others were discarded, the original and authentic ones are re-adopted), mythology and traditions are modified and reversed, and alternative bases of solidarity building are discovered to forge wider links with a view to evolving, articulate, aggressive, and viable identities.[62]

The crisis of identity happens whenever there is a break down of an old identity unable to cope with the changing situation. This is a common problem of minority groups, whose identities are threatened either in the interaction with a larger dominant group or in the modernisation process.

In the case of tribal people in NEI, a number of factors brought about identity crisis: when the British administration brought all the autonomous villages, ruled by their respective chiefs or leaders, together under one administration; when they were converted into Christian faith, and when they were exposed to the outside world during the First and Second World Wars. The tribals' conversion into Christian faith, unlike the sudden change of administrative system brought by British administrators, was a gradual process. It took about 60-100 years for the whole tribe to embrace Christianity.

The present identity crisis in NEI is different, however, from that of the earlier, British period The transition is no longer from isolated village community to larger tribal community, nor from primal religion to Christianity. It is a shift from tribal polity with its chieftainhood to nation-state democratic politics; from bare subsistence economy towards a

---

[62] S.C. Dube, *Tribal Heritage of India*, (New Delhi: Vikas Publishing House, 1977), p. 5

competitive market economy; from communitarianism towards individualism; from personal community towards impersonal society; from illiteracy to literacy; from dependent church to self-supporting and self-propagating church; from the integrity of one or two denominational churches to a diversity of denominations and multiplicity of sectarian groups. The traditional decisionmaking process by consensus has been changed to the majority vote of the modern politics. Old values have been replaced by new. Above all, the tribal people experience themselves as a small minority, ethnically, linguistically, culturally and religiously so different from the majority of the people. They often ask themselves, "Who are we?" as they are wrongly identified in all the cities of India and asked, "Are you a Chinese?" or "From which country do you come?" Sometimes, frustrated young people express themselves saying, "I am not an Indian."

The rapid social change brought by modernisation has run through all the fabric of tribal social life. The progressive change as such is what the people have been looking for, but the way the change has been brought about has created many problems. Sudden and disruptive change has created confusion and frustration in the struggle for transformation. VIK. Sarin rightly commented,

> The tribal society is undergoing a cataclysmic upheaval. It is in the process of transition from a primitive community based on shifting cultivation to a society better equipped to grapple with twentieth century ideas, technologies and ways of life. Such a transition was inevitable in a world where faster means of communication are not allowing any area to remain isolated, but it is regrettable that, due no doubt to the long years of neglect and repression, it is happening in a series of explosions rather than in a gradual manner. The effect of these convulsions has been to put the tribal society in a state of ferment and turmoil, which to a great extent contributed to the insurgency in Nagaland and Mizoram and the current spurt of violence in Meghalaya.[63]

The identity crisis caused by rapid social change and particularly by the development activities is due to the failure in the part of planners

[63] VIK. Sarin, *India's North East in Flame*, p. viii

and policy makers to take the cultural dimension of development seriously. The Planning Commission and the de-culturalised tribal elites[64] who are responsible for the planning of tribal development pay only lip service to Nehru's idea that tribals in India should be developed according to their own wishes and genius, in order to avoid causing cultural erosion in the process of development.

What part does culture play in the process of development? To answer this question it is necessary to clarify what we mean by this term. Culture is used here as "the sum total of the original solutions that a group of human beings invent to adapt to their natural and social environment."[65] Culture develops out of human beings' encounter with nature in a particular environment to meet their needs and to solve their problems and to live within the demands, restrains and potentials of their environment. Thus, culture is dependent on the conditionsof people's environment, and may change as the environment changes. But a critical study of development activities reveals that what the planners mean by culture is merely art, music, dance and literature. Their efforts are often limited to the inclusion of tribal colour in the development effort rather than rediscovering tribal models of development from their own traditional ways of conducting and living their lives. This type of development not only caused identity crisis and frustration, but failed as a development effort.[66]

The concern for culture to be considered as part of the development process is not about maintaining the status quo against modernisation as C. Nunthara suggested.[67] It is a sincere concern for

---

64 The vision of tribal elites for their own development is nothing but modernization towards Westernization. Since they are the instruments of the Planning Commission, they are responsible for failing to take their own culture seriously, and for the introduction of an alien system of development. V. Xaxa in his paper, "Tribal Development in North East India: Trends and Perspectives" admitted that the development experience of tribals in North East India is not different from the rest of India. *Tribal Demography and Development in North East India*, p. 28

65 Thierry G. Verhelst, *No Life Without Roots: Culture and Development*, (translated by Bob Cunning), (London: Zed Book Ltd., 1990), p. 3

66 *Ibid*, p. 19

67 C. Nunthara, "Social Aspect of Tribal Development," *Tribal Demography and Development in North East India*, *Op cit.*, p. 31ff

stability as well as progress, to create a participatory and sustainable society. Indeed, the success of the Village Development Board (VDB) in Nagaland, patterned according to the traditional village administrative set up, was acclaimed as an exemplary model of culturally related development.[68] Unfortunately that was disrupted again by political intervention and influence of the present development effort. However, an emphasis on culture does not mean uncritical endorsement of all aspects of indigenous culture. Rather culture should be critically judged by the way it assists the transformation of human society towards the realisation of the Kingdom of God. Some possibilities of such transformation through the tribal culture itself will be explored in the following chapters.

(e) Separatism : Separatism is one of the crucial problems for the tribals in their struggle for social transformation. They seek to come out from their isolated cells to build a larger and more powerful community. The tribals whose social relations have been limited within the village community or tribal community fround it difficult to come together to form a larger community for the common good and interest of a larger society. Most of the tribe in the past perceived their identity at the village level; only in recent years have they begun to see their identity at the regional or State level. Thus, the whole tribal movement in North East India has been widely interpreted as a separatist movement, in terms of seeking separation from India. As long as their identity was confined to the village, there was not question of separation from India. The present separatist movement is the result of the larger identity that has been developed over the past fifty years.

Separatism in no way is limited to the tribal movement alone. It is also found in the non-tribal movement in Punjab and Kashmir and Assam. In regard to North East India, however, 'separatism' has a more limited definition. For our purposes it refers to the tribal disunity and formation of many small groups which makes them vulnerable and insignificant. This problem is clearly seen in the proliferation of sectarian groups and denominations in the church, and in the formation of many political parties since the inception of democracy. It is a society not yet accustomed to

---

[68] D.P. Maitham and K. Haloi, "Implementation of IRDP: Nagaland Experience," *Journal of Rural Development*, Vol. 7(5), pp. 501-518

large scale groupings. The sense of being one unified group has not yet emerged.

(i) *Tribal separatism in party politics :* It was from the hill States of North East India that regional political parties began to emerge. Until the National Congress party swept through the hill States of North East India in recent years, regional parties had won elections most of the time. A complete list of regional parties is not necessary for our purpose, suffice it to say that there are many.[69] While some of them are no longer in existence, other parties are still active. Many of them ceased to exist never having won a single seat in the election. Some of the parties were founded on ethnic considerations rather than ideology, to protect minority interests. The proliferation of political parties is one of the evidences of neo-tribalism which has crippled politics in North East India.

No in-depth study on the impact of modern party politics on the tribal society has been done. The personal experience and limited research of the writer on this subject suggests, however, that party politics has brought radical change to traditional values and practice. It advocates, contrary to the tribal social ethics of *tlawmngaihna* (self-sacrifice and humility), self exaltation and condemnation of others. The traditional decision-making procedure by consensus in consultation with others has been replaced by majority vote, that has in turn changed the concept of rights. The harmony of the village community has been disrupted, dividing the community into several parties, sometimes creating tension and conflict among the simple villagers. Appointment to jobs, allocation of development funds and activities and the distribution of contract works are highly politicised and used by those in power to further their political purposes. In many respects, any political party in power fails to serve the interests of the people as a whole, as the ministry is concerned only for members belonging to their party.

---

[69] Some of the regional parties are the Eastern Indian Tribal Union (EITU), the All Parties Hill Leaders Conference (not exactly a party, more of a forum), the Mizo Union (MU), the Mizo National Front (MNF), the People Conference (PC), the Naga National Council (NNC), the Naga National Organisation (NNO), the United Front of Nagaland (UFN), Naga National Party (NNP), the National Socialist Council of Nagaland (NSCN), Kuki National Assembly (KNA), Hmar People's Convention (HPC), Tribal National Volunteer (TNV), etc.

The credibility of democracy for the tribals is thus highly questionable and problematic. As Gunnar has said, "Full democracy with universal fuffrage in the West has only been successfully tried out at an advanced stage of economic development, when there were relatively high levels of living and literacy and a fair amount of equal opportunity.[70]

(ii) *Tribal separatism in the church :* As mentioned earlier, the Christian church was instrumental in the emergence of a larger tribal identity and unity. Belief in the universal fellowship of the church initially broke down the barrier of tribalism. But the proliferation of sectarian groups within the church has disintegrated the churches planted by missionaries and has divided the society in general. This phenomenon is comparable with the proliferation of regional political parties in politics. Unlike political divisions, the division in the church is more institutionalised and often have a more profound effect in the life of society.

It is interesting to note that various theoretical interpretations of the cause of the proliferation of sectarian group in North East India identify such factors as dissatisfaction with the existing church, the tribal nature, the manifestation of tribal culture and a sign of selfhood in tribal Christianity.[71] Whether it is neo-tribalism, a manifestation of a repressed

---

70 Gunnar Myrdal, *Asian Drama: An Inquiry into the Poverty of Nations*, *Op cit.*, p. 124

71 The main cause of sectarianism for Vanlalchhunga is the dissatisfaction with the existing church's administration and false interpretation of the Bible. For C.L. Hminga, it is mainly due to the rapid social change and the free life style of tribal people; for James Dokhuma, a manifestation of Mizo traditional life in a different form; for Goswami and Stephen Fuch, a by-product of cultural and 'ideotional' confrontation with more powerful groups; for F. Hrangkhuma, a sign of selfhood and dynamism. Ref: C.L. Hminga, *The Life and Witness of the Churches in Mizoram*; (1987) Vanlalchhunga, *An Zirtirnate* (1984); James Dokhuma, *Zorum Kohhran Tualto Chanchinte* (1975); Stephen Fuchs, *Religious Prophets: A Study of Messianic Movement in Indian Region*, (1965); B.B. Goswami, "Hill Tribes of North East India: The Impact of Christianity", in *The Tribal World and Its Transformation*, (1980); The Christian census jointly conducted by the Presbyterian Synod, Baptist Union and the Mara Evangelical Church in Mizoram in 1980 identified 60 sectarian groups in Mizoram. However some of them were already extinct, some others are insignificant in number. There are 13 established churches and 14 sectarian groups and 5 other religious groups in Mizoram.

village mentality in a different form, or the expression of dissatisfaction with the existing established churches, or a sign of 'selfhood' in the history of Christianity in the hill regions of NEI, all of these, in one way or another indicate a search for identity in the new-found religion. Sectarianism in North East India, particularly in Mizoram is a search for self identity, mainly expressed by the poor people who could not integrate themselves into the new movement. Originally Christianity was a poor people's movement which later on became a respectable organisation. Now the poorer members of society are searching for identity and acceptance through Christian groups.

In fact, most of the people movements in North East India began as movements of the poor, including the Christian conversion and the first democratic movements. But within a very short span of time, the church became an institution of the new elite group who controlled the society. Sectarian groups comprised mostly frustrated poor people who found it difficult in adapt themselves to Christian movements. Sectarianism was in the main the result of frustration or a sense of crisis rather than an exercise of creativity.

Reasons for this frustration were both cultural and economic. In the cultural area, the Western model of trained leadership and style of worship were unacceptable for the common masses. The tribal leadership, particularly the priesthood, was a gift, a charisma, not artificially trained or certified by a college or a college. However, this does not mean that all the trained leaders are not charismatic leaders. It is not only the pattern of leadership which is unacceptable. Many tribal Christians felt like 'fish out of water' in the Western pattern of worship.[72] Most of the members of various sectarian groups were socially marginalised, educationally backward, economically poor, politically powerless and religiously neglected people within the tribal community. Those who are in the main stream of the church and society regard them as fanatical, unrealistic people trying to escape from life's struggle. Given these varying perspectives, it is clear that the proliferation of Christian sects and denominations in North East India, particularly in Mizoram, is an expression of an on-going identity crisis within the church.

---

[72] Lalbiaktluanga, "Theological Trends in Mizoram," *Towards A Tribal Theology: The Mizo Perspective*, (Aizawl: Mizo Theological Conference, 1989), p. 63ff

The impact of division in the church in the tribal context is disastrous. The image of the church is tarnished, the village community is disintegrated into pieces, huge amounts of money are wasted for the support of competing denominational interests, and the ministry of the church at large is accordingly crippled. If this separatist tendency could have been kept as a movement within the existing churches, it would have been less divisive and less wasteful.

We may recaptulate the problems of tribal society discussed in this chapter. We have accepted the fact that the process of modernization and detribalisation is irreversible in the hill regions of North East India, for which the British administration, Christianity and the process of modernization are identified as the primary causes. The question is whether this process will ruin or transform the society. While admitting the change as the need of society and irreversible process, we have also admitted that it has casued certain problems as discussed above. For Lalsawma, the problem is serious that it shakes the foundation of tribal society as it alienates tribals from their culture.[73] This is quite natural for a society under going rapid social change. The development effort in recent years has not only created dependency among the tribals, it has also stratified the tribal society into rich and poor classes. Modern politics has radically changed the social structure, decision-making process, and value system and divided society into different political parties.

D. THEOLOGICAL AGENDA

A theological approach to social problems would be goal-oriented, towards the realisation of the Kingdom of God. For this reason, a theological reorientation of the people to invoke their faith and deepen their commitment to the cause of social transformation as a valid manifestation of the kingdom values and practice will be our primary concern. Accoodingly, the theological orientation must be shaped by the problems and challenges. Some of the major social problems in the tribal society have been identified in this chapter. It has not been possible here to address every issue separately. However, all the problems are interconnected. As Downs suggested, identity crisis can be treated as a

[73] Lalsawma, "The Shaking of Foundation in Mizo Society," *Mizoram Today*, Vol. 1, No. 2, (January, 1975)

potentially integrative principle for understanding all other problems. This problem has manifested itself in many different forms in the social, economic and political life of the tribal people. The introduction of an alien system of development has created economic dependency which does not allow them to keep the integrity of their own identity so as to live with dignity. Separatism in the tribal society is a further evidence of identity crisis. To address this fundamental problem, it is important for the churches and the Central and State governments to take the culture of the people seriously in the effort for development. Likewise, for the purpose of theological reorientation, it is necessary for theologians to consider liberation motifs from their own traditions and experiences of liberation. Thus, in response to the findings of this kind socio-theological analysis, we can legitimately expect that some transformational motifs of the tribal traditions will be theologically rediscovered.

CHAPTER III

METHODOLOGICAL ISSUES IN TRIBAL THEOLOGY

Theological methodology is here understood as a working principle used by theologians in the articulation of theology with a view to achieving a theological vision of the community of faith or of the theologians themselves. The term method is derived from the Greek *methodos* which literally means "going after" or "a way of doing anything". A combination of *meta* = after and *thodos* = way implies that after a particular way or system has been found, it is followed by people. In the light of this, theological method may be defined as a regular, orderly, definite way or principle of doing theology. Bernard Lonergan defines it as a normative pattern of recurrent and related operations yielding commutative and progressive result.[1] In theological method, as in the method of any discipline, there is explicitly or implicitly an overriding rationale which coordinates the various avenues of approach and assigns to each its proper degree of emphasis. This is in accordance with the constructive role of reason, in its imaginative or architectonic function. We should not think of this methodological rationale as an arbitary presupposition, or as entirely as priori. It must indeed be sketch out at the beginning, if the inquiry is to proceed on consistent lines and is to be properly articulated.[2] As Tillich has argued that theologians might have an overriding rationale which integrate their theological articulations, they usually found the basic structure of their theology before they reflected on the method to be used.[3] He maintains the integrity of content and method.

> A method is a tool, literally a way around, which must be adequate to its subject matter. Whether or not a method is adequate cannot be decided a priori; it is continually being decided in the cognitive process itself. Method and system determine each other. Therefore, no method can claim to be adequate for every subject. Methodological imperialism is dangerous as political imperialism; like the latter, it breaks down when the independent elements of reality revolt against

---

1 Bernard Lonergan, *Method in Theology*, p. 4

2 John Macquarrie, *Principle of Christian Theology*, p. 30

3 Paul Tillich, *Systematic Theology*, Vol. I, p. 34

> it. A method is not an "indifferent net" in which reality caught, but the method is an element of the reality.[4]

It is not possible to separate method and contents of theology, they are like the two sides of the same coin. Since theological method is often determined by the context in which theology is constructed and the vision of theologians drawn from the context, there are many theologies and methods. It is evident in the history of Christian thought that the choice of method has been differed widely among the theologians depending on the social and historical context in which theology was constructed. For instance, while "corelation" is the method for Paul Tillich, "action-reflection" is the method for liberation theologians.

Both in science and theology, it is the presupposition or the vision developed from a particular social context which determines the choice of methodology. Anders Nygren expresses this well,

> In all sciences as in all experiences there are certain general presuppositions which we do and must make because apart from them no science and no experience whatever would be possible. Without these presuppositions everything becomes meaningless. Hence we are led from the question of meaning to that of method. In seeking to elicit these universal, inescapable presuppositions, philosophy has to emply, besides the general analysis of concept, a method particularly suited to its purpose, namely 'the logical analysis of basic presuppositions.[5]

What Nygren called 'presuppositions' may be legitimately called a theological 'vision'. For some theologians, particularly for liberation theologians, a theological method is not merely a means of arriving at logical truth, as in Nygren's statement. For them it is a means of articulating their vision of society. To a large extent, one's theological vision determines the way one does theology. It is therefore important

---

4 Paul Tillich, *Ibid.*, p. 60

5 While Anders Nygren regards method as the logical analysis of basic presuppositions, liberation theologians perceive it as a means of arriving at their thological vision. *Meaning and Method: Prolegomena to a Scientific Philosophy of Religion and a Scientific Theory*, (Philadelphia: Fortress Press, 1972), p. 227

to discuss the theological vision of the churches or theologians in this region.

A. Theological Vision

The question that confronts the churches in general and theologians in particular in the Northest is how, adequately, to define the purpose or goal of the contextual theology which we are inending to construct. What is the goal or vision in our attempt to develop a contextual theology? Are we seeking understanding to arrive at logical truth or trying to defend the interests and traditions of our respective Christian denominations? Whenever I asked y students, particularly the first year students, to write a brief essay on the topic "Why do I study Theology?", most of them expressed that they want to know more about God. It is evident that the traditional understanding of the task of theology as 'faith seeking understanding' is very strong in the minds of our people. While understanding is important and necessary in every study, it is not the goal in itself, it is a means of achieving the goal. Education does not aim at accumulating information and cultivating skill alone. True education is concerned with the application of whatever knowledge and skill have been acquired, to the transformation of human society. Similarly theological education is concerned with the transformation of social and individual lives towards the fuller realization of the Kingdom of God. Realization of the Kingdom of God here and now is the goal of theology. In concrete terms, this realization of the Kingdom of God here and now means building a just, free, participatory, progressive, harmonious and sustainable society. In order to arrive at this goal, we have to develop such a theological methodology which will help us construct a contextual theology to inspire and challenge the churches in this region that they may sincerely strive for the realization of the Kingdom of God.

B. Paradigm Shift In Theology

Paradigm is similar with methodology but larger in its scope. Paradigm in theology means an interpretative model commonly agreed and shared by the members of community. It is specific and realistic set of agreed collective ideals. Methodology, on the other hand, does not have to be necessarily shared or agreed collectively, it can be developed and used by individual scholars. However, a particular methodology of individual scholars can be developed into a new paradigm bringing about shift from the old paradigm. Basing on Thomas S. Kuhn's idea of paradigm, Hans Küng defines it as follows:

> For my own part I am equally happy to speak of interpretative models, explanatory models for understanding. By this I mean by the term 'paradigm' an entire constellation of beliefs, value and techniques and so on shared by the members or a given community.[6]

Obviously, in the history of Christianity, a shift of theological paradigm has taken place from time to time. Such a shift may be briefly outlined as follows: a eschatological paradigm of early church was overlapped with and followed by an apologetic paradigm, then came a meditative paradigm, a rationalistic paradigm, a reformation paradigm, a liberal paradigm, a contextual paradigm and then a liberation paradigm. We cannot but ask, why has the shifting of theological paradigms taken place?

A new paradigm of theology usually emerges due to a change of situation. It is quite evident from history, both in theology and natural science, that whenever an old paradigm becomes obsolete and inadequate to meet contemporary needs, a new paradigm emerges.[7] Whenever such a shift of paradigm occured, the old paradigm seldom disappeared completely. David J. Bosch rightly aserts that in the field of religion, a paradigm shift always means both continuity and change, both faithfulness to the past and boldness to engage the future, both constancy and contingency, both tradition and transformation.[8] It is the failure of traditional paradigm to address to the problems faced by the churches in North East India which necessitates a new contextual theological paradigm.

C. Major Issues in Contextual Theology

In the world of theology, the most significant development that has taken place in recent years is the emergenece of contextual theology.

---

6 Hans Küng and David Tracy (ed.), *The Paradigm Change in Theology: A Symposium for the Future*, (Edinburg: T & T Clark, LTD., 1989), p. 7

7 Hans Küng, "Paradigm Change in Theology: A Proposal for Discussion," *Paradigm Change in Theology, Ibid.*, p. 20 & 23

8 David J. Bosch, *Transforming Mission: Paradigm Shift in Theology of Mission*, (Maryknoll: Orbis Books, 1991), p. 366

Though contextualization has been the way of doing theology throughout the history of Christian thought, the introduction of the Theological Education Fund in the World Council of Churches is primarily responsible for the development of contextual theology in recent years. The role that WCC has played in the development of contextual theology is vigorously promotional. WCC by itself does not construct a contextual theology; it encourages and enables theological institutions and individual theologians in their efforts to develop theology in their own contexts.

The movement for self-hood in politics and the process of de-colonization that have given birth to new independent nations have at the same time created self-awareness among the Christians in the former colonies. This new reality eventually produced a contextual theology. Development of contextual theology in the Third World countries is a part of the larger movement of liberation and self-hood. In this development the Theological Education Fund of WCC has played a significant role. The Central Committee of WCC expressed its commitment to understand the implication of the gospel that both challenges and is challenged by the cultures in which it finds itself, in order that the churches and individual Christians may live and witness authentically.[9] Contextual theology is a theological expression of the movement for self-hood. In fact, supporting, self-propagating and self-governing, but not 'self-theologizing'. Emergence of contextual theology in the Third World can be interpreted as a sign of maturity of the churches.

We will now briefly discuss some of the major methodological issues of the contextual theology such as: *the meaning of contextual theology, its validity, its concerns, the relationship between the particularity and the universality in the contextual theology and its criteria.*

1. Meaning : What do we mean by contextual theology? Contextual theology may be broadly defined as a systematic and coherent articulation of how a community of faith confesses Christ in a particular context. Bevans more specifically defines it as a way of doing theology in which one takes into account: the spirit and mesage of the gospel; the tradition of the Christian people; the culture in which one is theologizing;

---

9 Cited by S. Wesley Ariarajah, *Gospel and Culture: An Ongoing Discussion Within the Ecumenical Movement*, (Geneva: WCC, 1995), p. i

and social change in that culture, whether brought about by Western technological processes or the grass-roots struggle for equality, justice, and liberation.[10]

In theological literatures, we often encounter terms like contextualization, inculturation and indigenization that, sometimes, create confusion. Inculturatio and indigenization are interchangeably used and are increasingly treated as more or less the same. They are theologizing methods which focus on articulation of the Christian faith for a particular culture.[11] As the members of the Theological Education Fund wrote when the term was introduced in 1972 :

> Indigenization tends to be ued in the sense of responding to the Gospel in term of a traditional culture. Contextualization, while not ignoring this, takes into account the process of secularism, technology and the struggle for human justice, which characterized the historical movement of nations in the Third World.[12]

Contextual theology is a departure from classical theology which conceived theology as a science of faith draw from scripture and tradition. What makes a contextual theology different from classical theology is primarily its locus. Contextual theology, without ignoring the importance of scriptures and tradition, considers culture, socio-economic and political issues and the struggle of people for their liberation as important sources of theology.

2. Validity : Contextualization of theology is the very nature of Christianity. As Duraisigh rightly stated that at the heart of Christian faith lies the affirmation that "the Word become flesh". This implies that God chose to reveal himself in a particular context and through a

---

10 Stephen B. Bevans, *Models of Contextual Theology: Faith and Culture*, (Maryknoll: Orbis Books, 1992), p. 1

11 Ruy O. Costa, "Inculturation, Indigenization and Contextualization," *One Faith Many Cultures: Inculturation, Indigenization and Contextualization*, (Maryknoll: Orbis Book, 1988), p. xii

12 Theological Education Fund, *Ministry in Context:* The Third Mandate Programme of the Theological Education Fund of WCC (1970-1977), (Bromley, Kent: New Life Press, 1972), p. 20

particular culture.[13] There is no question about the validity of the need for constructing a contextual tribal theology. Theology must be contextual because cultural differences are intrinsic to human nature.[14] Just as 'culture shapes the human voice that answers the voice of Christ',[15] so too the way we perceive the message of God in Christ is different from culture to culture. It is not possible to think of one theology for all ages and places. Constructing a contextual theology is therefore a theological imperative.

The age of "Euro-centric theology" has come to an end with the end of colonialism. Today, the churches planted by Western missionaries are beginning to look at what they have inherited as the gospel message and "Christian" culture. And they have a fuller awareness of the need to own the gospel anew in their own culture, and expressed it in an idiom and concept that make sense to their own people. There is a new self-confidence on the part of those who do theology from various cultural perspective as well as from the perspective of women and the marginalized in society.[16]

3. Concern : The fundamental concern of contextual theology is how to confess Christ authentically in different cultures. Confessing Christ in a particular cultural context cannot be universalised, for it is shaped by a particular culture. Therefore, confessing Christ in different cultural contexts certainly requires different theologies. When the confession of Christ in a particular context is articulated in the form of theology, it is the situation of the context in which one constructs theology which determines the theological articulation. That is necessary because the purpose of constructing a contextual theology is to help the community of faith in a particular socio-cultural context to understand Christian faith. A profound understanding of faith would enable the gospel to take root in the culture of the people in a way that will eventually lead them towards realization of the Reign of God.

---

[13] C. Duraisingh, "Forward," *Gospel and Culture: On going Discussion within the Ecumenical Movement*, (Geneva: WCC, 1995), p. i

[14] S.B. Bevans, *Op cit.*, pp. 1, 2, 10

[15] *Bangkok Assembly 1973, Minutes and Reports of the Assembly of the CWME*, (Geneva: WCC, 1973), p. 73

[16] S. Wesley Ariarajha, *Gospel and Culture: An Ongoing Discussion Within the Ecumenical Movement*, (Geneva: WCC, 1995), p. vi

We observe today that new ways of understanding the Gospels have emerged. The churches in Latin America, in the context of poverty and oppression of the masses, understood Gospel as liberation and developed a liberation theology. This theology, which methodologically has evolved from 'action-reflection' (praxis), regards the gospel primarily as "Good News to the Poor". Similarly the *Dalits* in India, who have been suffering from oppression in the caste-ridden society of India, developed a liberation theology of their own, known as *Dalit Theology*. For them Gospel is good news about the liberation of *Dalits* from the oppression of the caste system and from social stigma. Christians in Asia, living in the context of religious pluralism, have developed a theology which regards an inter-religious dialogue as the primary method of theology. Likewise, the tribals in North East India must develop a theology of their own if they want the Gospel to take root deep into their culture and become effective.

4. Universality andParticularity : The question that has been often asked in the construction of a local theology is how it should be related to Christian fundamental belief. The incarnation of God took place in a particular place in a particular time, yet it has universal meaning. Thus Christians universally confess "one faith in Christ" but the confession is shaped by local culture where it is confessed. The Assembly of CWME in Bangkok (1973) rightly said,

> The universality of Christian faith does not contradict its particularity. Christ has to be responded to in a particular situation. Many people try to give universal validity to their particular response instead of acknowledging that the diversity of responses to Christ is essential precisely because they are related to particular situations and are thus relevant and complementary.[17]

Today, the diversity of theological methods and reflections certainly creates confusion in some circles. It is certainly important that theologians from different cultural contexts should work together to develop a vital and coherent theology. However, working for a vital and coherent theology does not mean that the diversity should be minimized; rather it has to be held together as a mosaic to enrich

---

[17] *Bangkok Assembly 1973, Minutes and Reports of the Assembly of CWME*, p. 74

Christian theology.[18] Rather than distorting the gospel truth, diversity will reveal the rich complexity of the gospel truth. We are led, then, to confront the question of how to hold diversity together? To what extent should a contextual theology be allowed to be different? What should be the limit of diversity? What should be the criteria for constructing a contextual theology?

5. Criteria : It is not easy to work out criteria for judging the authencity of contextual theology. Contextual theology is concerned with the relationship between Gospel and Culture. We have noted that Gospel and culture debates in WCC had often been paralyzed by the effort of finding 'gospel criteria' to judge culture.[19] C. Duraisingh, Director of CWME, admitted in his report that, 'it is easier to note the crucial importance of the relationship of gospel and culture than to suggest ways to secure a creative interrelationship of the two'.[20] It is certainly difficult to work out criteria for contextual theology which has emerged from a particular social-cultural context. At the same time, we are aware of the problem that unless there are certain criteria to judge the orthodoxy of contextual theology, there is the danger that a contextual theology may be captivated by the context. This would mean contextualism, not contextualization of Christian faith.

The fundamental question of criteria for contextual theology is the question of "truth". Does uniersal truth exist? In other words, can we really talk about universal truth, essence, core value, metaphysical or moral principle? Is there anything we can define as a "pure gospel"? While Charles Kraft suggested that there is, Hyun-Kyung Chung would question the existing criteria known as "gospelcriteria" and ask, "Who has the right to decide that I am wrong, and on what basis?"[21] For her and many others, truth emerges from the context itself because God has created human beings with the ability to know and practise truth, even before they embraced Christianity. While I agree with the view that truth is relative, and the validity of the truth is perceived from its

18 S. Wesley Ariarajah, *Gospel and Culture: An Ongoing Discussion within the Ecumenical Movement*, (Geneva: WCC, 1994), p. 35

19 S.W. Ariarajah, *Ibid*, p. 38

20 Frederick R. Wilson, *The San Antonio Report: Your Will Be Done - Mission in Christ's Way*, (Geneva: WCC, 1990), p. 123

21 S.W. Ariarajah, *Op cit.* p. 16

function or applicability to a particular context, I cannot deny the existence of the essence or core value of the gospel. If this does not exist, we cannot speak of contextualizing faith, for there would be no faith distinct from what is already in the context to be contextualized. At the same time, I believe that the essence or core value does not exist out there in isolation, but it is to be found in the context itself. As the core value of the gospel pervades all culture, it is found in every culture, albeit in the imperfect form. That core value can be received from outside of one's own culture (Judeo - Western tradition) as well as from one's own culture. Our theological task is to re-discover the essence that has been present in the tribal culture and engage in the dialogue with the gospel. In other words, the method of contextualization is a dialogical interaction of the tribal culture and the gospel.

Whenever the gospel is received from outside of one's own culture, contextualization is necessary. Since the gospel is present in every culture in an imperfect form, re-discovery of the hidden gospel from one's own culture is necessary to interact with the gospel received from outside. Then only the Christian gospel will be contextualized. This is the reaso why I often use the term "re-discovery" of the gospel truth from my own culture and tradition. The fact is that the hidden gospel in my culture and tradition is not ex;icit until my faith in Christ encounters both me as an individual person and my community as a whole. In the light of my faith in Christ, I have begun to recognise the presence of Christ in my culture. Contextualization is therefore a process of interaction between the hidden gospel re-discovered from my own culture and the gospel preached to me by missionaries. In fact, when missionaries preached the gospel, they certainly did not write in the blank paper. The gospel was preached to the people who had their own culture and traditions. A dialogical interaction of the gospel and the culture of the receiving people is self evident. The tragedy is that in the process of interaction, the hidden gospel in the tribal culture was ignored, dominated and not theologically articulated.

We may conclude that the core value of the Gospel which Christ has proclaimed does exist, and the same Gospel is also found in every culture in an imperfect form. The interaction of the gospel and culture in a particular context helps people to understand the hidden gospel in their own culture. The articulation of faith in Jesus Christ with the help of that hidden gospel often makes theology more meaningful and effective. This is nothing but contextualization.

The question of criteria is concerned with how to rediscover the elements of gospel from one's own culture. How a theologizing is often determined by his/her theological agenda. Those who have the issue of identity as their primary theological agenda usually take their culture seriously, in some cases romanticize, even absolutize their culture. Instead of the gospel judges the culture, the gospel is judged by culture, in which case gospel is becoming captive to the culture. The Vancouver WCC Assembly expressed this concern that "we need to be aware of the possibility of our witnesses to the Gospel becoming captive to any culture, recognizing the fact that all cultures are judged by the Gospel.[22] Those who regard liberation as their primary theological agenda also take culture seriously but are critical of their culture and selective in the use of their culture. In fact, it is the theological vision or goal which judges the authenticity of contextual theology. Any contextual theology is judged by its contribution to the achievement of its goal which is realization of the Kingdom of God. For this I use "re-discovery of transformational motifs" from the tribal tradition as my method of constructing a tribal theology.

An authentic contextual theology has to be a reflection upon action which should lead to further action to transform human society and individual lives. However, all actions are not necessarily Christian in spirit and motive, so that any theological expression that leads to actions that are clearly un-Christian cannot be considered orthodox. Praxis must be validated by orthodoxy. It has to be "orthopraxis". For example, the present ethnic violence in North East India cannot be considered as orthodox because it is against the Christian basic value; it is a destructive but not transformative action.

The validity of any contextual theology depends on its inner consistency and relationship to the fundamental Christian values and beliefs. Every theology must be logically consistent. It must enable a coherent understanding of what it asserts about reality as a whole, about God and about Christian practice and as such it must be believable to any person who is open to it. The presentation may be narrative or

[22] Cited in *New Directions in Mission & Evangelization*, p. 55

logical, above all else, it must be coherent in its account of faith and in its relation to other dimensions of life.

Contextual theology must be translatable into worship. It must be incorporated into the preaching, the hymns, the prayers and the litanies of the Christian worship. If this is not possible, the validity of that particular contextual theology is questionable. Such theology will remain abstract and irrelevant.

Contextual theology myst be open to criticism and change. The nature of constant change is both the weakness and the strength of contextual theology. As the society in which we live is changing, a relevant theology cannot be static. It must be opened to critical re-evaluation and, if necessary, to re-construction to meet the need of the context.

D. Models of Contextual Theology

It is important to consider at least some major approaches of contextual theology that may help us to understand what we are doing. Models are certainly helpful for distinguishing various approaches, but they can not be rigidly classified and followed. It is, therefore, not possible to draw a precise boundary line between the models. They are often intertwined or overlapped one with another.

1. Transplantation model : This view represents the traditional missionary model which regarded the Western culture as the only valid expression of Christian culture, and considered every thing non-Christian as the product of deprived human existence under the control of Satan.[23] This view is based on a linear view of history which suggests the moder Western society as the goal for all human societies. From this view arose a theology of social Darwinism. The ignorance, insentivity and outright rejection of other cultures as "primitive", "pagan", "heathen" or "savage" has been well documented in the history of Christian mission. John Mbiti, an African theologian, strongly condemns this view :

> Missionary culture told Africans in effect, that unless you are circumcised you cannot inherit the Kingdom of God... Unless they become culturally Westernised, Lutheranised,

---

[23] John T Seamands, *Tell It Well: Communicating the Gospel Across Cultures*, (Missouri: Beacon Hill Press, 1981), p. 42

> Methoditised, Anglicanised, Roman Catholicised, Presbyterianised, Africans cannot inherit one centimetre of Christian faith.[24]

Here the issue of contextualization does not arise. For them the Western Culture is the only valid expression of Christianity, no other culture being sufficient to express Christian faith. There is no room for contextualization of theology. The theology that was constructed in the West has to be transplanted in a foreign soil, imposed on the people whether they understand it or not; whether it is meaningful or not, recipients have to learn and believe it. While this type of extremely negative attitude towards other cultures has almost disappeared and most of which Western missionaries themselves would reject, unfortunately it remains in North East India. The existing popular theology is built upon the foundation of Western imperial philosophy.

This model of theology is mainly practiced by conservative Christians. As they hold to the Christian traditions they first received, they are very skeptical about any new ideas and uncritical and literalistic in their interpretation of the Bible. As many lay leaders including some theologians who have graduated from conservative theological colleges and seminaries supported this view, it has become a great hurdle for development of contextual theology. Basically they are biblicist, not biblical, who believe in the verbal inspiration and infallibility of the Bible.

2. Fulfilment Model : This view, like the transplantational model, maintains that Christianity is above all other cultures, because Jesus Christ is the great hero of human culture. In him, it is believed, the best aspirations of men and women towards their traditional values are brought to a point of culmination. Jesus Christ confirms what is best in the past, and guides the process of civilization to its proper goal.[25] J.N. Farquhar, in his famous book, *The Crown of Hinduism*, argues that Christ provides the fulfilment of the highest aspiration of Hinduism. He is the crown of the faith of India.[26] Hendrik Kraemer, a leading figure in

---

24 John Mbiti, "African Indigenous Culture in Relation to Evangelism and Church Development," *The Gospel and Frontier People*, ed. R. Pierce Beaver, (Pasaden: William Carey Library, 1992), p. 82

25 H.R. Niebuhr, *Christ and Culture*, (New York: Harper and Row, 1951), p. 45

26 J.N. Farquhar, *The Crown of Hinduism*, (London: Oxford University Press, 1930), p. 45

the debate of the International Missionary Council, 1938, took seriously religious and cultural diversity, and advocated a certain measure of indifenization and adaptation but maintained the 'unbridgeable gulf' between Christianity and other religions.[27] Kraemer certainly recognised the presence of truth in other cultures, but for him, that is not same as the gospel truth. There is no link between the two, and certainly no continuity.

Many of the Christian leaders in North East India subscribed to this view. They are not completely negative to their own culture. They do recognise some good things in their own culture, but, like Kreamer, they believe that the good things are not compatible with the gospel in substance. They are only preparatory fo the gospel. C.L. Hmings, one of the church leaders of Mizoram, argues that the gospel has fulfilled and transformed the Mizo culture.[28] Hminga is quite critical about the Mizo traditional culture, but does not fail to recognise some good things in it like *tlawmngaihna* although for him it is only *praeparatio evangelii*. Similarly, O. Alem, in his book *Tsungremology: Ao Naga Christian Theology*, supports this view. He also considers Naga (Ao) culture as mere *praeparatio evangelii*.[29] Practitioners of this model are willing to do certain measures of indigenization but find fuller expression in Western culture. Subsequently they adopt the Barthian dialectical theology for their theological framework.

The problem with this view is the affirmation of the nation that Western culture is the only valid expression of Christian faith. It fails to evaluate critically the underlying philosophy of imperialism that influenced, and even shaped, Christian theology. The very consideration of tribal culture as *praeparatio evangelii* encourages a perspective that limits God's revelation and activities in the tribal culture. This view is not consistent with the Christian belief that Christ is the cosmic Christ whose salvific activities pervade the whole world.

---

27 Henrik Kraemer, *The Christian Message in a Non-Christian World*, (New York: Harper and Brothers, 1938), pp. 368, 56

28 C.L. Hminga, *The Life and Witness of the Churches in Mizoram*, (Serkawn: Baptist Church of Mizoram, 1987), p. 287ff

29 O. Alem, *Tsungremlogy: Ao Naga Christian Theology*, (Mokokchung: Clark Theological College, 1994), p. 12ff

3. Translation Model : Basically there are two methods of translation - (a) a literalistic, word-for-word translation and (b) a functional, dynamic translation which is concerned with dynamic equivalence rather than formal correspondence of word with word. In this model, 'translation' is used in the sense of dynamic equivalence. In this sense, translation does not mean a mere word-for-word translation, literally translating the theology constructed in the West into the tribal language in North East India. Rather, it is concerned with translating the meaning of theology into another language of different cultural context. Charles Kraft explains,

> Theological truth must be re-created like a dynamic-equivalence translation or transculturation within the language accompanying conceptual framework of the hearer if its true relvevance is to be properly perceived by them. Theologizing, like all Christian communication, must be directed to someone if it is to serve its purpose. It cannot be flung out into thin air.[30]

The fundamental assumption of this model is that Christianity contains an essential element, a supra-cultural message which can be separated from a culturally bound mode of expression. The supra-cultural element must be translated without alteration. In other words, the essence of the gospel is unchanging, above all cultures, and should not be altered. It can only be translated or communicated in the way that is understandable and meaningful to the hearers. Practitioners of this model are concerned with meaningful communication of the gospel, and meaningful communication requires encoding-decoding-encoding of the message. Contextualization of the gospel message also requires 'decontextualization' of the message that was already contextualized in a particular context for 're-contextualization'. Hesselgrave insists that decontextualization is needed in order to arrive at the supra-cultural message which is to be conveyed in a culturally meaningful form.[31] He says,

> Decontextualization is needed in order to arrive at the supracultural message which is conveyed in culturally

[30] Kraft, *Christianity in Culture*, p. 297

[31] D. Hesselgrave, *Communicating Christ Cross-Culturally*, (Michigan, Grand Rapids: Zondervan, 1979), pp. 67-86

> meaningful forms. The cultural wrappings must be folded back in order to get the gift of truth - the Western wrappings of the missionary's culture (where the missionary is a Westerner) and also the wrapping of biblical culture itself. When one come to the Scriptures, he must be especially cautious, for in the Bible God Himself chose the language and forms by which the truth came to be unfolded. The words are God's; as well as the truth... As for *contextualization* it is needed to make the message meaningful, relevant, persuasive, and effective within the respondent culture.[32]

This view is widely supported by evangelical scholars, including Pope John Paul. In the history of Christian thought, we noted that Brahmabandhav Upadhyaya, Bishop Appasamy and many others in India believed that Christian faith should be interpreted using the categories of the Indian religious and philosophical tradition.[33] Brahmabandhav Upadhyaya suggested that in India the philosophy of Aristotle could be replaced by the *Advaita* philosophy of Sankara, and the *Vedas* be used as a part of the Old Testament for the Indian church. [34] Similarly, Robin Boyd used *advaita* philosophy to interpret, redefine and to wrap the gospel in India.[35] However, this effort has been recently criticized by Dalit theologians because the use of advaita not only reaffirms but re-enforces Brahmanism which provides a philosophical basis for the caste system in India.

Most of the renowed theologians in North East India explicitly or implicitly support this model of contextual theology. Zairema, a church leader from Mizoram who has been greatly involved in the translation

---

32 Hesselgrave, *Communicating Christ Cross Culturally*, p. 86

33 Bishop A.S. Appasamy (1848-1926) and Brahmabandhav Upadhyaya (1861-1907) were church leaders as well as theologians who made significant contributions to the development of Indian Christian Theology.
M.M. Thomas and P.T. Thomas, *Towards Indian Christian Theology: Life and Thoughts of Some Pioneers*, (Tiruvalla: New Day Publications of India, 1992), pp 57-62, 71-76

34 J. Russel Chandran, "Development of Christian Theology in India: A Critical Survey:, in *Readings in Indian Christian Theology*, Vol. I, ed. by R.S. Sugirtharajah, (Delhi: ISPCK, 1993), p. 8

35 R.H.S. Boyd, *Khristadvaita: A Theology for India*, (Madras: CLS, 1977)

of the Mizo Bible, has long advocated the use of dynamic equivalence. To certain degree, he practised his method in the actual translation of the Mizo Bible.[36] Lalsawma, a Mizo theologian, lamented over the erosion of Mizo culture and held the conservative theology of missionaries to be responsible. For him the gospel is not inculturated in Mizoram and this has eventually shaken the foundation of Mizo society.[37] For him inculturation is nothing but a dynamic translation of the gospel.

Renthy Keitzar, one of the outstanding biblical scholars in North East India, advocates this model.[38] He, like Lalsawma, is critical of the popular theology and type of Christianity in North East India. For him, the message of the gospel has not sufficiently gone deep into the tribal culture; it has not taken root firmly in that soil.[39] In his early writings R. Keitzer has expressed that Christianity is not indigeneous to Nagaland, it has to be indigenized if its message is to be locally or regionally relevent to the Nagas. In his recent writings he also has admitted the process of indigenization that has been going on since the inception of Christianity in this region Keitzer's view is that although Christianity in North East India has been indigenized to a certain degree that is not sufficient, it has to be inculturated. Addressing the question of how the gospel should be made relevant in North East India, he expresses :

> The tribal thought forms, ideas, theological terms, life situations, and so on be adopted with adaptations in interpreting Christian ideas, so the gospel truth can be made relevant to whom it is proclaimed. The tribal way of thinking has some affinity with Hebrew and as such the biblical ideas can easily be translated (or trans-communicated) to the tribal languages. But, on the other hand, one should watch against the danger or tendency of assimilating animistic elements

36 Zairema, "Bible Translation in North East India," *A Trainer of Leaders: Essays in Honour of [illegible]*, Edited by Renthy Keitzar, (Jorhat. Eastern Theological College, 1989), pp. 16-19

37 Lalsawma, "The Shaking of Foundations in Mizo Society," *Mizoram Today*, Vol. I, No. 2, (21 January, 1975)

38 Renthy Keitzar has made significant contributions to the development of tribal theology in NEI. A collection of his articles is published in a book entitled *In Search of A Relevant Gospel Message*, (Guwahati: Christian Literature Centre, 1995).

39 Renthy Keitzar, *Ibid*, p. 63

into Christian faith because such intrusion may distort the gospel truth. Any tribal theological term or idea be used only as linguistic vehicle, a communication of the gospel truth through a medium of language.[40]

Like Kraft and Hesselgrave, Keitzar is concerned for communicating or interpreting the gospel in a way that is meaningful to the tribal people. Like any other Third World theologian, he identifies that Christian theology is not in NEI and acknowledges the need for tribal theology. He is aware of what Christianity is not in North East India, and confronted with the task of telling what it should be.

The method he suggests for constructing a contextual tribal theology is 'translational approach' i.e. an interpretation of the gospel's essence in the tribal context. The problem with those who advocate this model is to identify the essential elements or the core of the gospel as distinct from the culturally bound message. It is extremely difficult to distinguish the essential elements or the pure gospel messages from the culturally bound message. Though the task of identifying the core elements of the gospel is difficult, interpretation of the gospel for a particular context is one of the essential part of contextual theology.

4. Dialogical Model : This approach is primarily the contribution of Asian theologians in general and Indian theologians in particular. For many years, a few thinkers in India have been contemplating the problem of witnessing to Christ in the pluralistic context of India in which the Christian community has to exist in the midst of Hindu, Buddhist, Jain, Sikh and Tribal communities. Like any other communities, the Christian community also encounters different ideologies and new cultures emerging from moder science and technologies. Increasingly, they have been dissatisfied with the traditional missiological approach which condemned other religions and eventually disrupted the harmony of the community. With reference to a traditional missiological approach to other faiths, J. Samartha expresses that there is a hidden agenda in this approach to show the inadequacy of other religions.[41] Practitioners of

---

40 Renthy Keitzar, *Ibid*, p. 1

41 S.J. Samartha, "Dialogue in a Religiously Pluralistic Society" *The Multi-Faith Context of India: Resources and Challenges for Christians*, ed. by Israel Selvanayagam, (Bangalore: The Board of Theological Text Books Programme of South Asia, 1994), p. 5

dialogical model have recognized this approach as harmful and destructive to the harmony of Indian society. Such an approach, with its inbuilt injustice, is seen as obsolete and impracticable. So they have been engaged themselves in the search for alternative means of witnessing to Christ in the pluralistic context of Asia.

They are generally sympathetic and open to other religions. The change of attitude towards other religion has been taking place as the Western Christians were exposed to other cultures interacting with other faiths. It was openly expressed in the International Missionary Conference held in Tambaram (Madras) in 1938. William Hocking, a strong opponent of Kraemer in the Tambaram Conference, considered that *'the osmosis of cultures and religions'* would bring about a kind of synthesis of the 'unlosable essence' of religion in which a major theological task would be the reconception of certain cultures. Similarly the dialogical model assumes that God's revelation is not limited to only one particular religion; God's salvific activities operate in all religions and cultures. Raimond Pannikar argues that in all religions, Christ whom he calls the *Mystery* is already present in a hidden and imperfect manner. "There is a living presence of that *Mystery* which Christians call *Christ.*"[42] Similarly, Rusell Chandran argued from the perspective of creation in the Nairobi WCC Assembly that "The theology of creation affirms the presence and work of God in all cultures. Our confession of Christ as Lord is an affirmation that he is Lord, not only of Christians but of all peoples. He is the *Logos* who holds all things together."[43]

This approach has in fact been used in India, at least by a few radical thinkers, for many years. Robert de Nobili (1577-1656), the Mardras rethinking group (1880-1960) and P.D. Devanandan (1901-1962), to a certain content, had used this approach which is now being developed and expressed by a few scholars such as Raymond Pannikar, S.J. Samartha, Israel Selvanayagam and others. The present Indian Christian Theology, being studied in all the colleges under the Senate of Serampore, basically uses this approach.

---

[42] R. Pannikar, *The Unknown Christ of Hinduism,* (London: Darton, Longman & Todd, 1981), pp. 2, 49

[43] Russel Chandran quoted in the report of Section III: 'Seeking Community,' *Breaking the Barriers, Nairobi 1975.* The Official Report of the Fifth Assembly of the WCC, ed. David M. Paton, (London: SPCK, 1976), p. 71

The theological task in this approach may be summarized with the words of S.J. Samartha that, 'while Christianity with its faith in Jesus Christ as Lord and Saviour can help Hindu spirituality to recover a sense of the personal, the historical and the social, the Hindu insight into *the larger unity of all life* can help Christianity to overcome *a narrow view of revelation as confined to the historical, thus isolating it from nature and from human consciousness.*'[44] Samartha's contention is that the interaction between Hinduism and Christianity should be two ways traffic, both mutually transforming each other. The openness to other faiths with willingness to learn from others and allow ourselves to be changed, if necessary, is fundamental to its methodology. Pannikar suggests that an attitude of inclusion and a magnanimous attitude which admits positive and true values outside one's own tradition, will open the road for intra-religious dialogue.[45] The primary concern and goal of dialogical theology is mutual co-existence through tolerance, not the painful search for theological meaning. Samartha has said, "Dialogue stands for an attempt on the part of Christians in a post-colonial and pluralistic society to build up new relationships with their neighbours of other faith."[46]

The problems with this approach is its objective which is primarily mutual co-existence in the pluralistic society. The mission of the Christian church, whether it is in the pluralistic situation or not, is not merely harmony of the society, but realization of the Kingdom of God. As long as Hinduism legitimizes the caste system without recognising the existence of social-structural sin within Hinduism itself, should the 'harmony of society' be used as the goal of dialogue? Similarly, as long as Christians hold on the uniqueness of Jesus Christ, is genuine dialogue possible? Since dialogue has to do with other faiths, would it be possible to translate into worship in the congregational level, apart from occasional experiments in theological seminaries and conferences? The usual Christian worship is monologue, certainly not dialogue. If it is not translatable into the Christian worship, should dialogue be treated as a method of a contextual Christian theology?

---

44 S.J. Samartha, *The Hindu Response to the Unbound Christ*, (Madras: CLS, 1974), p. 12

45 Raymond Pannikar, *The Inter-Religious Dialogue*, (New York: Paulist Press, 1978), pp. xiv-xix

46 S.J. Samartha, "Dialogue in a Religously Pluralistic Society", *Op cit*, p. 6

There are several questions that have been raised concerning dialogue. What is the place of conversion? Samartha certainly would say that conversion is a vertical conversion, not horizontal. In other words, it is turning to God, but not changing the community. Would a conversion really be complete until the 'turning to God' has resulted in 'turning to the community', the church? In fact, a vertical aspect of conversion is incomplete without a horizontal dimension of conversion. Christians, of course, have been talking quite seriously about dialogue, but people of other faiths are not serious about it. In the absence of reciprocity, is genuine dialogue possible? Until recently when Israel Selvanayagam and others started developing a theology of dialogue from the Dalit's perspective, dialogue in India has been largely from the Brahmanical perspective which does not contribute towards the liberation of Tribals and Dalits. There was for along time a strong and indeed pervasive tendency in the dialogical approach to integrate whatever is true and good in non-Christian religions into Christian theology. S. Kappen criticised this as imperialism under a new guise, seeking to annex the non-Christian world through an act of "ideological agreesion."[47] While practitioners of dialogue regarded themselves as 'risking Christ for Christ's sake', some saw them as escapists who avoided any confrontation.

A dialogical interaction of gospel and other cultures happen wherever the gospel is preached. Dialogue is obviously an integral part of evangelism, but the advocates of dialogue are critical of the Christians; attitude to other faiths which simply condemned other faiths and eventually disrupted the harmony of society. As they are concerned building a harmonious society in the pluralistic society through mutual learning from one another, they are opened to see the truth in other faith and willing to learn from others; but the actual dialogue often focus on the commonalities of Christian faith and the faith of dialogue partners, rather than analysing one's own faith critically. Unless dialogue is shifted from 'commonalities' to 'critical evaluation of one own faiths', it will not bring about radical social transformation.

47 S. Kappen, "Towards an Indian Theology of Liberation," *Readings in Indian Christian Theology*, Vol. I, edited by R.S. Sugirtharajah and Cecil Hargreaves, (1993). p. 33

No evidence has been uncovered in my research, up till now, of any substantial effort having been made in North East India to apply a dialogical model for the construction of theology. Practitioners of dialogue have not seriously thought about dialogue with primal religions. Certainly interaction between tribal religion and Christianity had happened, but that was not a conscious effort at dialogue. The interaction between the tribal culture and Christianity over the past one hundred years was spontaneous and natural, such interaction is more significant as far as construction of contextual theology is concerned. It would be more accurate to explain the interaction between tribal culture and Christianity with reference to the "synthetic model".

5. Synthetic Model : The fundamental assumption of this view is not different from the dialogical model mentioned above; both hold the view that culture is good and valuable, both take it as axiomatic that it is within human culture that God has been working and revealing divine truth, which is experienced and perceived in many different ways. Revelation is understod as something discovered in the context itself, not brought from outside. Christ is to be found in the values, symbols and behaviour patterns of a culture, and in the situations and events which effect culture.[48] Hence Christ is present in all cultures in a hidden and imperfect manner. However, a synthetic approach is different from the dialogical model in that the truth in any culture in itself is not regarded as adequate unless it interacts with the truth revealed in Jesus Christ. In other words, the hidden gospel in any culture is not adequate for faith until it is activated by the gospel of Christ. The encounter of these two, the revealed and the hidden gospels, may be explained with Gadamer's ideas of 'fusion of horizons' or Buber's "I-Thou" relationship.

A synthetic model is concerned with a relevant theology as any of the other contextual theologies. The source of theology is the fusion or interaction of the Judaeo - Christian tradition which came to us via Wester culture and with the recipient culture, for us, a tribal culture. To this extent it is the same as dialogue. While dialogue is looking for common ground and concerns with other faiths, a synthetic model is searching for a new theology resulting from the synthesis of the two, or the fusion of the two horizons. It is an honest and painful interaction as

[48] S. Bevans, "Models of Contextual Theology", *Missiology: An International Review*, Vol. XIII, No. 2, (April, 1985), pp. 185-202, p. 197

it seeks to disclose the inadequacies and fallacies of Christianity and other religions. As a result, a new form of Christianity or theology emerges which is what a synthetic model is searching for. The diagram given below may relfect the interaction of the two horizons.

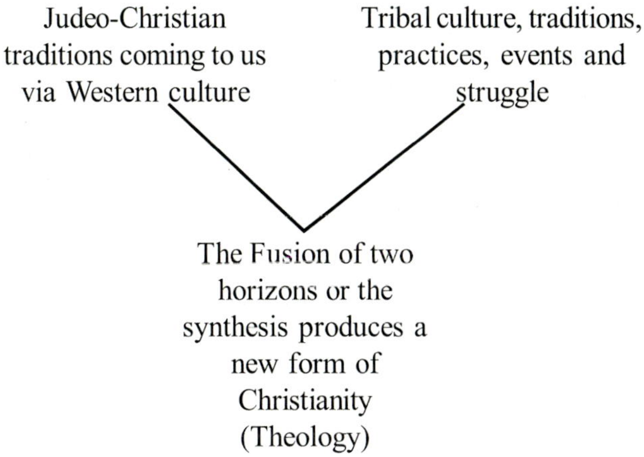

One may ask whether this is really possible. The answer is "Yes". It has happened, though not necessarily as the result of conscious effort. F.S. Downs, a missionary of the Board of International Ministries of the American Baptist Churches, who was born and brought up in North East India, argues that the type of Christianity in NEI is not merely a Western duplicate, it has taken a certain form of tribal culture.[49] It is a common knowledge among the church's leaders and theologians that a certain degree of indigenization had taken place. Renthy Keitzar, S.C. Daniel, Juanita War and Julian Marak have expressed the view that the interaction between Christianity and traditional tribal culture has been mutually compatible and salutary, especially in terms of sublimating their faith, and preserving tribal identities and their social-cultural traditions.[50]

---

49 Frederick S. Downs, "Christianity and Cultural Change in North East India", *Christian Faith and Multiform Culture in India*, edited by Somen Das, (Bangalore; United Theological College, 1987), p. 101

50 Renthy Keitzar, "A Study of the North-East India Tribal Christian Theology", S.C. Daniel, "Khasi Religion and Christianity. A Comparative Study"; Juanita War, "Family Structures, Customary Laws and Christianity: the Khasi Context"; Julius L.R. Mark, "Traditional Marriage Customs of the Garos", in *Religion and Society*, Vol. XXXIX, No. 4, (December, 1992).

Thus the structure of the Church in Mizoram is one which has evolved from the interaction of one type of Western ecclesial structure and the traditional tribal structure. It was the direct outcome of conscious effort on the part of pioneer missionaries to Mizoram. J.H. Lorrain wrote,

> Our experience has taught us that the *Lushais* (now known as Mizo) are born Methodist .... We are not here to make them Eastern duplicates of Western Baptist .... but ... to so guide them that they shall develop along their own national lines (cultural lines) into a strong Lushai Church of God, ... We look forward to the time when the Lushai Church shall be a happy blend of all that is best in Baptist, Presbyterian and Methodist, with something added perhaps which no Western denomination can supply.[51]

Different denominations have been existing in Mizoram, but all of them, the Presbyterian, the Baptist, the United Pentecostal Church, the Evangelical Church of Maraland, including the Salvation Army, have a similar ecclesial structure. The existing structure is a blended structure of the Western Methodist ecclesial structure ad the Mizo traditional social structure in which the chief and his elders were responsible for the administration of a village.

The revival was one of the primary factors, particularly in the Mizo society, for the inculturation of Christianity.It was the revival movement which swept through Mizoram several times, that brought the traditional drum, once rejected as Satanic instrument by missionaries, back into the Church.As a direct result of the revival movement, Mizo converts who used to sing only the translated hymns started composing songs and hymns of their own. The most interesting characteristic of these new songs and hymns is the tune which is neither exactly the Western tune nore the traditional Mizo tune; a synthetic new tune has emerged which really satisfies the Mizo believers. With these songs they could express their feeling and emotions, and be satisfied.

When I talk about contextualization of theology, I have been expecting that the same thing of what had happened in the development of songs and music would also happen in theology. But that has not taken place. The problem now is that the theology and dogmas of the

---

[51] *BMS Printed Report* for the Year 1914, p. 122v

Churches in NEI continue to remain alien to the culture. A genuine incarnation has not taken place. This could be one of the reasons that Christianity, although more visible in NEI then in any other part of India, does not take root deep in the culture and remains, in stead, superficial.

6. Praxis Model : If the dialogical and synthetic models focus on the cultural identity of the context, and the translation model focuses on communicating the given gospel or supra-cultural message, what distinguishes the praxis model is its focus on transformation or liberation of individuals as well as society. Differences in these various models are perhaps be best exemplified in the way revelation is perceived. While revelation is perceived in the dialogical and the synthetic models as hidden in every culture, in the translational model it is perceived as a supra-cultural message. The praxis model perceives revelation quire differently as God's on-going activities in history, manifested in daily individual and societal situations.

The terms "praxis" and "liberation" are interchangeable used in theology to describe the model that we are now to discuss, I prefer "praxis" for the simple reason that it is neutral and inclusive. When a certain stage of liberation is achieved in the struggle, the term "liberation" may no longer be helpful or meaningful. The method of ***praxis*** as "action-reflection" cannot be rejected as long as we try to construct a contextual relevant theology. Since praxis is the very method of liberation theology, it has been extensively discussed by prominent liberation theologians, and therefore enormous material for the subject is available.[52] The English word, "practice" is not an adequate translation of praxis,

---

[52] Some of the material which deals with Praxis Model of theology are: G. Gutierrez, *A Theology of Liberation* (1973); "Liberation, Praxis and Christian Faith", *Frontier Theology in Latin America*; Dermont A. Lane, *Foundation of Social Theology: Praxis and Action*, (1979), Clodovis Boff, *Theology and Praxis* (1978); R.J. Berstain, *Praxis and Action* (1979); N. Lobkowiz, *Theory and Practice: History of a Concept From Aristotle to Marx* (1967); H. Assamann, *Practical Theology of Liberation* (1973); Resbery, "Theological Method: Praxis and Liberation", *Communio: International Catholic Review*, Vol. 6, pp. 133-134 (1979); Anslem K. Min, "Praxis and Theology in Recent Debate"; *Scottish Journal of Theology*, Vol. 39, pp. 529-549; M. Gaiogh L. Nassan, "Liberation Praxis. Challenge to Lutheran Theology" *Dialog*, (Minnesota), Vol. 25, pp. 124-128, (1986), Glyn Richards, "Faith and Praxis in Liberation Theology, Bonhoeffer and Gandhi", *Modern Theology*, Vol. 3, (1987), pp. 359-373

especially when practice is used with its common meaning, as in "putting theory into practice." A proper understanding of praxis requires a different understanding of the relationship between 'practice' and 'theoty'.[53] They are twin moments of the same activity, dialectically united in praxis. Instead of theory leading to practice, theory becomes or is seen sas the reflective moment in praxis, and articulated theory arises from that praxis to yield future praxis.[54] Thus, theology become a critical reflection on action. An 'action-reflection for further action' is the hermeneutical circle which is spirally moving as indicated below :

---

53 For Aristotle, there are three ways of knowing truth - theory, praxis and *poiesia*. These represent speculative life, practical life and the productive life of human beings. A 'theoria' way of knowing is the quest for truth by a contemplative, reflective process. A 'praxis' way of knowing is by reflective engagement in a social situation. A 'poiesia' way of knowing is based on finishing product. For Hegel, praxis is self activities of Geist (spirit), the overall controlling principle of the universe. In Hegel there is unity of theory and praxis, a self-reflective form of theoria. (Berstaein, *Praxis and Action*, p. 34). For Karl Marx, the over-arching reality is not *Geist*, as Hegel claimed, but humankind in relationship with history particularly with economic production. The moving power is not divine providence but humanity's self-constitutive labour. Thus for Karl Marx, praxis is a self-initiated and a self-creating activity of human beings that is intentionally and reflectively done to transform social reality in the direction of human emancipation. Praxis for Marx is human praxis not *Geist* praxis. It is agency in history for freedom and emancipation. A praxis epistemology is central to Marx's understanding. The production of ideas, of conceptions, of consciousness "does not determine life, but life determines consciousness," K. Marx, 'German Ideology' (1845) in *Writings of Young Marx on Philosophy and Society*, edited by L.D. Easton and K.H. Guddat, New York: Doubleday, 1976, pp. 414-415. Liberation theologians have certainly adopted Marxian concept of praxis.

54 Thomas H. Groome, *Christian Religious Education: Shaing Our Story and Vision*, (San Francisco: Harper & Row Publisher, 1980), p. 152

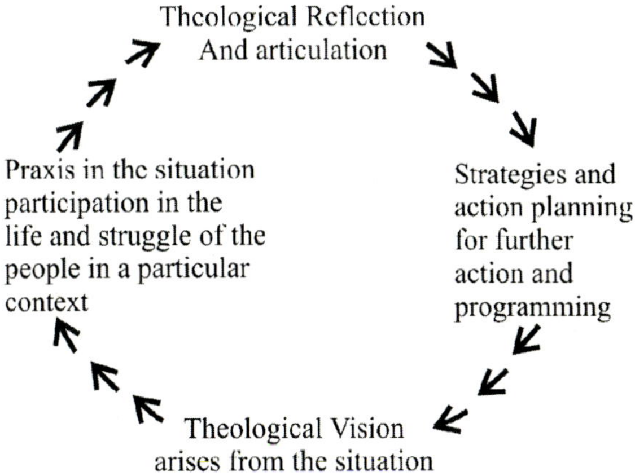

This approach takes the culture of the people seriously because people are the subject of theology. Since the primary criterion for juding the authencity of theology is how it transforms both individual and social lives, no culture is uncritically accepted or rejected. Theology in this approach is a reflection on action for further action. By definition, then, theology cannot be static. It must be dynamic, progressive and processive. What matters is praxis - the praxis which acts as a corrective to theory and brings about change in theory. Praxis, though inspired by theory, is the norm of theory, it exercises a critical function vis-a-vis all theory.[55] Thus praxis becomes the source and criterion of theology. The praxis model understands the objective of theology not so much as the development of the right formulas of "right thinking" (orthodoxy), but rather it sees as the ultimate goal of theology "right doing" (orthopraxis).[56] As most of the practitioners of this model address concrete social problems, social analysis has become an integral part of the method. Our theological task in this approach is both involvement in and reflection on people's struggle for their liberation.

In North East India no substantial theological reflection on the struggle of the people has been made. V.K. Nuh's book *Nagaland Church and Politics* is one of the non-academic reflections on the Naga people's struggle for liberation.[57] Wati Aier who is very much

---

55 Dermont A. Lane, *Foundation of Social Theology: Praxis, Process and Salvation*, (London: Gill and Macmillan, 1984), p. 63

56 Bevans, "Models of Contextual Theology", *Missiology*, p. 193

57 V.K. Nuh, *Nagaland Church and Politics*, (Kohima: V. Nuh and Bro., 1986).

influenced by Latin American Liberation theology has made a theological reflection on the struggle of the people in Nagaland.[58] It is more or less a Naga version of the Latin American liberation theology. Though it is not a theological reflection, J.V. Hluna discussed the contribution of Christian church for the restoration of peace and tranquility in Mizoram.[59] For research scholars the paucity of literature on the North East Indian perspective of praxis model is quire disappointing, but it is interesting and significant that the preaching from the pulpil in recent years deals increasingly with liberation themes. A shift of emphasis in the sermons from 'born again' to 'social justice' is taking place, although most of the sermons on social justice continue to be theologically and sociologically conservative. They are more of a (prophetic) condemnation of the existing social order, corruption, nepotism, exploitation and drugs. Among charismatic Christians these social problems are often interpreted as one of the signs of the Last Days. They are regarded as warnings to get themselves ready for the Second Coming of Jesus Christ. They make no effort to change the situation. Conservative evangelicals, for their part, regard them as ethnical problems which must be dealt with. The best solution to the problems is a change of heart of every individual person by being borne again. It is also interesting to note that the underground Nagas and Mizos interpret their struggle for political self-determination as the will of God and for Christ.[60] Some charismatic leaders have supported this view.

Within the umbrella of the praxis model, a few feminist and ecological theologians are making an effort to develop the tribal approach. While the feminist theologians focus on the liberation of woemen from male domination, the ecological theologians focus on the liberation of the whole ecological system from exploitation of human beings.

[58] Wati Aier, *Future of Nagaland: A Socio-Politico-Theological Vision for the Nagas*, (Mokokchung: Author, 1988); *A Cry From the Rice Fields*, (Mokokchung: Author, 1989).

[59] J.V. Hluna, *Church and Political Upheaval in Mizoram: A Study of Impact of Christianity on the Political Development in Mizoram*, (Aizawl: Mizo Academy of Letters 1985).

[60] This view was obtained from my students who wrote assignments on this issue and with whom I conducted several discussions on the issue at the Eastern Theological College, Jorhat.*Government and Politics in Mizoram*, (New Delhi: Northern Book Centre, 1987), p. 98

(a) Feminist Approach : The feminist theologians in North East India, like any other feminist theologians in other parts of the world, identified the prevalence of sexism in this region. They remain convinced that women are oppressed, alienated and discriminated against on the ground of sex. Though they have not make in-depth analysis of the tribal society to identify the root cause of sexism, the following factors are commonly held as the root causes of sexism :

(i) Patriarchal social structures in which men dominate the social, economic, political and religious affairs, (the Khasis and Garos who belong to a matrilineal society are exception).

(ii) Some of the tribal traditions are responsible for shaping the attitude of the society towards women.

(iii) The traditional theology which advocates the superiority of men over women had shaped the attitudes of missionaries, and eventually leaders of the church in this region.

(iv) Traditional interpretation of the Bible.

R.L. Hnuni, a professor in Old Testament, is concerned with feminist hermeneutics. She is critical of the existing structures of the church which have deprived women of equal participation in the ministry and decision-making bodies.[61] Hnuni thinks that re-interpretation of the Bible is necessary in order to bring about change in the church. Miss Rini Ralte has critically examined the traditions which she thinks responsible for the subjugation of women. She also observes that Christianity reinforced the subordination of women in Mizoram. The first woman ordained in the Council of Baptist Churches in North East India, Rev. Noksangchila insists that the role of women must be changed along with socio-cultural change. The change must take place in the realm of religion, society and in the realm of Christian ministry and

61 R.L. Hnuni, "Women in the Context of the Bible and Mizoram", *Towards a Tribal Theology: The Mizo Perspective*, edited by Thanzauva, (Aizawl: Mizo Theological Conference, 1989), pp. 72-79, "Spirituality from the Feminist Perspective", *Spirituality and Theological Education*, edited by H.S. Wilson, (Bangalore, Board of Theological Education of the Senate of Serampore, 1986), pp. 47-59, "Issues of Women in Ministry" *Feminism: A North East Indian Perspective*, edited by Kim Vaiphei, (Imphal: Women Department of Manipur Baptist Convention, 1995), pp. 54-64

mission.[62] Kim Vaiphei's efforts to apply inclusive language have provoked the anger of some church leaders. Most of these women theologians see the structure of church as oppressive and this has to be changed.

(b) Ecological Approach : The reality of global ecological deterioration, which has reached an alarming situation, has challenged the competitive market economy and traditional theology which places human beings at the top of the pyramid with a right to exploit other creatures for their own selfish benefit. Theologians who are aware of the problems began to reflect theologically and see the possibility of the salvation of all creatures in the economy of God's salvation. Thus, a holistic understanding of liberation has emerged which includes the liberation of the whole creation. Against the utilitarian view (for some it is an anthropocentric) of creation which judges creatures from their untility for human benefit, the World Council of Churches develops a new understanding of creation which advocates the integrity of all creatures. Here we noticed the paradigm shift from an utilitarian approach to a creation centered approach in which theology emphasizes the unity of human beings and nature.

In North East India, Wati Longchar, who is now teaching at the Eastern Theological College, looks at the issue from the tribal perspective. He advocates the centrality of creation in which he emphasizes the integrity of all creation. He has rediscovered the tribal concept of nature rather than applying the ecological theology developed in the West to the tribal context. He writes :

> The sanctity of life and oneness with the nature and the divine is the basic affirmation of tribal religion. According to our creation stories it was the divine intention that people, nature and divinity from one community.[63]

For Wati, liberation of creation requires in the tribal context reaffirmation of their traditional belief.

---

[62] Noksangchilla, "The Place of Women in the Socio-Cultural Changes", *Feminist: A North East Indian Perspective*, edited by Kim Vaiphei, pp. 108-114

[63] A. Wati Longchar, *Tribal Religious Tradition*, pp. 10-24

Classification of methodology in various models is helpful and necessary, but we should be aware of the fact that there is no rigid boundary between various models. In the actual construction of contextual theology, models often overlap one another. Moreover, no single method is perfectly adequate for the construction of a contextual theology. However, as a theological construction has to be guided by certain principles, the choice of a methodological principle is necessary.

E. Choice of Methodology for North East India

Usually the choice of method depends on the theological vision of a theologian and the situation in which theology is constructed. The theological vision stated earlier has arisen from the situation in North East India where identity crisis, economic dependency, tribalism, ecological crisis and social injustice become the main theological agenda. In respond to this complex situation we are concerned to integrate both social transformation ad inculturation of the Christian gospel. It is these concerns which compel me to combine the Synthetic and Praxis models, both of which take the culture of the people seriously and, at the same time, emphasize social transformation. In the attempt to develop 'vital and coherent theology, the Vancouver WCC Assembly rightly pointed out that, "a coherent theological approach will incorporate traditions and methods of reflection which represent the concrete needs and call of each and all members of the ecumenical movement towards unity of life and faith."[64] My choice of the approach which i called "Synthetic-Praxis" in no way means that all other approaches are irrelevant for the North East, but simply a matter of the choice of a working principle without discounting others.

1. Synthetic-Praxis : We have indicated earlier that the synthetic model is concerned with the development of a new and relevant theology from a synthesis of gospel and culture in a particular context of preserve the cultural identity of the people, and to confess Christ in the way they understand him. The praxis model is concerned with the transformation of society towards the realization of the Kingdom of God, and emphasizes liberation, social justice and wholeness. It challenges the structure and system of any society responsible for poverty, discrimination, exploitation and injustice. The combination of these two

[64] Gill, ed., *Gather for Life*, p. 251

models is necessary in a society like outs, suffering as it dues from a crisis of identity and at the same time struggling to catch up with others. Therefore, we cannot neglect indigenization or inculturation as long as we are culturally alienated and impverished. At the same time, in a situation where people have been neglected and marginalised, where the development effort has stratified the tribal society into rich and poor classes, where social injustices and corruption are endemic, we need the praxis model of contextual theology with its concern with the transformation of these social realities towards the realization of the Reign of God.

2. Implications of Synthetic-Praxis Method : As I have mentioned above, no single method is perfectly adequate. No single model can cover all the areas, therefore our theological construction in the context of North East India should include :

- Evaluation of the interaction of Christianity and tribal culture over the past one hundred years;
- Social analysis to identify and set our theological agenda;
- Reflection on the people's struggle - the causes, manifestations, outcomes;
- Rediscovery of liberative elements from traditional values.

(a) Evaluation of the Interaction between Christianity and Tribal Culture : Almost all those who work on contextual theology in North East India have evaluated the interaction between Christianity and Tribal Culture though the depth and method of evaluation may have differed from person to person. To identify the mistakes, achievements and specific problems of missionaries working in this region, an evaluation of the interaction of the two traditions over the past one hundred years is necessary. F.S. Downs has made significant contributions in all this. For Downs, more than any other factor, Christianity prevented a process of detribalization from taking place, while at the same time helping the tribes come to term with the process of modernization.[65] Along the same line, O.L. Snaitang argues from the context of the Khasi and Jaintia tribes, that in a situation where radical changes were taking place,

---

[65] F.S. Downs, "Christianity and Cultural Change in North East India", *Op cit.*, p. 100

Christianity provided institutions, a new life style and an ideology which actually protected the society from the inherent danger of detribalization with the consequent detribalization and loss of identity.[66] On the other hand, persons like Renthy Keitzar, Lalsawma and others, though they are grateful to missionaries for what they have done, admitted that the types of Christianity introduced in this region is responsible for the erosion of tribal culture. The fact is, of course, that tribal culture had multiple interactions with other cultures and ideologies, first it was with the British administration; with the Western Christianity and its missionaries; with the plain people in India and finally with the ongoing modernization process and its technologies. Along with the changes, a certain degree of detribalization is bound to happen. The assumption of this book is that the tribals were rapidly and radically deculturalised to the extent of creating a crisis of identity. Though Christianity helped the tribals to cope with the process of modernization, it is, at the same time, one of the factors responsible for the alienation of tribals from their culture. Therefore, rediscovery, reconception and transformation of tribal culture is necessary to construct authentic indigenous Christian theology.

(b) Social Analysis : Social analysis is an integral part of a praxis approach to a contextual theology. Since all theologies arise from certain social milieus in human history to address their contemporary challenges, no meaningful construction of any contextual theology is possible without an analysis of society for which a theology is constructed. In the context of Northeast India, we have to analyse the tribal situation so as to determine the right theological questions to be addressed in the actual construction of a contextual theology. Social analysis asks question about and suggest the root causes of problems and makes agenda for theology. For example, Why are some people poor? What is the root causes of poverty? In the same way we can ask the question: why did the Nagas and Mizo people start armed struggle? Was the traditional practice of head-hunting really responsible? Are there some other factors which compelled them to take up arms and revolt against the Government of India? The root causes identified in the analysis of various issues become the theological agenda for us in North East India. Today, from the general

---

66 O.L. Snaitang, "A Study of the Role of Christianity in Social Change among the Khasi and Jaintia Hill Tribes of Meghalaya from 1841 to the present", United Theological College, D.Th. Dissertation, (1990), p. 264

observation, the following issues are identified as the social problems that have to be studied and addressed:

- the attitude of dominant groups towards the tribals.
- economic dependency,
- alienation tribal culture and land
- identity crisis,
- social injustice, corruption, exploitation
- disunity manifested in the forms of denominational groups, proliferation of charismatic sects, numerous political parties, etc.
- technical backwardness, lack of infrastructure, etc.

These are often identified as the major problems in North East India. They may be genuine problems, but what really matters is the method and the quality of analysis. Social analysis using the praxis approach requires involvement in the actual life struggle of the people. It is participatory research.

(c) Reflection on People's Struggle : Unless theology responds to the issues and the actual life problems, it becomes irrelevant and useless. This is the reason why theological reflection on the actual life struggle of the people is necessary. The struggle for liberation in North East India has not yet been the subject of theological reflection. However, more and more books and articles written in the vernacular on the vision and struggle of the people for their liberation are appearing. Much of this material deals with the present social problems from the Christian perspective. Some of the publications such as *Tea Garden Labourers of North East India* by the Vendrame Institute, some booklets published by the Synod Social Front, Mizoram, and quite a few thesis at B.D and M.Th levels have reflected upon the struggle of the people.

In the praxis approach to theology is not merely an academic discipline. It is the people themselves who do theology. It is a theology by the people for the people, not a theology by theologians for the people. The task of theologians is to do theology *with* the people and to enable them to articulate their own theology. As professional theologians, our role is to be involved, to listen, to enable and to articulate with them.

(d) Rediscovery of Traditional Values : The fundamental assumption of the re-discovery of traditional values is that human beings as created in the image of God have the potential to transform their own lives.

Every society has its own way of solving problems and doing development. An imposition of a foreign ideology, technology and development approach will not enhance real development unless they are incarnated or indigenized. In other words, any theology or ideology, unless it takes root in the culture of the people, will not be effective. Confusion, frustration and resentment among the people are the inevitable outcome. Any ideology, including theology, must be first of all incarnated in the culture of the people. When we think of constructing a contextual theology, rediscovery of traditional values does not mean 'culturalism' or 'contextualism' in which culture is romanticized and venerated above the Bible; rather culture is judged from its proven contribution to social transformation. No culture should be uncritically accepted or rejected. 'Rejection', 'Adoption' and 'Transformation' become integral components of the necessary filtering process of culture and of the method of inculturation.

Rejection : Some dehumanizing and oppressive elements of culture must be rejected as imcompatible with the gospel. There are dehumanizing elements in tribal culture as well as in the Christian traditions which came to us via Judaeo, Greek and Western cultures. They must be rejected. For example, sacrifice offered to evil spirits, black magic, head-hunting, discrimination of women, etc. must be rejected from tribal culture. Similarly, the dehumanizing elements of the Western culture which wrapped the Christian gospel such as extreme form of individualism, imperialism, subordination of women etc. must be striped off.

Adoption : There are liberative elements in tribal culture as well as in the West, which must be adopted, affirmed and articulated in the contextual theology. For example, the tribal altruism (*tlawmngaihna* in Mizo society), communitarian life, communitarian ownership of land, the tribal understanding of God-Self-World relationship, etc.

Transformation : In the process of interaction, both Christianity and tribal culture are mutually reshaped and transformed. Some of the cultural lements are neither completely rejected nor adopted, they are transformed. For instance, the tribal world-view, the practice of community singing and dancing, festivals, tribal understanding of creation and concept of spirits, etc.

This is certainly a difficult and painful process. However, it is necessary for the development of an authentic tribal theology.

CHAPTER IV

TRIBAL HERMENEUTICS
Alienation as the Tribal Hermeneutical Paradigm

A. Tribals and the Bible

The tribal religion, known today as primal religion, does not depend on a written Scripture but on the experience of the peoples' encounter with their environment in their day to day life. Rather than reading written Scriptures, tribals read nature and what happened to their own lives in order to understand God's intention for them. Their conversion to Christianity brought about radical changes in their lies. In fact translation of the Bible into tribal languages making them available to major tribes is one of the important factors for the emergence of a new tribal identity. We shold be aware of the fact that translation of the Bible has both negative and positive impact on tribal society. While reading the Bible in one particular dialect contributed towards the emergence of a larger tribal identity, it is also responsible for the present identity crisis.

Publication of the Bible into the tribal languages is not merely making a written book available in the tribal language; it means much more than that. Since belief in *mana* (impersonal supernatural power) is the core of religion, the Bible also came to be regarded as *mana*, having impersonal supernatural power. In fact, the Mizo[1] called it *Pathian Lehkhabu* (the Holy Book of God) and venerated it so highly that 35% of the fund raised in India for the Bible Society of India came from a tiny state of Mizoram. Having this notion of the Bible, it is not surprising that the tribal churches readily accepted a doctrine of verbal inspiration of the Scripture. The Bible for the tribal Christians is a propositional truth about God and human life supernaturally communicated to human beings by the Holy Spirit.

---

1 The Mizos, one of the tribal communities in North East India, respect and dearly love the Bible that is reflected in the composition of a few Bible songs. A verse in of one of the songs says,

> Oh Bible the source of life,
> Only in the Bible I find redemption,
> Because it shows me the way to heaven.

As mentioned above, the translation of the Bible into tribal languages has had both positive and negative impact on the tribal society. A few concrete examples of the positive impact may be narrated. A new common history for the tribals was created as they shared the same faith and the same story through the Bible. This broke the barrier of narrow village mentality and "tribalism", and paved the way for the emergence of a new and larger tribal identity. The translation of the Bible introduced a common dialect for some tribes, and this has to some extent helped them to overcome liguistic differences..[2] Reading one Bible in one language was an important factor in the development of a larger tribal identity, and if a common dialect had not been developed in this way, the tribals in North East India would have been compelled to speak and use Bengali.[3] Indeed, it was through the efforts of the missionaries, and tribal Christian themselves, to enable the Christian community to read the Bible that the literacy rate is significantly higher among the tribal Christians than their neighbouring peoples. It was this concern which led church leaders in the Khasi Hills to take the decision that no convert would be granted full membership in the church until he/she could read.[4] The translation of the Bible, therefore, had made significant contributions towards social transformation.

Having acknowledged the significant contribution of biblical translation, it is also important to acknowledge the negative impact as well. The translation of the Bible, which once time had linguistically integrated different dialects creating a larger tribal identity, is also increasingly used for asserting tribal identity which might had been absorbed into a larger identity if Bible was not translated in their own

---

[2] The *Awe* dialect was used for the Garo tribe in Meghalaya, the *Cherrapunji* dialect for the Khasi tribe in Meghalaya, the *Ukhrul* diaclect for the Tangkhul Nagas in Manipur, the *Changki* dialect for Ao Nagas in Nagaland, the *Duhlian* dialect for the Mizos in Mizoram, the *Serkawr* dialect for the Mara tribe in Mizoram and so on

[3] Since the British administrators had learned Bengali and trained the Benglai people, they had a policy to introduce Bengali as a court language. It was the Christian missionaries who developed and reduced the tribal dialects to written form.

[4] F.S. Downs, *History of Christianity in India, Vol. 5, Part 5: North East India in the Nineteenth and Twentieth Centuries* (Bangalore, Church History Association in India, 1992), p. 200

dialect. Now, with the pretext of concern for communicating gospel, each tribal group, however small it may be, made an effort to have Bible in their own dialect. This has fragmented the tribal society and hindered unity in the church and society. The tribal concept of inspiration and authority of the Bible has also created enormous problems in biblical hermeneutics. The tribal Christians are mostly biblicists who try to use the Bible as a magical book to provide ready-made answers to solve their problems. In the context of North East India translation of the Bible was certainly an important instrument in the search for their own identity, but it also alienated them from their own culture. Considering the positive and negative impacts, we may conclude that a fresh hermeneutic could once again produce a social dynamic and liberating influence on the tribal Christian community which had experienced the liberating influence of the Bible.

B. Need for Tribal Hermeneutics

With the emergence of various contextual theologies from Third World countries, people of different cultures are beginning to find the new way of reading the Bible in their respective contexts. Similarly it is also necessary for the tribal Christians to find a new way of reading and understanding the Bible. Paul Ricoeur, with his idea of the autonomy of the text and its surplus meaning, provides an appropriate philosophical basis for a contextual hermeneutic. As opposed to oral discourse, texts achieve a 'semantic autonomy'; they can mean more than what the author intended. "The (author's) intention is often unknown to us, sometimes redundant, sometimes useless, and sometimes even harmful as regards to the interpretation of the verbal meaning of his work."[5] There is a distancing of the text from the original audience, and this autonomy from the original readers opens up a range of potential readers and potential interpretations.[6] This approach makes possible to develop a new tribal hermeneutics.

The older (and even many of the present) habits of biblical interpretation amongst the tribals do not, in fact, take the tribal, social and cultural conditions into consideration. As a result, the Bible continues

---

5 Paul Ricoeur, *Interpretation Theory: Discourse and the Surplus of Meaning* (Forth Worth: Texas Christian University, 1976), p. 76

6 Ricoeur, *Ibid.*, pp. 29-32

to contribute towards alienation of tribals from their culture. This problem of adequately addressing the present social and economic problems, has been only dimly perceived in the past.

1. Evidence from Missionary Experience : In retrospection of their first ten years' experience in Mizoram, the two Baptist missionaries, Rev. J.H. Lorrain and F.W. Savidge, expressed in their report,

> Our first message, as soon as we could speak the language, was to proclaim a Saviour from sin. But the people had no sense of sin and felt no need for such a Saviour. Then, we found a point of contact. We proclaimed Jesus as the vanquisher of the Devil as the One who had bound the "strong man" and taken away from him "all his armour wherein he trusted" and so had made it possible for his slaves to be free. This to the Lushais (now known as Mizos) was "Good News" indeed and exactly met their great need.[7]

It is evident from the statement above that what was considered a meaningful message, for missionaries trained in England, was no longer meaningful when it was preached to a different culture. The task for the two missionaries was to reinterpret the gospel in the context of Mizoram.

2. Inadequacy of Historical Critical Interpretation : With the exception of fundamentalist circles, historical criticism remains a dominant method for interpreting the Bible in all the theological seminaries. In this approach rationalism reigns supreme, demanding the subjugation of the biblical texts to a critical examination apart from the dogma of ecclesiastical authority. The result has generally been a low estimate of the reliability of the biblical texts, since the world view implied by the texts seem so inferior to the contemporary perspective.[8] H.S.

---

7 J. Herbert Lorrain and F.W. Savidge, "After Ten Years: Report for 1913 of the BMS Mission in the South Lushai Hills, Assam", In *The Annual Report of BMS on Mizoram* 1901-1938 (Serkawn: Mizoram Gospel Centenary Committee, 1994), pp. 93-94

8 For further study see W.G. Kummel, *The New Testament: The History of the Investigation of Its Problems* (trans. S. Maclean Gilmour and Howard Clark Kee; Nashville: Abingdon, 1972); Hans W. Fei, *The Eclipse of Biblical Narrative: A Study in Eighteenth and Nineteenth Century Hermeneutics* (New Haven: Yale University Press, 1974).

Reimarus and H.E.G. Paul, for example, sought to reconstruct a purely historical life of Jesus, free from the "simple-minded supernaturalism", of the first century.[9] While some scholars emphasized historical factuality of the biblical texts, some entertained the notion that the biblical narrative could be factually erroneous and yet religiously meaningful.[10] This result in hermeneutical method of demythologization by the liberals and the historical reconstruction of events by the conservatives. Neither of these approaches helped the tribal Christians in their self-understanding, mission and ministry. Rather they seemed to make Christianity more and more irrelevant, precisely because they reflected Western cultural dynamics in response to the Enlightenment.

3. Inadequacy of Dialogical Interpretation in India : P.D. Devanandan, Raymond Pannikar, Bishop A.J. Appasamy and others have responded to the religious and ideological pluralism in India. In recent years, Paul Gregorios and Stanley Samartha have argued that we should not take authority of the Christian Scripture as self-evidently valid, rejecting other scriptures; this would simply invite counter claims from other religious groups. In such a situation, so it is argued, the task of hermeneutics is to work out a larger framework of neighbourly relationships within which the insights of different sacred texts can be related to each other for mutual enrichment, yet without denying their particularities.[11] Similarly, R.S. Sugirtharajah advocates that biblical scholars must be sensitive to the scriptural texts of others faith and the spiritual sustenance they provide for many adherents. They should re-read some of the biblical materials in the light of the multi-faith context. All of these writers are concerned with discovering truth from other Scriptures and synthesizing it with Christian truth found in the Scripture, a process which might be called dialogical hermeneutics. This represents

---

9 Larry Chouinard, "Gospel Christology: A Study of Methodology", *A Journal for the Study of New Testament*, Vol. 30 (1987), pp. 21-37. Albert Schwitzer, *The Quest of the Historical Jesus: A Critical Study of Its Progress from Reimarus to Wrede* (New York: Macmillan, 9th Printing, 19680, pp. 13-67

10 *Ibid*, p. 12

11 S.J. Samartha, *The Search for New Hermeneutics in Asian Christian Theology* (Bangalore: Board of Theological Education of Serampore College, 1987); Paul Gregorious, "Hermeneutics in India Today in the Light of the World Debate", in R.S. Sugitharaja and Cecil Hargreaves (ed)., *Reading in Indian Christian Theology*, Vol. I (Delhi: ISPCK, 1993), pp. 176-185

a radical shift from the approach of "decoding" the biblical texts for people of others culture to a synthetic approach.

While dialogical hermeneutics may be appropriate in pluralistic contexts, it is not directly relevant in the tribal context. The idea of Scripture, first of all, is itself alien to the tribals. Moreover, the Hindu, Muslim and Buddhist Scriptures, will be further alienating since these derive from the dominant cultures which impinges on the tribals. This is the reason why *Dalit* and Tribal theologians are critical of the present Indian Christian Theology largely based on Brahmanism. If we are going to discuss interpretation of Scripture at all, Bible is certainly familiar with the tribals and has been internalized. As they read the Bible in their own context, it is also important to note that they are also reading the new "Scriptures" being written by God in their day-to-day struggle for authentic existence. The fusion of the Bible and the new "Scriptures" in the heart of the reader produces an authentic interpretation of the Bible.

C. Hermeneutical Principle in Tribal Theology

The question which confront us in the construction of tribal theology is how to interpret the Bible in the context of North East India. Juan Luis Segundo rightly warned his colleagues that without the connection between the past (biblical text) and the present (the context), there would be no theology of liberation in the long run. He said that "a theology dealing with liberation might be developed, but without biblical basis its methodological naiveté would fatal." It is the same case with the tribal Christian theology. As Moltmann has rightly expressed "reading the Bible with the eyes of the poor is a different thing from reading it with the eye of the man with full belly",[12] there are different ways of reading the Bible. The tribal people read the Bible in the context of alienation from their land and culture. The way they read the Bible cannot be the same as that of those who do not face the same problems. Their context requires a re-interpretation of the Bible to address the problems that encountered their lives. Unless the tribals are allowed to be different in their interpretation of the Bible, the Bible will not only lose its significance, Christianity will remain superficial without really

[12] J. Moltmann, *The Church in the Power of Spirit* (London: SCM, 1977), p. 17

taking root into the tribal culture. In fact, Christianity is quire visible and popular in the tribal society of North East India, and to a great extent it appears indigenized. But an in-depth study, however, reveals that Christianity has not taken root deep within the tribal culture. It is the task of Tribal Theology to develop a hermeneutical principle to fill this lacuna.

1. Tribal Hermeneutical Paradigm : The concern of tribal hermeneutics is not merely understanding the ancient text objectively, but how I know myself in the process of knowing God through the text, and how will I, as individual person and my society, be transformed by that knowledge? The older (and even many of the present) habits of biblical interpretation among the tribals do not, in fact, take the tribal, social and cultural conditions into consideration. As a result, the Bible continues to contribute towards alienation of tribals from their culture. This problem, of adequately addressing the present social and economic problems, has been only dimly perceived in the past.

An authentic interpretation involves reading the texts with sensitivity to the reader's own context, to the horizons of the texts and that of the readers' fused together, this alone will generate a new meaning of the text. This approach abandons any historical-critical concerns for historicit or demythologization and engages wioth the evangelists' forms of the text. We are therefore proposing a multi-task hermaneutics, encouraging people to understand themselves in the process of understanding the text, that they may be inspired to respond to the issues that confront them. As F.S. Downs points out, the struggle of tribes in India is mainly for *liberation from any form of alienation in order to preserve* their unique identity.[13] In the light of this struggle, the tribal theologians resist traditional interpretation of the Bible which tend to make an "integrationist" approach to minority cultures: we are no more interested in being integrated into an homogeneous hermeneutics than we are into that form of nationalism which tries to integrate diverse culture into one nation. The attempt to create a tribal hermeneutics is an on-going struggle for autonomy both in politics and in the interpretation of the Bible.

---

[13] F.S. Downs, "Identity: The Integrating Principles", *Journal of Social Sciences and Humanities of North Eastern Hill University*, Vol. 9/3 (1991), p. 7ff, italics are mine)

In the search for authentic and meaningful interpretation of the Bible, the basic community, the community of the poor in Latin America began to suspect the traditionsl interpretation as well as the interpretation of experts (hermeneutics of suspicion) and read the Bible through the eyes of the poor and the powerless. In their new way of reading the Bible, the **exodus** has become the hermeneutical paradigm.[14] Ben Dominguez who looks to the New Testament for "integrating perspective" suggested **travails** for Asian hermeneutics.[15] However, Samartha who takes seriously the presence of scriptures of other faith in Asia, proposes **dialogue** as a Asian hermeneutical paradigm which seems to be a dominant hermeneutical principle in Asia. This paradigm is concerned knowing truth rather than finding out the meaning of the text for the context in which it is going to be read. In the search for truth, he argues, one should admit the fact that Bible alone does not contain truth, truth in the scriptures of other faith should also be discovered to enrich our understanding of God's intention for humanity.[16] A.P. Normal suggested **pathos** (suffering) as an organizing principle and hermeneutical paradigm for the Dalit Theology.[17] For Tribal Theology I suggest **alienation** as the hermeneutical paradigm, for the tribals have been a lienated people throughout the history. Their history is a history of alienation. They have been alienated from their culture, land, economic development and politics.

2. Liberation of the Aliens as the Tribal Hermeneutical Paradigm : The fundamental problem of tribal society in India is **alienation**. In that situation the hermeneutical paradigm has to be drawn from the experience and suffering of the ***gerim*** **(aliens)**. I need not prove that tribals in India are alienated people. It is self-evident that we have been sufficiently experiencing alienation in the railway stations, in the schools and hostels by our children, in the street of our cities, in the offices, in the politics and in the business. The reasons for being aliens may be briefly explained: (a) we do not belong

---

14 Anthony R. Ceresko, *The Old Testament. A Liberation Perspective*, Bangalore. St. Pauls, 1993, p. 11ff

15 Ben Dominguez, *The Human and the Holy*, ed. Emerito P. Nacpil and Douglas J. Elwood, New York: Orbis Books, 1980, p. 97

16 J. Samartha, *The Search for new Hermeneutis in Asian Christian Theology*, Bangalore: BTESS, 1987, pp. 21-33, 45ff

17 A.P. Nirmal, "Doing Theology from A Dalit Perspective", *A Reader in Dalit Theology*, edited by A.P. Nirmal, Madras: Department of Dalit Theology, UELCI Gurukul, pp. 139-150

to the dominant racial group of the Aryans and Dravidians; (b) we do not belong to the major religious communities of the Hindus and the Muslims; (c) we are vulnerable minority; (d) some of the tribes are landless; (e) we are dependent upon the assistance of the Central Government, and (f) our physical appearance is different. For all these reasons we become victims of alienation, oppression and exploitation. When I study the Bible with this experience, I begin to see the whole history of God's people as the story of aliens.

D. Aliens in the Bible (*gerim*)

R.L. Hnuni argues that the issue of alien occupies an integral part in the Old Testament especially in the legal collections.[18] This is probably true that Biblical tradition places the beginning of Israelite history with a story of the patriarch who first appeared as a 'sojourner' in the scene, his descendants continued to be *gerim* both in Canaan and Egypt until their settlement in Canaan. Since then the Israelites themselves became hosts to different groups of aliens until the exilic period when they again fell in the hands of Babylonians as 'aliens'. The history of Israel is, therefore, a history of 'aliens', and it is no wonder that aliens play an integral part in the Old Testament. F.A. Spina who has extensively dealt with the identity of alien (*ger*) defines as follows :

> ...*ger* in the Hebrew Bible refers to people who are no longer directly related to their original social setting and who have therefore entered into dependent relationships with various groups of officials in a new social setting. The *ger* was of another tribe, city, district or country who was without customary social protection or privilege and of necessity had to place himself under the jurisdiction of someone else.[19]

---

[18] R.L. Hnuni, "Legal Protection of the Poor in Ancient Israel and Its Significance for Mizo Society", A Doctoral Thesis submitted to the Senate of Serampore College in 1995, p. 99

[19] F.A. Spina, "Israelite as *gerin*, "Sojourner in Social and Historical Context," *The Word of the Shall Go Forth: Essay in Honour of David Noel Freedman*, ed. C.L. Meyer and M. O'Connor, Winnona Lake In; Eisen Brouns, 1983, p. 324. This definition is agreed also by Y. Osumi that a *ger* may be an Israelite from different tribe or district or a foreigner who came to live in the land for some period.

The above lines offer a comprehensive explanation that covers the wide range of **alien** (*ger*) through the changes of the history of Israel. This explains the argument and different views connected with the identity of the ***ger***. A full monograph on aliens is given by Christiana van Houten[20] and I do not intent to present a full account of aliens. My purpose here is to find the affinities with the tribals in India to provide a hermeneutical paradigm for tribal theology.

1. The patriarchs and the Israelites were aliens : The patriarchs themselves are portrayed as aliens both in Canaan and Egypt in the so-called 'historical credo'.[21]

> And you shall response before the Lord your God, 'A wandering Aramean was my father; and he went down into Egypt and **sojourned** *(wayyagar)* there, few in number; and there he became a nation, great, mighty, and populous. And Egyptians treated us harshly, and afflicated us, and laid upon us hard bondage. Then we cried to Lord the God of our fathers, and the Lord heard our voice, and saw our affliction, our toil and our oppression; and the Lord brought us out of Egypt with mighty hand and outstretch arms, with great terror, with signs and wonders; and he brought us into this place and gave us this land, a land flowing with milk and honey. (Deut. 26:5-9)

This text explicitly explains that patriarchs who were aliens in Egypt were ill-treated by the Egyptians. This reflects that aliens have been alienated and oppressed from the ancient up to this time. Oppression has become their identity.

It is quite obvious from the biblical references that Israelites were aliens (Exod. 22:21; 23:9; Deut. 24:18, 22). "You shall not wrong a stranger (alien) or oppress him, for you were strangers in Egypt." Spina tries to find the possible connection between the Israelites as Hebrews

---

20 Christiana van Houten, in her monograph *The Aliens in Israelite Law*, 1991 gives a thorough treatment of aliens in ancient Israel and in extra biblical literature.

21 F.A. Spina, "Israelite as gerim", *Op cit.* p. 322

and Israelites as aliens.[22] He argues that the words *aliens* and *Hebrews* refer to the same social type, to individuals or groups who are alienated from their original social context.[23]

2. Aliens among the Israelites : The Israelites were themselves once aliens in the land of Egypt. In later period after Israel's settlement, *gerim* refers to those non-Israelites who have found a home in Israel. The presence of *gerim* among the Israelites was not unique to them as there were also analogies in ancient Near Eastern literature.[24] It is the commandment of God that they should not oppress the aliens within their own community. Houten observes that the perception of aliens among the Israelites changed. She said,

> One may belong to a tribe or a city or district or country, and through Israel's history the primary group to which an Israelite belonged changed. The *ger* in the period of the Judges was anyone from another tribe or village, while the *ger* in the monarchical period was a citizen from a foreign country.[25]

---

[22] The issue on the possible connection between Hebrews and Israelites position as aliens was raised and discussed in Spina's "Israelites as *gerim*", pp. 330-331 cf. C. van Houten in her *The Alien in Israelite Law*, p. 41. Spina notes that the presence of *habiru* is no longer attested after 1500-1200 B.C.E and no group of people were called *apiru* throughout the period of Israelite's history though *ger* continued to be used to describe certain tribes or individuals. The possible reason for this was because the terms *apiru/habiru* were not epithets by which these people used for themselves but insiders to outsiders. Spina thinks that the term Hebrew is used frequently by non-Hebrews except when the word refers to their ethnic identity or when talking to foreigners. Spina thinks that the term Hebrew is used frequently by non-Hebrews except when the word referes to their ethnic identity or when talking to foreigners. See also M.C. Astour, "Habiru", *Interpreter's Dictionary of the Bible, Suppl. Volume*. Nashville: Abingdon Press, 1976, pp. 382-385 for further reading on hapiru/habiru.

[23] F.A. Spina, *Ibid.* pp. 331-332

[24] The Mesopotamian law collections - the laws of Eshnuna, the code of Hammurabi and the Middle Assyrian laws each contained only one law pertaining to alien (Pritchard, *ANET*, pp. 162, 171, 183). cf. Christiana van Houten, *The Alien in Israelite Law*, pp. 34-42

[25] Christiana van Houten, *The Alien in Israelite Law*, p. 20

3. Identity of the Aliens : The ***ger*** occupies an intermediate position between a native (ezrah) and a foreigner (nokri), lives among people who are not his blood kinship and thus lacks legitimate rights and protection which a citizen enjoys.[26] As they remain on the fringe of the society, and did not enjoy the full rights of citizens, maintenance of livelihood is not easy.[27] Though ***gerim*** might not be always poor, but on many occasions, they would be the least of the poor for they did not have equal opportunities as the average, poor, adult, male Israel had.[28] An alien was dependent on the good will of others because they had no natural ties to the social structure. He/she was a person 'who did not belong' because of being different from the rest. Their distress sometimes included poverty because "it would be easier for them to become poor than any other group for it was easy to cheat them and their options were so few."[29] They had no inheritance when they first settled in Israelites' country and depended on some landowners even for a place to live.[30] They must have been economically vulnerable. As they were bereft of their cultural and economic security and fellowship, along with the poor, widows and orphans aliens were granted special protection in the Old Testament specially in the legal collection.

4. Protection of the Aliens : The laws in Deuteronomy are more comprehensive than those in the Book of Covenant, especially in relation to the protection of aliens, therefore we can get a more comprehensive picture of the legal treatment of aliens in Deuteronomic law.[31] In Deuteronomy we find that since the Israelites themselves were once aliens, they must care for the aliens in their own land (24:18, 22; cf. Exod. 22:22; 23:19). The aliens should be helped (Deut. 5:12-15), they should be allowed to participate in Covenant ceremonies and worship (29:9, 10; 31:12). Justice must be done to the aliens (Deut. 24:14, 17, 19, 21, 22).

---

26 D. Kellerman, "GUR", *Theological Dictionary of the Old Testament*, II, p 443

27 D. Patrick, *Old Testament Law*, (Atlanta: John Knox Press, 1985), p. 86

28 D.E. Gowan, "Wealth and Poverty in the Old Testament" *International*, Vol. 41, 1987, pp. 341-355

29 D.E. Gowan, *Ibid*. p. 344

30 D.E. Gowan, *Ibid*. p. 345

31 Reference to aliens in Deuteronomy are : 1:16; 5:14; 10:18; 19; 14:21, 29; 16:11, 14; 24:24, 17, 19, 20, 21; 26:11, 12, 13; 27:19; 29:11; 31:12.

E. Hermeneutical Significance of Tribals

The hill tribes in North East India will tell a similar story and way as deuteronomists had said, ' a wandering hunter was my fathe and he went down to Myanmar and sojourned there, there his descendants were multiplied and became great in number. They were oppressed and exploited by the Burmese. The king of Myanmar (Siampahranga) forced them to work very hard in the construction of his palace. When the burden became too heavy for them, they left Myanmar in search of a new land. Then they came to the present habitat and lived in peace. But the British invaded them and made them aliens. For the convenience of their administration, the British rulers divided them, since then they became a divided people. Now they are scattered in Myanmar, Bangladesh and India. Their dream and aspiration to become one nation remains as an ideal hope, but in reality they continue to remain as aliens.

The tribals in North East India are aliens in India. It is not our choice. Our choice is to be left alone for which we have been struggling more than fifty years. If Government of India wants to keep us, it has responsibility for the protection and development of tribals in this country. Therefore the Government policy towards tribal communities should combine both legal protection of their rights and concern for development. The British administration adopted a policy of protection, isolating and tribal communities to protect them from the interference of others in their affairs. This policy has been continued until recently. The Central Government's intention today is lift the "Inner Line Regulation" - introduced in Arunachal Pradesh, Nagaland and Mizoram for the purpose of protecting the tribal people from others - could well lead to even greater hardship for the tribals. This will be a radical change in the tribal policy. Any weaker section of any society will need a certain degree of protection, without which no emancipation will take place. Protection must be seen as an integral part of the development process.

Protection, however, important as it may be, is not sufficient in itself. True protection means empowering the people - caring, teaching, training and organizing the people to enable the tribal community to protect themselves; certainly not to keep them inside the fencing. It should aim at empowerment of the tribal community. Empowering the tribals would also involve letting them participate in the formulation and execution of the laws. Empowering tribals to protect themselves involves economic development, because economic vulnerability is one of the primary factors for tribal exploitation and oppression. Policy for the tribals has to be changed from isolationistic protection to empowerment which may take us beyond the legal vision of Deuteronomy to encompass Ezekiel's radical exhortation to allot resident aliens an inheritance within the boundaries of the land (47:22-23), thereby allowing aliens to participate in the promise land.

Within the tribal community, there are aliens such as the Chakmas and people of other tribes. They should not be oppressed and exploited. They should not be deprived of justice. Thre are also the poor, the marginalized women who are almost in same status with the aliens. As much as we demand protection and development from the Central Government of India, they should also be protected and developed.

F. Other Hermeneutical Clues

A few more hermeneutical clues are indicated here to show the possibility of tribal hermeneutics. Our purpose in introducing these examples is not to provide a detail treatment of the interpretation of the selected texts, but simply to indicate the possibility of tribal hermeneutics.

1. Promise Land : Alienation from tribal land is a common problem throughout India. Transfer of tribal land to non-tribals is now prohibited, yet this legal strategy fails to protect Tribals; the laws are easily circumvented. Many of the tribes have been reduced to landless wanderers. This situation has to be understood in the context of two competing views of land: while the tribals treat land as an essential part of their communal identity (land can only be "owned" by becoming a member of the community who live in the land), the non-tribals regard it as property which can be owned by legal fiction - bought, sold and claimed

In this context, the tribals may re-read the following biblical passages concerning the promise land: they may put themselves into the role of the Israelites who have been afflicted and humiliated (cf. Deut. 26:5ff); they also might receive the promise of God which came through Joseph: "God will visit you one day, bring you back to the land which he swore to your fathers, Abraham, Isaac, and Jacob" (cf. Gen. 50:24); they might see an analogy with their own experience when God called the tribal leader Moses and asked, "Go and gather the elders of your own tribe, and say to them. The Lord the God of your fathers has appeared to me, saying, 'I have observed you and what has been done to you in this land, and I promise that I will bring you out of this affliction,'" (cf. Exod. 3:16-17).

Abraham, Jacob, Joseph and Moses are all landless, but they are caught up in a journey towards the promise land. Their story can shape the tribals' struggle for homeland. Most of the tribal movements in India today - such as the *Jarkhan* movement in Bihar; the *Gurkha* movement in Bengal, the *Bodo* and *Karbi* movement in Assam, the *Kuki* movement in Manipur, the tribal movement in Tripura - are fundamentally struggle for a homeland in their own land. Unlike the patriarchal story, this Indian tribal experience represents the hope of returning to a land that was, at an earlier time, already theirs. But the idea of promised land can become an impetus, or a motivating analogy, for the tribal struggle.

2. Pentecost that Revives and Empower (Acts 2:1-17) : The coming of the Holy Spirit on the day of Pentecost revived and transformed the disciples of Jesus Christ. In spite of the fact that the Pentecost movement was the origin of the Christian church, today the revival or charismatic movement has gained very little room in the mainline churches. While the mainline churches have had a very low opinion of revivalism, it is one of the distinctive characteristics of the tribal churches. In spite of constant critiques and objections from missionaries and theologically trained leaders, this element remains. Renthy Keitzar, and a few other scholars in this region, have rightly observed that the revival movement among the tribal churches in fact an expression of suppressed traditional animistic religion.[32] Keitzar observes that missionaries in Nagaland were able to suppress tribal emotionalism and traditional religious practice. But in Mizoram, this was not the case; the tribal emotionalism has always been a feature of religious practice from the beginning of Christian influence until today. Instead of suppressing this movement, we shold guide and transform it. In this context, it is necessary to re-discover and re-read the texts concerning the gift of the Holy Spirit on the day of Pentecost and in the subsequent history of the Church.

---

[32] Renthy Keitzar, "Common Features of Theological Trends in North East India", *ETC Journal*, Vol. 4, 1991, p. 28

The re-reading of texts concerning the gift of the Holy Spirit needs to be undertaken without rational prejudices which so often underlie Western biblical interpretation. The same Holy Spirit is received by different people, and manifested differently, depending on the culture, environment and nature of the society. As far as the scriptural texts are concerned, the Holy Spirit inspires and guides kings, prophets, Jesus Christ, the disciples, the church and individual believers. Here I would like to discuss briefly the work of Holy Spirit in the tribal context of revivalism.

(a) Revival as inculturation : Today inculturation or indigenization is a central concern of churches in the Third World countries. Efforts towards inculturation have been made in India since the inception of Christianity by missionaries like De Nobili, William Carey and many others. While De Nobili tried to identify himself with Hindu Brahmins and used Brahmanical language to present the Christian gospel, Carey translated Bible into the vernacular languages. Some of the Christian intellectuals, such as Chenchiah, Chakkarai and others, used Hindu philosophical categories to interpret the Christian gospel. Similarly, Robin Boyd used *advaita* philosophy. The success of these efforts has been limited; the churches remain alienated and Christianity remains a foreign religion in India. Comparatively, the tribal churches in the hills appear much more indigenized. Christianity has become their new identity, and this is reflected in some of the tribal churches who mostly sing their own indigenous Christian songs. It is beyond doubt that the revival movement is the primary factor which internalized Christianity in tribal society. In the tribal context, Christianity does not remain as a foreign religion. However, this does not mean that Christianity is perfectly indigenized in the tribal areas; it is *comparatively* indigenized. We have to move beyond this situation to contextualize Christianity more fully, for which task a tribal hermeneutics is necessary

(b) Revival as Praxis : Just as the disciples were empowered on the day of Pentecost to witness, so the first Christians of the tribal community - who felt inferior to others and longed for their old ways of life - were empowered by the revival movement. It was the revival movement that enabled the new converts, a marginalized group of the society, to accept themselves with self-esteem and to take up their mission. In much of the debate about mission in India, the priority of praxis has been emphasized, but most of the churches stand still. It is time to realise that real praxis begins with revival or renewal of the churches.

These are just some hints to show the possibility of re-reading and re-interpreting the Bible in the tribal context in India. Rather than contributing towards the alienation of the tribal people, proper biblical hermeneutics done in the context of the tribals and the Bible's social and spiritual visions could empower them in their struggle for social transformation.

CHAPTER V

TRIBAL CONCEPT OF HUMANITY
Communitarianism as the Tribal Concept of Humanity

A. Meaning of Communitarianism

Anyone who knows the tribal community well will admit that the strength of tribal people is the community. Communitarianism is obviously one of the transformational motifs which has to be rediscovered from the tribal culture for theologizing. Communitarianism is a concept and life principle of tribal community in which a homogeneous people live together sharing their joy and sorrows in mutual love and care. The fundamental idea of Communitarianism is that human beings are, by nature, social beings. They are not simply isolated individuals who choose to come together in society only because it is necessary to do so to protect their individual rights and freedom, and to fulfil their economic interest.[1] To be truly human requires as to be in communion with others. Living in community is not the same as living in society.

Ferdinand Tonnies' distinction between *Gemeinschaft* and *Gesellschaft* may be helpful to explain the difference between community and society, though they are best understood as a continuum and cannot be sharply distinguished. *Gemeinschaft* cannot be accurately translated. It refers to the community of feeling, a kind of associative unity of ideas and emotion that results from likeness and from shared experiences. Natural will predominates in the "*Gemeinschaft* relationships", which may be best illustrated by kinship. In *Gesellschaft* (society) relationships, "everybody is by himself and isolated, and there exists a condition of tension against all others ... intrusions are regarded as hostile acts ... nobody wants to grant and produce anything for another individual ... all goods are conceived to be separated, as are their

---

[1] Leonard Weber, "Land Use Ethics: The Social Responsibility of Ownership" *Theology of the Land*, edited by Bernard E. Evan and Gregory D. Cusak, (Collegeville: the Liturgical Press, 1987), p. 28

owners."[2] Tonnies has been criticised for assigning the names of his ideal types of actual periods of history, but his distinction between society and community nonetheless remains a valid and useful tool. These categories, however, are highly general. By contrast Robert Redfield explained the characteristics of tribal community which he called "The Folk Society" as follows :

> Such society is small, isolated, non-literate, and homogeneous, with a strong sense of group solidarity. The ways of living are conventionalised into that coherent system which we call "culture". Behaviour is traditional, spontaneous, uncritical, and personal; there is no legislation or habit of experiment and reflection for intellectual ends. Kinship its relationships and the familial group is the unit of action. The sacred prevails over the secular; the economy is one of status rather than the market.[3]

Redfield rightly points out the bad and good aspects of tribal society, but by using modernisation as the sole criterion to judge tribal society, he failed to appreciate the good aspects of tribal society as such. If one looks at the tribal society from the post-modern perspective, recognising the failures of modernisation as well as its gains, one would certainly see the lost treasures of human society to be discovered from the tribal society. Accordingly the concern here is rediscovery of tribal

---

2 Ferdinand Tonnies, *Community and Society (Gemeinschaft and Gesellchaft)*, Translated and edited by Charles P. Loomis, (East Lansing: Michigan University Press, (1887), 1963), p. 231. What Tonnies saw as the period of 'society' emerged, he believed, as the result of the growth of city life based on trade and contractual relationship. Industrialisation and the rational manipulation of capital and labour are accompanied by the growth of the state and national life. Cosmopolitan life, toward which Tonnies thought society was moving, would be based on the ultimate expressions of rational will - science, informed public opinion, and controlled by "the republic of scholars". Horace M. Miner, "Community and Society Continua" *International Encyclopaedia of the Social Sciences*, Vol. 3 and 4, Edited by David L. Dills, (New York: Macmillan Company & The Free Press, 1968), p. 175

3 Robert Redfield, "The Folk Society", *American Journal of Sociology*, Vol. 52, (1947), p. 293

communitarian life as one of the transformational elements from the tribal society.

One of the common characteristics, in a wide range of tribal societies, is the practice of a communitarian way of living together in the village level in which people know each other sharing their joys and sorrows. The local community in tribal society is the seed bed of all statism. In face to face relations in the daily round of life, it is the first group beyond the family to which personal loyalty is attached. In the *esprit de corps* of the local group lies the germ of patriotism. It was presumably the only territorial unit of society known to early humanity.[4] Anthropologists often describe it as kinship, meaning a system of dyadic relations between person and person, regulated by the community.[5] Though communitarianism is intrinsic to human nature, it is notably the way tribal people adjusted themselves to their own situation and respond to their environmental needs.

Since the members of a community live together under a common culture, they share their patterns of living and ideas in common to a large extent. Community, thus, means commonality in which diversity exists but unity previals in the long run. Community means that the feeling of oneness, a sense of entity, an *espirit de corps*, extends to the whole territorial society. Community means that the culture sets values that orient behaviour in the direction of common as well as individual or sub-group interests. The common interest is what constitutes political interest. The community is the polity. Political organisation, therefore, is that part of culture which functions to direct the activities of the members of the society towards community.[6] Community is not a society of individuals in which the relationship is inter-dependence, though it will involve this element. It is a personal communion in which each member, in the midst of diversity, works for the common good.

Anthropologists are critical about idealizing the tribal society as an egalitarian society. Thus, K.S. Singh argues that almost all tribal

---

4 E. Adamson Hobel, *Man in the Primitive World: An Introduction to Anthropology*, (New York: McGraw Hill Book Company, 1958), p. 487

5 A.R. Radcliffe Brown, *Structure and Function in Primitive Society*, (London: Routledge & Kegan Paul, 1952), p. 52

6 E. Adamson Hobel, *Man in the Primitive World: An Introduction to Anthropology*, p. 487

communities have divisions and a notion of hierarchy based on ecology, descendent, ranking, status and so on.[7] While admitting the existence of hierarchy in the tribal community, we should also recognise the great difference between the tribal community and the society structured on the basis of class and caste. Even today, we would rarely find any beggar in the tribal communities in North East India, not because they can survive without the help of others, but because the community takes cae of the sick, the widows and the poor. Sine the community assures the sustenance of their future life, the Life Insurance Corporation makes no progress in the tribal areas. Comparatively speaking, the traditional tribal community is much more caring and harmonious than society at large. S.C. Dube rightly observed that 'if the tribals are not egalitarian, they are at least non-hierarchical and undifferentiated.'[8]

Our purpose here is neither to return to a primitive communism, in the way some communists have thought human beings are destined to return to an original social pattern;[9] nor to idealise such a concept of community. It is an attempt to rediscover the essence of tribal communitarian life for an alternative doctrine of humanity for transformation of tribal society, with a view also to making a contribution to the wider Christian community in the on-going search for all over the world a community. The writer is aware of the difficulty of applying the exact form of the tribal communitarian life to modern society. But the essence of communitarianism is applicable to and important for modern society. Technological advancement, secularism, industrial development, centralisation of political power, with is underlying

---

[7] K.S. Singh, *The Scheculed Tribes*, *Op cit*. p. 7

[8] S.C. Dube (ed), *Tribal Heritage of India*, (New Delhi: Vikas Publishing House, Pvt. Ltd., 1977), p. 2. The attempt of Roy Burman to categorise the traditional political system of North Eastern tribes into authoritarian and republican types of organisation is a superficial formulation from the perspective of the modern political theory. Roy Burman, "Integrated Area Approach to the Problem of the Hill Tribes of Northeast India", *Tribal Situation in India*, edited by K. Suresh Singh, (1972), p. 75

[9] *Ibid*. pp. 441-442. The idea of returning to the original pattern of human society would theologically negate the dynamics of God's creativity and advocate a "closed system of creation". At the same time, uncritical acceptance of the practice of privatization or private ownership as an indication of civilised society is unacceptable.

philosophy of individualism, have created a yearning and widespread quest for community in modern society.[10] Communitarianism cannot be discarded as a primitive philosophy of life useless for modern society. It is, rather, intrinsic to human nature and essential for human beings to be truly human. This could be the reason why people in the culture of rugged individualism are longing for community.[11] John Macquarrie rightly observed that it is right for an individual to have a certain measure of privacy and autonomy. But belonging in an equally primordial way to the very structure of existence is the need for community and an inescapable interdependence among existents, together with the privacy and separateness of each existent who in some regards cannot be other than lonely and isolated.[12]

The outcome of modern individualism is clear particularly in the Wester society. Physically people work together in factories and offices, but they are separated. Students live together in the hostel and people go to the club, but they remain lonely and isolated. This situation is described by Robert A. Nisbet that the outcome of Western individualism is "not the free individual but the lost individual; not independence but isolation; not self discovery but self-obsession; not to conquer but to be conquered; ..."[13] Likewise, Reinhold Niebuhr also observed that, "it is this autonomous individual who really ushers in moder civilisations and who is completely annihilated in the final stages of that civilisation."[14] The destructive effect of modern individualism so widely observable in modern world is a further reminder of the need for establishing a true community.

One may raise the question, "Should we regard modern communism as an attempt to rediscover the tribal communitarian life? If so, does communism provide a better alternative to the existing system of human relationship based on capitalism competitive market?" One

---

10 Robert A. Nisbet, *The Quest for Community*, (London: Oxford University Press, 1953), (reprint of 1978), p. 4

11 M. Scott Peck, *The Different Drum: The Creation of True Community - the First Step to World Peace*. (London: Rider & Co., 1987), p. 59

12 J. Macquarrie, *Principles of Christian Theology*, (London: SCM, 1966), pp. 57 & 58

13 Robert A. Nisbet, *Op cit.* p. 12

14 R. Niebuhr, *The Nature and Destiny of Man*, Vol. I, (London: 1941), p. 59

helpful way of responding to the questions may be to compare communitarianism, Capitalism and Modern Communism and their respective implications and purposes. The following table outlines such a comparison.

Communitarianism	Capitalism	Modern Communism
(1) Village community	Society of multiple individual persons	State society
(2) Isolated and closed society	Larger and more open society	Larger and more regulated society
(3) Inter-personal relationship	Inter-dependent relationship	Inter-dependent relationship
(4) Natural will dominates human functions and relationship	Rational will operates in human functions and relationship	Rational will operates in human functions and relationship
(5) Chieftainhood	Democracy	Totalitarianism
(6) Decision by consensus	Decisionby majority vote	Decision by leaders
(7) Subsistence economy	Market economy/ Mixed economy	Labour intensive
(8) Principle of participation	Principle of competition	Principle of planning
(9) Well-being of the community	Well-being of individuals and groups, supported by state welfare system	Classless society

Though this is not an exhaustive comparisom of the three systems, it indicates that tribal communitarianism is quite distinct from modern communism.

The collapse of communism in Eastern Europe should not be uncritically used to reject any idea of communitarianism. Rather rejecting the ideal of communism, it is more important to investigate why modern communism has failed. The Third World Theologians identified the 'non-democratic forms of government, the imposition of a centralised economy and the denial of people's participation' as the basic causes of the collapse of the historical expression of socialism in Eastern Europe.[15] In fact, these things were not found in the tribal comunitarian life. Of course, as our table illustrates, the tribal communitarianism is far more limit but comparatively more democratic than modern communism. However, the tribal communitarianism requires a reconstruction as any other traditions do.

B. Rediscovery of Communitarianism for Theology

The collapse of the historical model of socialism in Eastern Europe certainly does not signal the demise of the values, goals and concerns of communitarianism. Some of its core values concern for the well-being of the community, participation of the people in the decision-making process, as well as in their own development; mutual care, trust and openness to one another; sharing of joy and sorrow - these resonate with the fundamental principle of Christian social thinking.

True community is born from love that risks the sorrow of rejection for the joy of acceptance. Community implies participation; participation means being open, and therefore vulnerable to one another. Love casts out fear, and fear is the root cause of hostility and war. Communitarianism is not social determinism in which individual freedom is subsumed; rather true community includes members with many different points of view and creates an atmosphere of freedom to express themselves. Incorporating the dark and the light, the sacred and the profane, the sorrow and the joy, the glory and the mud, its conclusions are well rounded.[16] It is a community where individual freedom is safeguarded and every one participates as a part of the whole. It is a place for mutual acceptance where there is no caste system nor class system. We must, of course, avoid romanticizing it. It is simply as egalitarian or non-differentiated a society as is possible.

---

15 "A Cry for Life: the Spirituality of the Third World, A Statement from the Third General Assembly of the Ecumenical Association of Third World Theologians, Jan. 5-16, (1992), Nairobi, Africa", *Asian Journal of Theology*, Vol. 6, No. 2, p. 345. But the conference did not accept capitalism as an alternative to communism and acknowledged the contribution of communism towards elimination of absolute poverty, economic democracy, full employment, development of science and sports.

16 M. Scott Peck, *Op cit*. p. 65

Such a true community is marked by humility, because different persons see themselves more clearly in the mirror of the living relationship with others. A genuine and profound self-understanding makes a person humble. "Meekness in itself is nothing else than a true knowing and feeling of a man's self as he is. Any man who truly sees and feels himself as he must surely be meek."[17] In this community of self-realisation human beings become realistic, honest and open to one another, for fear is dispelled.

A sense of security among the members goes on healing and binding the community together. The widow, the sick and the handicapped, all are taken care of by the community. As a community they build their houses together, labour together in their *jhum*, mourn together and celebrate together if there is anything to celebrate. In the Mizo society rich people used to compete to be *thangchhuah*.[18] This requires giving public a feast at least four times, culminating in throwing much of their valuable prossessions to the crowd, who scramble after them.[19] This means that there was no chance for accumulation of wealth, the rich shared all what they had. The meaning of celebration in the tribal community is sharing the blessings they have received with others.

The sense of community is so strong that they give priority to their community in their thinking and actions, rather than to their individual personal needs. Ultimately they deeply identify themselves with the village needs. The village community becomes their own identity.[20] People tell the name of the village rather than telling their name because the village community is their own identity. When some one met a stranger, he would ask the name of his village insteadof asking his name. In reply he would tell the name of his village.

---

17 Ira Progoff, *The Cloud of Unknowing*, (New York: Jullian Press, 1969), p. 92

18 Thangchhuah is an honourable title given in the Mizo community to rich persons who either killed ferocious animals or gave public feasts at least four times culminating giving away the treasures in their possession.

19 Zairema, "The Mizos and Their Religon", *Towards A Tribal Theology" The Mizo Perspective*, edited by K. Thanzauva, (Aizawl: Mizo Theological Conference, 1989), p. 42

20 When someone met strangers they usually asked the name of their village instead of asking their names. In their reply they usually said, "I or we belong to so and so village."

Having described the concept of communitarian living, it is now crucial to ask what is its theological validity and significance for tribal society today. Can this concept be a part of a theological model for social transformation in the context of North East India?

C. Theological Validity of Comminitarianism

The three fundamental bases of the theology of community are : the doctrine of the trinity, i.e. the divine community; the doctrine of the human person who is created to live in community; and the doctrine of the church - the community of believers. Thus, Christian theology is primarily a theology of community as it seeks to reflect and articulate the faith experiences of the community of believers and their understanding of 'God-Human-World' relationship.[21]

The doctrine of trinity is an affirmation of the idea that living in community is the fundamental nature of all living beings including God himself. It tries to elucidate the picture of God who live in unity with others. The divine community known as trinity is a symbolic expression of the reality of life. God then placed co-agents (persons) and created them such that they could be fulfilled or realise their nature only by entering into a community of love with God and other persons.[22] Similarly, for Karl Barth creation in the image of God means co-humanity. He said,

> Man has plurality like God, who is plural. Being man means being in togetherness: man and wife ... Image has a double meaning: God lives in togetherness with himself, then God lives in togetherness with men, then men live in togetherness with one another.[23]

Communitarian life is intrinsic human nature. Any person who undermine or negate community, whether they know it or not, acts in

---

[21] For examples of various treatments of this theme, see John Macquarrie, *Principles of Christian Theology*, (London: SCM, 1996), p. 1-2; R. Bultmann, *Jesus Christ and Mythology*, p. 68; John Cobb, *Christian Natural Theology*, p. 252; G. Guttierrez, *A Theology of Liberation*, pp. 3 & 6

[22] Frank G. Kirpatrick, "Toward A Metaphysics of Community", *Scottish Journal of Theology*, Vol. 38, (1985), p. 572

[23] J.D. Godsey (Recorded & Edit), *Karl Barth's Table Talk*, (Richmond Virginia: John Knox Press, 1962), p. 57

opposition to his/her own ultimate fulfilment and against his/her very nature.[24] Biblical concept of human is essentially communitarian. The primal reality here is not the individual, but the group the enduring entity to which the individual has his root. Therefore we must delight in each other, make others' conditions our own, rejoice together, mourn together, labour and suffer together, always having before our eyes our community as members of the same body. Likewise the church is a community of believers. Any ecclesiology which does not keep *koinonia* as its central theme cannot be an authentic ecclesiology. The World Council of Churches has repeatedly emphasised *koinonia*, using it to express and also illustrate the Christian concept of unity.[25] We see that communitarianism mirrors a fundamental doctrine of Christian church.

Our task is to build a just and haarmonious community free from discrimination, where women are free to live out the gifts God has given them, to respond to their calling, to share fully in the life and witness of the church. We are called to build a community where love dominates human relationship, where the widows and weaker section of the community are taken care, where the poor have hope for future emancipation and living with dignity. Communitarian humanity is a theological task involving action towards realization of God intended life for human community. Our theological task of building a harmonious community can be pursued in many different directions, however, our discussion in this chapter will mainly focus on its implication for tribal development.

D. Theological Significance for Social Transformation

The goal of development in the context of tribal community in North East India and other parts of India is not merely modernisation. It is recognised today that high rates of economic growth, necessary and essential though they may be, do not by themselves guarantee the easing of urgent social and human problems. Indeed in many countries high rates of economic growth have been accompanied by increasing unemployment, rising disparities in income both between groups and

---

[24] *Ibid.* p. 573

[25] The Canberra Assembly 1991 consistently used *koinonia*. The Fifth Assembly of Faith and Order Commission (WCC) has *koinonia* as its central theme.

between regions, and the deterioration of social and cultural conditions. A new emphasis is thus being placed on the attainment of social and cultural goals as part of development.[26] Tribal communitarianism essentially suggests that the goal of development is the common good for all members of community. This means community itself is both the goal and the means of development.

1. Community as the goal of development : In the context of the displaced and alieanted tribals in India, the reconstruction and empowering community is the basic step towards authentic development. The tribals themselves are aware of the importance of keeping the cultural and social integrity of their own community for their existence and development. The primary purpose of tribal struggle in India, particularly in North East India, has been to prevent their community from disintegration and to safeguard their cultural identity. It has not, however, been seen as the essential and primary step for development by policy makers and the so-called experts in tribal development.

The community development programs of various kinds, such as Rural Development, Rural Reconstruction, Rural Welfare, Social Welfare, Tribal Development and Integrated Rural Development Program (IRDP) perceived community as the unit and target of development in India and in other parts of Asia.[27] Since the primary concern of these various programs is economic development, the community is regarded as a "given". The community is treated as an *object* of development, where developmental activities should take place according to the programmes designed by experts. In this approach of development, people are expected to understand and appreciate the programmes and get themselves actively involved in the development process that the Government's programmes will be successfully implemented. Since the community is not seen as the very subject of

[26] M.P. Todaro, *Economic Development in the Third World, Op cit*. p. 8; See also the social teaching of the churches in the first chapter; *Human Development Reports of U N D P 1992* which states that economic growth does not automatically improve people's lives, either within nations or internationally. The U.N. advocates a human oriented approach of development, (New York. Oxford University Press, 1992), p. 3

[27] E. Desingu Serry, "Field Approach to Integrated Rural Development", *Journal of Rural Development*, Vol. 7, No. 6, (1988), pp. 676-677

development, a reconstruction and empowerment of community has not always been understood as the fundamental task of development.

The idea of community as a *goal* of development implies a holistic approach to development in which a community is politically empowered, educationally enlightened and made technically competent, socially reconstructed and organised, and made personally free and responsible for their own development. The political implications of community reconstruction at the macro level, are difficult and painful; but they are necessary for genuine development. Whether it is in America, Australia, Africa or Asia, a genuine activity in the area of tribal development must give serious consideration to political reconstruction and empowerment of tribal community. As far as India is concerned, the most advanced tribal groups are those of the communities who keep their own identity intact. This does not mean that isolation of tribals in itself will bring about advancement to the community; the displaced and alienated community must be reconstructed and politically empowered to rebuild self-esteem, confidence, hope for the future and to heal the trauma of genocide and the wounds of oppression and exploitation.

2. Community as means of development : This is an affirmation of the idea that *people* are the means and goals of development. The underlying assumption of this view is that human beings have the strength, potential and wisdom to learn from one another the fundamental beliefs, value systems and necessary skills to transform their social condition. This implies participation of the community in their own development process. In fact, the spirit of Community Development Programmes (CDP) in India and IRDP in general is that the community should be the unit and target of development, and all segments in the community should have opportunity for their development and should participate in the planning as well as in the implementation of various stages of development programs.[28] Samuel Paul defines community participation as "an active process by which beneficiary/client groups influence the direction and execution of a development project with a view to enhancing their well-being in terms of income, personal growth, self reliance or other values they cherish.[29]

---

[28] Kuruganty R. Sastry and C.P. Vithal, "Participatory Dimension in Rural Development: The Case of Panchyati Raj", *Journal of Rural Development*, Vol. 7, No. 6, (1988), p. 691, and E. Desingu Setty, *Ibid*. p. 678

[29] Cited by K.R. Sastry and C.P. Vithal, *Ibid*. p. 690

Though the ideal of IRDP is people's development programmes with government's participation, it remains largely a government administered program with people's participation. The program has been more target-oriented and there has been too much emphasis on achievements of targets and less emphasis in following the right menas, methods and processes to bring about change in the attitudes of the people.[30] It is for these and other reasons that government efforts in community development in India since 1952 has failed to achieve their vision. However, it has been found that wherever community development was taken seriously, the quality of the implementation of development was decidedly better.[31] A number of attempts have been made to review the functioning and performance of *Panchayati Raj* in India. It may be germane to point out that the emphasis of various committees, reviews, commissions and studies has been not that the *Pachayati Raj* should be scrapped but that it could be made more effective.[32]

A shared praxis, or a participatory approach is fundamental to effective community based development. It is a development effort not merely for the poor, but with the poor people. It aims at re-generation, utilisation, elaboration and consolidation of knowledge in order to help people understand their condition and appropriately respond to it. It felicitates as well as encourages people's action towards the transforation of their own society. It is a process of awakening and of continuing life education of communities, bringing them squarely on the path towards not only participation in, but also articulation of the community's self-knowledge, towards building self-confidence and esteem, and towards taking responsibility in the planning and management of their own development, discovering and re-evaluating of traditional beliefs and indigenous methods for dealing with needs, challenges and problems.

30 E. Esingu Setty, *Ibid*. p. 676

31 K.R. Sastry and C.P. Vithal, *Op cit*. p. 693

32 *Ibid*. Some of the notable commissions are: *Working Group on District Planning* (1984) which recommended that people's involvement should be encouraged at every stage of planning including pre-planning, strategy setting, scheme formulation, monitoring and review and not merely at the time of plan finalisation; Singhvi *Committee's Recommendations* (1987) suggested to constitutionalize *Panchayati Raj*; *Sankaria Commission* (1988) suggested that the local body should be strengthened in respect of recources and administrative matters.

CHAPTER VI

TRIBAL SOCIAL ETHICS:
A. "Tlawmngaihna" as the Tribal Social Ethic

We have dicussed the tribal community in the preceding chapter. One may wonder how did such a communitarian society actually operate in the complex "mix" which is life - be it in primitive or sophisticated. In deed we may question whether the nature of community described in the preceding chapter is a reality of the past; or a romanticised construct; or simply the naive dream of post-modernists. Though that was more of the past practice, it is more than a reality of the past, it is to a certain extent to actual life of the tribal community today. It is quite obvious that unless a certain principle of life or philosophy provides the basis, no society can practice such a communitarian way of living. This underlying principle of the tribal communitarian society is called *tlawmngaihna* by Mizos and *sobaliba* by the Ao Nagas. *Tlawmngaihna/sobaliba* is a social-ethical principle of the tribal community which provides the basis for a communitarian society to exist and function effectively. In othre words it is a philosophical and ethical foundation of communitarian society.

B. Meaning of *Tlawmngaihna*

Tlawmngaihna is a Mizo term which literally means resistance to being helped by others by helping others who are in need. The emphasis is on a denial of self rather than an effort to be independent.The purpose of this self-denial is to serve the community and any person in the community who are really in need of help. It is an act of charity whrein self-interest is subordinated to the interest of community, and the self sacrifices for the need of others is to come in sponteneously as a natural part of one's life. Without the pinciple of *tlawmngaihna* a communitarian society cannot function. Without the principle of *tlawmngaihna*, it would not be possible to build a harmonious society where members of the community practised 'decision by consensus', sharing their joy and sorrows and caring one another. The capitalistic as well as the modern communist systems do not have this kind of basis on which to build community. For tribal society, such a basis is provided by *tlawmngaihna*.

Several attempts have been made to define *tlawmngaihna*, both by the Mizos themselves and the non-Mizos who know the Mizo culture.[1] Definition, though it cannot be avoided, is often misleading and inadequate to explain accurately complex concepts and practices. Many of the definitions indicated in the footnote refer to a 'moral code' or 'code of morals' which are used not in a restricted sense of right conduct but in the sense of a principle or philosophical framework, held by a particular community regarding right or wrong relationships with others. For this book "social ethical principle" is preferred, to make clear the social nature of *tlawmngaihna* on the one hand, and its ethical nature on the other.[2]

The problem of defining and translating *tlawmngaihna* into English is clearly reflected by the many vocabularies and phrases employed by J.H. Lorrain, who tried to explain *tlawmngaihna* : as (a) to be self-sacrificing, unselfish, self-denying, persevering, stoical, stout-hearted, plucky, brave, firm, independent, loath to lose one's good reputation, prestige, too proud or self respecting to give in, etc.; (b) to persevere, to endure patiently, to make light of personal injuries, to dislike making a fuss about anything; (c) to put one's own inclination on one side and do things which one would rather not do, with the object either of keeping up one's prestige or of helping or pleasing another or of not disappointing another etc.; (d) to do whatever the occasion demands

---

1 While Mr. Sangliana defined it as the Mizo code of morals and good form, C.L. Hminga put it as the Mizo ethical code and good form. C.L. Hminga replaced 'morals' by 'ethics'. Rev. Challiana defined it as a strong moral code enforced by a strong public consensus permeating the whole section of the community and its social life. A.C. McCall, one time a superintendent of Mizoram, regarded it as a system of community oblication implying public service. N.E. Parry also defined it as a good moral code enforced solely by public opinion. See P.L. Lianzuala, "Towards A Theology of Tlawmngaihna", *Towards A Tribal Theology: The Mizo Perspective*, p. 55, C.L. Hminga *The Life of Witness of the Churches in Mizoram*, p. 30; J.M. Lloyd, *History of the Church in Mizoram, Ibid*, p. 4

2 Here ethics, as its Greek root 'ethos' refers to the customs or character which distinguishes a particular people, is used as a critical reflection of the morality of the norms and the practice of the people. Hunter P. Mabry, "Introduction", in *Christian Ethics: An Introductory Reader*, (Kottayam. Indian Theological Library, 1987), pp. 3 & 5

no matter how distasteful or inconvenient it may be to oneself or to one's own inclinations; (e) to refuse to give in, give way or be conquered, (f) not to like to refuse a request, to do a thing because one does not like to refuse or because one wishes to please others, (g) to act pluckily or show a brave front.[3]

Tlawmngaihna is the social principle as well as the norm for good conduct of the people in the community. The tribal moral ethos is based on good deeds for the welfare of the community, on putting the interest of the community above one's own individual interest. Thus, the tribals in their judgement of conduct would say, "it is shameful" rather than saying, "it is wrong". Doing anything that the society does not accept, whether wrong or right, is shameful. Parents forbid children doing certain things not necessarily because it is wrong to do them but shameful. In a society where community is placed above individuals, this kindof ethical judgement is inevitable. It is both moral and logical.

Tlawmngai is an attributive adjective form of *tlawmngaihna* to describe a person who practices *tlawmngaihna*. In order to become a *tlawmngai* person, one must be courteous, considerate, helpful, unselfish, courageous, industrious and ready to help others even at considerable inconvenience to oneself. M. Kipgen explains a *tlawmngai* person as one who is obedient and respectful to the elders; courteous in dealing with the weak and the lowly; generous and hospitable to the poor, the needy and the stranger; self-denying and self-sacrificing at the opportune moments in favour of others; ready to help those in distress; compassionate to a companion who falls sick while on journey or become victims of a wild beast in the hunt by never abandoning him to his fate; heoic and resolute at war and in hunting; stoical in suffering and in facing hardship under trying circumstances; and persevering in any worthwhile undertaking however hard and daunting that might proved to be.[4] A *tlawmngai* person (one who practises *tlawmngaihna*) whatever the occasion demands no matter how distasteful or inconvenient that might be to oneself or to one own inclinations; vie with others in excelling in sports or any other corporate labour; and try

---

3 J.H. Lorrain, *Dictionary of the Lushai Language*, (Calcutta: Royal Asiatic Society of Bengal, 1940).

4 M. Kipgen, *Christianity and Mizo Culture*, (Aizawl: Mizo Theological Conference, 1997), p. 65

to surpass others in hospitality and doing his daily task independently and efficiently.[5] A *tlawmngai* person will always try to ensure that he or she does not stand in need of help from others, and will strive to surpass others in doing his or her ordinary daily tasks efficiently for the sake of others.

Tlawmngaihna embraces various types of human qualities and activities, and manifests itself in various forms and aspects of community life which can be summed up as "community over self", wherein self-sacrifice for the need of others is the spontaneous outcome. A person who practices the precepts of *tlawmngaihna* is highly respected in the community.[6] It is *tlawmngaihna* that turns the steep mountains and the dense forests with all the toilsome labour of *jhum* cultivation, poverty and hardship into a pleasant dwelling place.[7] It is because of *tlawmngaihna* that poverty, misfortune, death, sickness has not traumatise the people. Every one in the community has been taken care of by the practice of *tlawmngaihna*. It is because of *tlawmngaihna* that every one tries to be self-sufficient in order to avoid receiving help from others.[8] It has been said,

The Mizo code of ethics revolves around *tlawmngaihna*, a composite term standing for such basic human qualities as kindness, courage and helpfulness. It indicates that compelling moral force which expresses itself in selfless service to society. *Tlawmngaihna* lies at the basis of the Mizo attitude of life. In war or peace, in private or public life, the Mizos are guided by the spirit of *tlawmngaihna*.[9]

While P.L. Lianzuala in his article "Towards a Theology of Miz Tlawmngaihna" argues that *tlawmngaihna* was created by social necessity in the Mizo society, he also makes the observation that while a number of Mizo cultural practices were annulled in the process of change by the other cultures,

---

5 M. Kipgen, *Ibid*. p. 65

6 Cited from Sangliana by J.M. Lloyd, *Ibid*. p. 4

7 K. Thanzauva, "Mizo 'Tlawmngaihna' and 'Niskama Karma'", *United Theological College Magazine*, (1984), p. 18

8 *Ibid*., p. 17

9 Director of Information and Publications, *Mizoram: Era of Peace and Progress*, (Aizawl: 1987), p. 11

C. Critical Analysis of *Tlawmngaihna*

Though we uphold with honour the spirit and objective of *tlawmngaihna*, we need to point out that the principle of *tlawmngaihna* does have both positive and negative aspects. It is the *tlawmngaihna* teaching of self-lessness which makes the Mizo people reserved, slow to express themselves even to the extent of telling a lie. A starving Mizo is reluctant to tell his want of food. Even a seriously sick patient, on the verge of death, will tell a doctor that he does not feel pain. The major weakness of *tlawmngaihna* is lack of a critical basis of assessment of its own actions. Since it has been so much socialised and people simply assume that what is expected in and by the society is right and good. Tribals are generally, and indeed traditionally, uncritical. *Tlawmngaihna* was conventionalised into the system of society. The same is true of contemporary Christianity. There is a strong tendency to consider everything done in the name of Christian faith as justifiable.

Tlawmngaihna is based on the principle of self sacrifice. It is not merely a system of social control for equilibrium, as some sociologists have suggested. 'Social control' implies seeking to contain individual or group resistance within tolerable limits.[11] *Tlawmngaihna* certainly contributes to social equilibrium, but it is not merely social obligation in terms of social control, as suggested for example by McCall.[12] Since the principle of *tlawmngaihna* prohibits criticism against others, *tlawmngaihna* could be one of the indirect causes of rampant corruption in the Mizo society today. Rather than challenging the wrong structures and misdeeds of the rulers, the principle of *tlawmngaihna* avoids pointing out the wrong doing of others.

Another weakness of *tlawmngaihna* is that its practice in the actual life is limited to those who understand the meaning of *tlawmngaihna*. The Mizos who are expossed to other cultures have realised that it is practicable only within the society where it is understood

---

[11] Peter L. Berger, *The Sacred Canopy: Elements of A Sociological Theory of Religion*, (New York: Doubleday & Company, 1968), pp. 29 & 24. Berger's distinction between socialisation and social control is used to distinguish tlawmngaihna from social control of the authoritarian type.

[12] A.G. McCall, *Lushai Chrysalis*, (reprinted), (Aizawl: Tribal Research 1977), p. 47

and practised by the people. First of all it begins in the village community, then expanded its circle to the larger Mizo society but rarely crossed beyond the boundary of Mizo society.

D. The Concept of *Tlawmngaihna* in Other Communities

As mentioned above, the principle and practice of *tlawmngaihna* is not confined to the Mizo society alone. A similar principle of social ethics has been found in all societies, particularly in the tribal societies. It is the basic principle of tribal life. While the universal nature of *tlawmngaihna* is admitted, the way it has been perceived and practised in the Mizo society is different. The term and concept of such social ethics is comparatively more explicit in Mizo society.

1. *Tlawmngaihna* and *Sobaliba* : The Ao Nagas' concept of *sobaliba* is quite similar to that of the Mizo *tlawmngaihna*. The term *sobaliba* embraces the traditional etiquette, social conduct, virtues and concern for others. It means honesty, integrity and denial of oneself for the sake of one's community. In the Ao community, as in other tribal society, the welfare of community is of first and foremost importance. The principle of *sobaliba* makes this vision of a just, harmonious and participatory society a reality. In short, it means total surrender of one's life to the cause of the whole society.[13] In explicating *sobaliba* Wati lists several terms and phrases such as extending help to the poor and needy, a willingness to share ones' belongings with others, respect for elders and parents, selflessness, truthfulness, self-control, integrity and obedience, being hospitable, industreousness, vicarousness, tackfulness, dedication, commitment, frugality, simplicity, sustainable use of resources, sociable and so forth.[14] Wati's definition of *sobaliba* is comparable with that of Lorrain's description of *tlawmngaihna*. The *tlawmngaihna* may be more commonly and expicitly used among the Mizos as it has been expressed in many songs, even an award of tlawmngaihna was instituted for those who practised and lived a life of *tlawmngaihna*.

2. *Tlawmngaihna* and *Niskama Karma* : It is quite evident that this kind of social ethics has been prevailing in most of the tribal

---

13 Wati Longchar, "Sobaliba" *Good News for North East India*, edited by Renthy Keitzar, Guwahati: Christian Literature Centre, (1995), p. 126

14 Wati, "Sobaliba". *Ibid.*, p. 126-27

societies. A similar idea of *tlawmngaihna* known as *niskama karma*, desireless action is also found in Hinduism. According to the common understanding, *karma* is actions which determine the condition fo a person in the cycle of rebirth (*samsara*). *Niskama karma* is a re-interpretation of *karma* in the Bhakti school, based on the teaching of Bagatvad Gita. It has been hailed by many scholars in Hinduism as one of the most important contributions of the Bhavadgita to ethical philosophy. Distinction can be made in the description of two tpes of actions : the traditional understanding of *karma* as desire for "fruit" and *niskama karma* as a desire for action itself. *Niskama karma* is the theory of non-attachment which demands self-sacrificial action without any desire of reward. Vivakenanda put it "Every act of charity, every thought of sympathy, every action of help, every good deed, is taking so much self importance away from our little selves as the lowest and the least; and therefore, it is all good."[15] B.G. Tilak holds that this concept is a perfect synthesis of the opposing tendencies in the moral life. Similarly, for P.N. Srinivaschari, "the Gita, theory of disinterested work is based on a synthetic view of human nature and harmonises its contradictions; it does not suppress the senses and their activities, but sublimates them to spiritual purpose."[16]

The distinctiveness of Mizo *tlawmngaihna* from *Niskama karma* is not so much in its teaching as in the degree of its impact upon the society.[17] While *Niskama karma* remains a religious ideal without having much impact on the society, the Mizo *tlawmngaihna* is the life principle which pervades the Mizo society and is essential for understanding the Mizo cultural life. Once again we must ask what is the significance of this concept for a contextual theology of social transformation for tribal community in North East India.

E. Reconstruction of *Tlawmngaihna* for Theology

We have already made the point that a theological rediscovery of *tlawmngaihna* in the changing situation demands re-interpretation and reconstruction of the traditional concept of *tlawmngaihna*. Let us pursue

---

15 Cited by Thanzauva, "Mizo 'Tlawmngaihna' and 'Niskama Karma'", *United Theological College Magazine*, (1984), p. 17

16 P.M. Thomas, *Op cit.*, p. 64

17 Thanzauva, *Op cit.*, p. 17

this issue. Re-interpretation of certain traditions and beliefs including Bible itself become inevitable if they are to be relevant and meaningful in our changing world. As tribal society is moving from personal towards an impersonal society where the right system becomes more important than personal *tlawmngaihna*. In fact, the present social, economic and political problems become increasingly complex which can be no longer solved with personal *tlawmngaihna*. The need of creating a social, political and economic system which should enhance justice, peace and harmony in the tribal society is an urgent and important task. In this situation, the issue of *tlawmngaihna* has to be shifted from "personal *tlawmngaihna*" to "social *tlawmngaihna*" which means creating a social economic system which should do the functions of *tlawmngai* persons to take care of the poor and the needy. The *tlawmngaihna* approach to social need is a charitable approach which has its own role, but is inadequate to deal with the modern tribal society which is becoming increasingly complex.

In other words, the traditional *tlawmngaihna* must be incorporated in the social system in which the structure, the planning for development and the legal system of the society must be made *tlawmngai*. However, a right system in itself is not adequate unless it is made function and effective, for which *tlawmngai* persons are needed to execute. Seeing the need of reinterpretation of traditional *tlawmngaihna*, it is necessary to incorporate the universal concern of Christian teaching for love and justice into *tlawmngaihna* to meet the challenges of today. Then only *tlawmngaihna* in modern society will be the insighful praxis of love to protect and uphold the marginalised, and to create a just, harmonious, progressive, participatory and sustainable society. Protection and upholding of the marginalised and commitment to the cause of the community today can no longer be confined to charitable service. It requires involvement in the struggle against all exploitative systems and structures which spoil the harmony of community. Doing justice overcoming evil with good must be perceived as an important element and necessary outcome of *tlawmngaihna* because this is a more effective way of caring the poor and marginalized.

Tlawmngaihna advocates individual freedom but rejects individualism as it puts society over individual. *Tlawmngaihna* is a tribal praxis in the sense of practicing its theoretical teaching of living for others Helping others is part and parcel of the principle of self-reliance. In other words, in the teaching of *tlawmngaihna*, helping others is the means by which one should become self-reliant. It is similar with the principle "give and you will be given". In fact, the Mizos have a saying that "those who eat by themselves will die, those who share with others will live." Life for them is living for others; selfishness is death. In sharing of their joy and sorrow, they find life that is the life of a true community.

F166. Theological validity of *Tlawmngaihna*

Tlawmngaihna is a message of Jesus Christ hidden in the tribal culture. It is an active love or love in action. If Love is the essence of the Gospel teaching, *tlawmngaihna* is the hidden gospel written in the hearts of the tribal people even before they embraced Christianity. The affinity of *tlawmngaihna* with love may be seen more clearly if one replaces the Pauline definition of love in I Cor. 13:4-7 with *tlawmngaihna* as follows : "*Tlawmngaihna* is patient and kind; *tlawmngaihna* is not jealous or boastful; it is not arrogant or rude. *Tlawmngaihna* does not insist on its own way; it is not irritable or resentful; it does not rejoice at wrong, but rejoices in the right. *Tlawmngaihna* bears all things, believes all things, hopes all things, endures all things." While love is arguably more comprehensive, with different shades of meaning, for examples, *tlawmngaihna* does have a connotation of communal love. *Tlawmngaihna* is a self-giving love which sets aside self-interests and seeks the betterment of others.

Though operates in both social and inter-personal relationships, in the main it is demonstrated in social or community life. For its societal nature, one may think that the Greek *philia* is a more appropriate term than *agape* for *tlawmngaihna*. But when the profound impact of *tlawmngaihna* upon the society is properly analysed, *agape* is more appropriate. Among the Mizos, there are a number of stories of those who laid down their lives for the cause of *tlawmngaihna*.[18] Such a love

---

[18] Taitesena, Khuangchera, Zampuimanga, Changbawla, Vanzema, Vanapa and others were said to lay down their lives for the cause of tlawmngaihna. Taitesena and Khuangchera were the martyrs of tlawmngaihna highly venerated by the Mizos. Vanapa was not a martyr of tlawmngaihna like the other two, but he was regarded as an embodiment of tlawmngaihna. These are the heroes of the Mizo people even today. The Mizo National Army, the military wing of Mizo National Front, named their battalions after Vanapa, Khuangchera, Taitesena and Zampuimanga. The Aizawl town hall is called Vanapa Hall.

is depicted by Jesus himself as the highest form of *agape*. “No one is greater love (*agape*) than this, to lay down one’s life for one’s friends.” (John 15:13)

If Jesus Christ is the expression and embodiment of God’s love, the incarnation, the ministry and the cross of Jesus Christ may be perceived as paramount act of *tlawmngaihna*. This may provide a basis for a Christological understanding of *tlawmngaihna*. The mythical heroes of the Mizo people were neither their warriors nor powerful chiefs but the *tlawmngai* persons who laid down their lives for the service of the community. Jesus Christ might thus be seen as the embodiment of *tlawmngaihna*, who transcends the tribal *tlawmngaihna*. Jesus is the *tlawmngai* par excellence.

G. Theological Significance for Social Transformation

The theological significance of *tlawmngaihna* can broadly be discussed in four categories :

1. *Tlawmngaihna* is a social ethic essential for the sustenance of harmony and integrity of the tribal community. For the tribals, harmony and sustainability of the society has been regarded as the primary objective of development. Thus, the goal of development envisaged in this book is not mere economic growth, it is the well-being and symbiotic progress of the society. In other words, the vision of society in this book is a shalomic society. *Tlawmngaihna* is an essential principle for the establishment and enhancement of such community. The principle of *tlawmngaihna* is in essence a “Kingdom principle” and is essential for the realization of the Kingdom of God in North East India and all over the world.

2. *Tlawmngaihna* is voluntarism which theologically advocates and empowers the voluntary organisations to bring about social transformation. Traditionally, voluntarism was regarded as charitable work within the system for the purpose of keeing social equilibrium. It was not expected to bring about a radical change. But the underlying assumption of voluntarism today is that people are the primary subject of change and have the power and responsibility to change their own situation.[19] The rapidly increasing number of voluntary organisations of various types in India is, in fact, a search for an alternative model of development in the face of the failures of the macro-organisations to initiate positive development.[20] However, this phenomenon is regarded by scholars of the privileged groups as the outcome of the apocalyptic vision of the middle class, developed in the process of their own struggle to climb the social ladder.[21] The active participants, particularly in action groups of a political nature, are regarded as deviants who are creating instability in the system, because the sociological perspective of the privileged groups is concerned with equilibrium and stability - often ignoring that most of the time what prevails in society is coercive equilibrium.[22] However, it can be observed that there is a shift of understanding and attitude towards voluntary organisations and movements. Increasingly the voluntary movements of various types - development groups, charity groups, action groups, support groups, political groups, etc. are perceived by sociologists as vehicles of innovative and creative ideas. Prof. T.K. Oommen observed that, "social movements are increasingly viewed as creative confrontation propelled by collectivities in search of a society based on a qualitative collective conscience.[23]

In the context of today, *tlawmngaihna* is concerned both for equilibrium as well as social transformation through various voluntary organisations and movements. In fact, voluntary organisations in Mizoram are known as *tlawmngai pawl* (*tlawmngai* association or organisation). The principle of *tlawmngaihna* should not be confined within static institutions or organisations, important though they are. It

[19] T.K. Oommen, "Mobilisation for Social Development: The Indian Situation", *Op cit*. pp. 1-16; D.L. Sheth, "Grass-roots Initiatives in India", *Economic and Political Weekly*, Vol. 19, (No. 6, 1984), pp. 259-262

[20] Harsh Sethi, "Groups in a New Politics of Transformation", *Economic and Political Weekly*, 19, (No. 8, Feb. 11, 1984), p. 305

[21] *Ibid*, p. 311. Organisations with a political nature are composed mainly of sensitised or radicalised middle class youth, working for and with the oppressed and exploited groups with a view to transform society. Their idea of self-denial and commitment to the cause is perceived by those who emphasized equilibrium as illusory and untrue.

[22] T.K. Oommen, *Op cit*., pp. 1 & 2. Social movements of both political and economic organisations in India are voluntary movements.

[23] *Ibid*., p. 2

should pervade all the fabric of the society, as it did in the past, in order to bring about transformation to the society. The church, as a voluntary organisation, is an institution of *tlawmngaihna* or love. But *tlawmngaihna* cannot be contained in the institutional church; rather the church is one of the instruments of *tlawmngaihna*.

3. *Tlawmngaihna* is 'praxis of love' or 'love in action'. We have read earlier I Corinthians 13:4 replacing "love" with "*tlawmngaihna*" that has reflected the similarities of *tlawmngaihna* and Christian love. "*Tlawmngaihna* is patient, kind, neither jealous nor boastful, nor arrogant, nor rude. *Tlawmngaihna* does not insist on its own way; it is not irritable or resentful; it does not rejoice at wrong, but rejoice in the right. *Tlawmngaihna* bears all things, believes all things, hopes all things, endures all things." *Tlawmngaihna* is the essential characteristic of divine nature from which the tribal *tlawmngaihna* is derived. It was the divine *tlawmngaihna* which sent Christ to take human form and die for the redemption of sinners. The love of God is qualified by sending his own son, Jesus Christ. Without the sending of his son, God's love would remain abstract. The act of love is what the Mizo called *tlawmngaihna*. The motif in the tribal *tlawmngaihna* is love for the community rather than concern for justice as in the Latin American liberation theology. This is as explained earlier, its weakness as well as its strength.

4. Tlawmngaihna is a communitarian discipleship, a commitment to the cause of community. It was a community which called the people to be *tlawmngai* or to be self-sacrificing for the sake of the community. Today in the Christian community, it is Jesus Christ who calls people, the believing community, to follow him in the mission of God - the establishment and extension of the reign of God. The call to be *tlawmngai*, before the advent of Christianity in Mizoram, was also the call to that same mission through the community. The calling as such, be it in the pre or post-Christian era to serve the interest of God within the community is the same. Thus, we may say that *tlawmngaihna* before the arrival of Christianity was a "discipleship" of Christ in a different form.

Discipleship for D. Bonhoeffer is obedience and commitment to Jesus Christ the one who called, not a confession of faith in Jesus Christ. Therefore, the disciple (*tlawmngai*) is drawn out of his or her vested interest into a selfless life, a life for others. Living for others to many people means suffering, insecurity and poverty. However, the true disciples (*tlawmngai persons)* experience the joy of suffering for others and for the just cause. It is nothing else than bondage to the community, completely breaking through every program, every ideal, every set of law. For Mizo people discipleship is nothing but *tlawmngaihna*. Following Jesus Christ means serving others, for he came not be served but to serve, and to give his life a ransom for many (Lk. 10:45). They are *tlawmngai* for Christ. *Tlawmngaihna* is the hidden law of the Cross in the Mizo society.

The norm for Christian existence for all ages must be self-giving love, an expression of a radical obedience to Jesus Christ. Discipleship is essential to participate in the establishment and extension of the Kingdom of God, which is central to the mission of Jesus Christ. The disciples in the Mizo context are the *tlawmngai* persons. The social transformation envisaged in this book is a transformation towards the realisation of the Kingdom of God. The disciples of Jesus Christ are the *tlawmngai* people for the cause of the Kingdom of God. Charles Scriven rightly observed that the transformation of culture is Christ's true purpose and his true means is the witness of radically obedient disciples.[24] *Tlawmngaihna* is commitment to the cause of society as discipleship is to the cause of the Kingdom of God. Realisation of the Kingdom of God here and now would certainly require Christian *tlawmngaihna*, which is nothing less than discipleship. Though the term is not used commonly inside the church, the medical, educational and all other charitable works of the church are the acts of *tlawmngaihna*. The success of social work heavily depends upon the commitment (*tlawmngaihna*) of active participants - the commitment of discipleship. *Tlawmngaihna* is a social ethics of the cross which seeks neither victory nor success, and is willing to suffer any loss or seeming defeat for the sake of obedience to Christ.

---

24 Charles Scriven, *The Transformation of Culture: Christian Social Ethics After H. Richard Niebuhr*, (Scottdale: Herald Press, 1988), p. 65

CHAPTER VII

TRIBAL ECCLESIOLOGY

"Community Home" as the Basic of Tribal Ecclesiology

As the Christian community requires the institution of the Church as a base for its authentic existence, a **community home** is essential for the tribal community to put the principle of **tlawmngaihna** into practice. In brief, **a community home** is an institution of **tlawmngaihna**. It is a common practice of various tribes to construct a large house in the village for the community, particularly for bachelors to sleep together. Different renderings have been used for this institution when translated into English, such as community house, dormitory, bachelor house, village house, community hall. *Morung*, the Assamese name, is commonly used in Nagaland. My study of its function led me to use **community home** which to me most accurately reflect the nature and function of the institution. This institution is similar to a hostel but again different from a hostel both in regard to its role and in the way it was run. A hostel is meant for a single purpose to do study whereas a community home is for multiple purposes as explained below. In the community home senior bachelors act like parents and teachers.

A **community home** is a social institution commonly found in most of the tribal societies all over the world. S.E. Peal observed that the sytem of a community home in the tribal society was found to exist from Bhutan to New Zealan and from the Marquesas to Nigeria.[1] Most of the tribes in North East India used to have a community home, though with their own names; *Kichu* for Angamis, *Ariju* for Aos, *Dikhu Chang* for Semas, *Longshim* for Tangkhuls, *Champo* for Lothas, *Smadi* for Lalungs, *Nokpante* for Garos, *Zawlbuk* for Mizos, etc. The Mizo term *Zawlbuk* is used for a **community home** mainly for bachelors. It literal meaning is a 'flat hut', (*Zawl* menas flat, *buk* is used for a hut). The detailed practice of various tribal groups differed from tribe to tribe. While some tribes have a separate building for ladies and bachelors

1 S.E. Peal, *The Communal Barrack of Primitive Races*, cited by Khasim Ruivah, "Long Shim (Dormitory) of the Tangkhuls", *Tribes of North East India, Op cit.*, p. 170

respectively, some have one only for the bachelors; while some were more organised others were informal.

Since it is not possible in this book to discuss the **community home** of each tribe, I will confine myself to which I know best. The Mizo **community home**, was usually constructed by the united, voluntary labour of the village community. It was usually located in the heart of the village, near the chief's house. In the **community home** all the young men slept at night.[2] In some big villages each locality, usually inhabited by the people of same clan, had a separate **community home**.[3] The then Major J. Shakespeare who subdued Mizoram and became the superintendent from 1897 to 1905, gave a vivid picture of a community home in Mizoram :

Zawlbuk is generally built on rather a steep hillside, so that the natural fall of the ground may allow ample room for animals under the raised floor and ensure good drainage. It is built, as are all other buildings in the village, of timber and bamboos, tied together with cane and thatched with either cane leaves or grass - if the former, then the ridge of the roof is straight and gable-ended; if the latter, it is far higher in the centre, whence it curves down somewhat abruptly to each gable. Access to the building is obtained by a platform of rough logs at the uphill end, where the front wall commences some 3.6 feet above the platform. Having stooped under this wall you are confronted by a low matting partition, surmounted by a huge log, the whole some 3 feet high, over which you scramble and find yourself in a large bare room varying from 15 to 50 feet long and 15 to 30 feet wide, according to the size of the village, with a square earthen hearth in the centre on which a few logs are always smouldering, and at the far end is a raised sleeping platform extending the whole width of the building. The young boys of the village

---

2 N.E. Parry, *A Monograph on Lushai Customs and Ceremonies*, (First edition in 1928 and reprinted in 1976) (Aizawl: Tribal Research, 1976), p. 8

3 Lt. Colonel J. Shakespeare, *The Lushai Kuki Clans*, (1912, reprinted in 1988), p. 20. Shakespeare narrated that the Lushai villages were well planned for the purpose of security. When Colonel Lister in 1850 captured the village of *Shentlang* he was so impressed with the regularity with which the villages within sight were laid out that he was easily led to believe that these were cantonments inhabited solely by warriors.

have to keep up the supply of firewood for the *Zawlbuk*, this duty continuing till they reach the age of puberty, when they cease sleeping in their parents' houses and join the young men in the *Zawlbuk*.[4]

The administration and regulations of a community home were recorded by N.E. Parry, a superintendent of Mizoram from 1924-1928, who consulted 56 chiefs of Mizoram and wrote that the community home had a regular system of self-government, very much in the same way as in a public school in England.[5] The *Val upa* (senior bachelors) were responsible for the administration of community home to arrange for all works to be done by inmates in the event of war, death, celebrations and accidents of the villagers. They made decisions concerning the admission of the boys into full membership. They also appointed three or four monitors to look after the boys and ensured that the boys did their duties.

Discipline was strictly enforced in all **community homes** and no interference from outside in the affairs of a community home was tolerated, except by the chief who might call the *Val upa* (senior bachelors) and discuss the affairs of a community home. The chief alone was allowed to throw a stone on the roof of a community home to caution the inmates in the event of a noisy or unpleasing scenes. Theft from a communal home was regarded as a disgrace and the punishment was a fine of Rs. 40, regardless of the article stolen, which had to be returned.[6] (Value of forty rupees in those would be not less than five thousand rupees). If a boy overheard a conversation between two young men in the community home and repeated it outside, he was fined Rs. 5 unless he was so small as to be considered incapable

---

4 J. Shakespeare, *Ibid.*, pp. 20-21

5 N.E. Parry, *A Monograph on Lushai Customs and Ceremonies*, (Aizawl: Tribal Research Institute, Reprint in 1976 of the first edition 1928), p. 9. The *Val upa* (senior bachelors) were experienced bachelors including a few exceptional married men who were acting as leaders and responsible for administration. The *Tlangval* (bachelors) were bachelors eligible to court girls and competent for all kinds of work. Most of the inmates were of this group. The *Thingfawm Naupang* were the boys who collected firewood under the supervision of monitors.

6 N.E. Parry, *Ibid.*, p. 11. In those days, to earn Rs. 40 one had to labour not less than 40 days.

of knowing that he had committed an offence.[7] Drunkenness in a **community home** was strictly prohibited.

B. Function of the Community Home

The function of the institution of a **community home** was multiple. The main functions may be briefly described as (a) Protection of the Village, (b) Training Young People, (c) Forum for Discussing Issues, (d) Recreation and Fellowship.

1. Protection of the Village : The primary function of the **community home** was to ensure the security and peace of the village. In the situation of inter-village feuds, head hunting, sudden attack of wild animals upon their domestic animals and human beings as well, an institution like the community home was a social necessity to ensure the security of the village. It enabled young men to keep vigil and protect the village at night. It also kept them assembled, as it were, for emergency to attend the needs of the village such as going to a distant village in the event of death and serious sickness, to call the relatives of sick persons and to render service when the storm or fire destroyed houses.

2. Training Young People : It was essentially a training institute for young men and boys to learn the arts of wrestling, singing, dancing, oratory, handicrafts and technique of war; for instruction about sex, manners, traditions, customs and etiquette and for learning religions and all the essential things for their lives in their own context.[8] It was a tribal education institution which provided different kinds of training necessary for villagers to live in the society and be self-sufficient. The *Zawlbuk* education aims at all-round development.

3. Forum for Discussing Issues : The *Zawlbuk* provided villagers a forum to discuss various issues pertaining to village welfare, security, relationship, hunting, inter-village feud, head hunting, jhum cultivation, and their own history. The village elders used to come in their free time to share thei experiences to the bachelors and chit chat; sometimes they narrated to them their myths, about *tlawmngai* persons and heroes of the village or tribe. It was in the *Zawlbuk* that they discussed, debated and resolved certain issues. Informal consultations

---

7 *Ibid*, p. 11

8 K. Thanzauva, "Theology of Zawlbuk", *Towards A Tribal Theolog*: *The Mizo Perspective*, p. 100

and seminars seemed to go on everyday. Young people learned their myths, folklores, songs and their own history.

4. Recreational Centre : It was in the Zawlbuk that villagers gathered together to sing, dance and do wrestling. Village comedians would tell funny stories and made all kinds of fun by acting and imitating others.

Over and above these, strangers from other villages who had no friends or relative in the village were usually entertained in the **community home** of the village and the news of the neighbouring villages were shared by the visitors to the inmates. When the first missionaries came to Mizoram, it was in the **community home** that they often preached the gospel and taught Christian humns.[9]

The Mizo *Zawlbuk* was exclusivel;y for men. However, the practice of different tribes differed. While entry to a **community home** was a taboo for women in the Mizos and Garos societies, the Aos and Tangkhuls had separate **community homes** for women and men. Exclusion of women from *Zawlbuk* reflects the relationship of men and women in the Mizo society. This exclusion of women has a lasting consequence that women have been excluded from decision-making bodies both in the church and society. It is important that when we incorporate *Zawlbuk* into ecclesiology, certain discriminative and oppressive elements should be rejected and others may be reinterpreted. Only the liberative elements, which is the method adopted in this book, should be adopted ecclesiology.

The fundamental principle of a **community home** was *tlawmngaihna*. As already suggested it could be called an institution of *tlawmngaihna*. Here *tlawngaihna* was theoretically taught and practically demonstrated in all the activities. It was in the communal home that *tlawmngai* (persons who practised *tlawmngaihna*) were

---

9 Rev. Edwin Rowlands reported in 1900, "About a mile from the Mission House there is a large *Zawlbuk* ... Lushais from distant village working for Government put up there. Sometimes there are 80 or more at the same time. This was visited twice a week, and sometimes views with the magic lantern were exhibited. In this way many from distant and scattered villages had an opportunity to hear the gospel, and they were continually changing", *Printed Report of Welsh Mission*, 1900-1901), p. LXi

recognised and venerated. The *Tlawmngai No* (a cup of rice beer) was instituted to be presented to the *tlawmngai* persons, in a special function or in a social drink, in honour of the contribution and sacrifice on had made for the community as a whole and for individual members of the community who are in need of help. A cup of rice beer was so simple but the attainment of the title *tlawmngai* was so difficult and greatly honoured in the Mizo society.

N.E. Parry, after consulting 56 chiefs, came to the conclusion that the villages that had community homes were coparatively better disciplined, more industrious and keener hunters than the villages where there was none.[10] A similar observation was made by S.T. Das that it was an excellent institution and a distinctive feature of every effective tribal village. In this situation young boys had to serve and obey older young men. Besides being associated with agriculture, social and almost all other activities of the village community were instilled into the youth, as well as respect for and obedience to elders and a spirit of service to the community.[11]

C. Rediscovery of Community Home for Ecclesiology

As with all social and cultural symbols, whenever an institution loses its significance in the changing world, it gradually dies out. D.N. Majumdar rightly observes that every institution in a society has its function, either practical or symbolic, to serve and maintain the society's ethos, mores and culture. Significant change often erodes the function as well as the form of an institution, and when an institution entirely loses its function, it loses its right to exist.[12] Thus it was with the tribal community home. Considerable effort was made in Mizoram by N.E. Parry in 1927-28 to revive the practice of a **community home** but that was fruitless.[13] Did the **community home** completely die out from

---

[10] N.E. Parry, *Op cit.*, p. 9

[11] S.T. Das, *The Tribal Life of North Eastern India*, (Delhi: Gain Publishing House, 1986), p. 51

[12] D.N. Majumdar, "A Decaying Institution - What Has Happened to the *Nokpante*? A Study Among the Garos", *The Tribes of North East India*, p. 306

[13] Liangkhaia, *Mizo Chanchin* (Mizo History), (Aizawl: Mizo Academy of Letters, 1976), p. 115

tribal society? The writer here argues that the physical structure and traditional form of a **community home** certainly died, but the Christian church and the educational hostels. In the process of transformation some essential substance was lost, which must be rediscovered and incorporated into the existing ecclesiology. A comparison of the Christia church and the tribal **community home** may be helpful to see the lost elements which need to be rediscovered :

Compare and Contrast the Community Home and Christian Church

(1) A community home is limited in its membership and concern; membership is open only to the villagers but inclusive in the sense that it admitted all the bachelors, in some cases even the ladies in the village.

The church is universal in its concern and membership. Its membership is open to all, and it is concerned for a wider human community but exclusive as it rejects non-Christians and members of other denominations.

(2) A Community home is the custodian of tribal culture, traditions and values, and an instrument for the welfare of the village community.

The church is the custodian of Christian faith and an instrument of the Kingdom of God.

(3) The community home is a big building at the heart of the village, near the house of the village chief. It is a community home where a village community becomes integrated.

The church is a big building at the heart of the village used to worship. It integrates its members who attend the church.

(4) The community home contributes towards integration, peace, security and harmony of the village community.

The church contributes towards integation of its own denomination and Christian community. Due to the existence of various denominations, it has increasingly become an instrument for the disintegration of the tribal community.

(5) The community home is an institution for training boys and young men and women in some cases to equip themselves with all the essential skill for living an independent life.

It is in the church that the spiritual life of the community of believers is nurtured. It also educates a number of students through its educational institutions. Women as well as men are included in this education.

(6) The community home keeps up a high ethical principle of *tlawmngaihna* and strict disciplines.

The church also teaches ethical life and imposes strict rules for its members.

From the above comparison it may be observed that the institution of a **community house** lacks an universal concern, but its contribution towards the harmony, welfare and peace of the village community was greater than the contribution of the church. The limitation of a **community home** and its exclusivist nature, due to the tribal world-view, has to be broadened. At the same time the Christian church should also realise that the local community, where the church really exists, matters most. The church is not a mystical institution existing beyond the realms of its human social environment. It is a believing community formed out of and existing in the concrete local community. In this context, the calling of God to be the instrument and sign of the Kingdom of God means to be an agent for the transformation of the local as well as universal human community, or rather to be an agent of transformation towards universal human community through transforming the local community.

Many wonderful statements and resolutions have been made by the World Council of Churches, the Roman Catholic Church and the Evangelical Movement expressing the need for creating a just, participatory and sustainable society. Many of their findings and resolutions remain in the realm of ideals, often without trickling down to the grassroots level. All those who are seriously thinking about how to translate those wonderful visions and statements into reality recognise the important responsibility of local communities to transform their own situations. No transformation will take place without the active participation of the local community. The tribal ecclesiology of a **community home** suggests that the local church should be an instrument of God for the well-being, harmony and development of the local community where it exists, without losing its universal nature.

D. Theological Validity of Community Home for Tribal Ecclesiology

The term 'ecclesiology' is here used as the doctrine of church, expressed systematically and coherently in order that the believing community may understand the true nature of extension, an ecclesiology which regards the local congregation as the true sign and instrument of the Kingdom of God. Bishop Lesslie Newbegin rightly said, "Positively, I think it is true that we must regard the local church (congregation) as having a certain real primary among the various units into which we may think of the church as being divided."[14] Hans Küng argues that the local church is in no way to be seen as a sub-division of the real church (universal church). The whole Church can only be understood in terms of the local church and its concrete actions. The local church is not a small cell of the whole, which does not represent the whole and which has no purpose in it. It is the real Church, to which in its local situation everything is given and promised which it needs for the salvation of humanity in its own situation: the preaching of the Gospel, baptism, the Lord's supper, different charisma and ministers.[15] For Leonardo Boff the local basic ecclesial community is a reflection of a true New Testament Church.[16] It is, for Sobrino, a 'resurrection' of the church. However, by resurrection he does not mean that the church is dead. Resurrection rather implies a new way of being church, manifesting a newness of substance and life more in conformity with the spirit of the early church.[17]

While stressing the primacy of local church, it is important to know that the New Testament does not undermine the universal church.[18] The emphasis on the primacy of the local believing community is made here mainly because it has been too often neglected in favour

---

14 L. Newbegin, *The Household of God*, (London: Friendship Press, 1954), p. 117

15 Hans Kung, *The Church*, (London, Search Press, 1973), p. 85

16 L. Boff, *Ecclesio - Genesis: The Base Communities Reinvent the Church*, (New Maryknoll: Orbis Books, 1986), p. i ff

17 John Sobrino, *The True Church and the Poor*, (Maryknoll: Orbis Books, 1984), pp. 85 ff

18 1 Cor. 9:4, 12:29, 15:9; Eph. 1:22, 3:10, 21; 5:23, 27, 29, 32; Matt. 16.18, Heb. 12:22-23; Gal. 1:13; Phil. 3:6.

of universal church or a massive institutional organisation with a powerful hierarchical structure. Each local ecclesial community is a microcosm of the whole ecclesia; the local ecclesia and the universal ecclesia are the two sides of the same reality. The local ecclesia in its visible form and structure has to manifest the inevitable, structureless dimension of the universal church.[19] It is sad that the churches in Mizoram have an orderly centralised structure, to the extent of squeezing out the financial resources of the local churches to serve the interest of the centre.[20] It is imperative to rediscover the tribal **community home** as a metaphor for an authentic ecclesiology for North East India.

The institution of a community home can be seen as a forerunner of the Christian Church. Therefore, ecclesiology for the tribal community does not have to be imported from the West; the authentic ecclesiology for tribal Christians has to be a synthesis of the community home and the traditional concept of church.[21] The pioneer missionaries to Mizoram, J. Herbert Lorrain and F.W. Savidge, rightly envisioned the Church in Mizoram and expressed as follows :

We are not here to make Eastern duplicate of Western Baptist, but to bring them to Christ and to so guide them that they shall develop along their own national lines into a strong Lushai Church of God which shall be a living witness of the Power of Gospel to change savages into saints and head-hunters into soul-hunters. We look forward to the time when the Lushai Church shall be a happy blend of all that is best in Baptist, Presbyterian and Methodist, **with something added perhaps which no Western denomination** can suppy.[22]

---

[19] G.R. Singh, "The Local Congregation - Some New Testament Insights", *The Local Congregation: Its Mission in India*, (Delhi: ISPCK, 1982), p. 2

[20] The Presbyterian administrative system was regarded by the missionaries as the most similar to the Mizo traditional administrative system. It was successfully introduced and adopted by all denominations. That certainly solved the economic problems and enabled the churches to be not only self supported and also enabled to spare huge amountof fund for mission and other projects. But my own field study revealed that the local churches are struggling for their own survival while the central headquarters is prospering.

[21] K. Thanzauva, "Theology of Zawlbuk", *Op cit.*, p. 104

[22] *The Annual Report of BCM on Mizoram 1901-1938*, (compiled and published by the Mizoram Gospel Centenary Committee) (Serkawn: Mizoram Gospel Centenary Committee, 1993), p. 99

In fact, the structure of Baptist Church of Mizoram is more or less a synthctic structure, a blend of the Baptist, Presbyterian and Methodist ecclesiology with the traditional social structure. What a pioneer missionary meant by "something added perhaps which no Western denomination can supply" seems to be the traditional village administrative structure where the council of elders with the chief planned for the village, decided and executed in Mizoram, the Presbyterian, the Baptist, the Pentecostal, the Seventhday Adventist, etc. have adopted a structure in which the council of elders along with a pastor does everything. But the objectives and functions of **community home** have not been incorporated into the mission and ministry of the church.

E. Theological Significance of Community Home for Social Transformation

The theological significance of the ecclesiology of **community home** is quite evident from the preceding discussion on the function of the institution in tribal society. The Christian church is an institution through which theology is put into practice, as a **community home** was an institution for *tlawmngaihna* in the Mizo society.

1. The Community Home as the Instrument of the Kingdom of God : The "ecclesiology of a **community home**" propounds that the local church should be committed to the cause of the well-being, security, development and harmony of the local community for the realisation of the Kingdom of God in a concrete situation. This ecclesiology also implies reconsideration of the traditional concept of the nature and function of the church. The church in the tribal ecclesiology is perceived as the servant and guardian of the believing community. It is an instrument of the Kingdom of God, and its mission is holistic. The essence of the tribal ecclesiology is that the Church is a community of believers responsible for the realisation of the Kingdom here and now. They share their joy and sorrow in the atmosphere of true *koinonia*, reflecting their problems together and participate in the planning of their own development, and labour together in the execution of work with the hope of transforming their own situations. They are brought together neither by ideology nor self interest, but by their love for their community, because loving God for them is loving the community which is the very body of Jesus Christ. Worshipping together in the **community home** (church) means celebration of life with each other and with Jesus Christ.

The emergence of basic Christian communities in Latin America is one of the concrete historical expressions of the ecclesiology of a community home in recent years.[23] Development of the Basic Christian Community was found to be imperative in the context of the Roman Catholic Church of Latin America, where the church is hierarchically structured. Leonardo Boff described the basic church communities as a specific response to a prevailing historical conjecture. Theologically they signify a new ecclesiological experience, "a renaissance of the very church, and hence an action of the Spirit on the horizon of the matters urgent for our time."[24] However, while this may be new for the Roman Catholic, it is not new for the tribal people and for some of the Protestant churches.

The basic ecclesial communities are not merely weekly discussion groups. They are believing communities striving to form a support group, sharing each others' concerns and problems as they reflect on the Bible. They consitute the poor, simple, marginalised and oppressed persons in their own society, similar to the New Testament Church. In the process of "action and reflection" in their struggle, they also recognise their potentials for organising together to work for social change.[25]

2. The Community Home as the Sign of the Kingdom of God : Formation of a shalomic community is seen as the means and goal of development. A **community home** in itself is a community as

---

23 A brief description of the development of these communities can be found from: Guillermo Cook, *The Expectation of the Poor: Latin American Base Ecclesial Committees in Protestant Perspective*, (Maryknoll: Orbis Books, 1990), and *New Face of the Church in Latin America: Between Tradition and Change*, (Maryknoll: Orbis Books, 1984), E. Clearly, *Crisis and Change: The Church in Latin America Today*, (Maryknoll: Orbis Books, 1984).

24 L. Boff, *Ecclesio-Genesis*, (Maryknoll: Orbis Books, 1986), p. i

25 A.F. McGovern, *Liberation Theology and Its Crisis*, (Second Orbis Books, 1990)m o, 202

well as an instrument for the formation and existence of a harmonious and sustainable community. The fellowship in the communal home was a true koinonia, a fellowship of mutual trust, heart-to-heart sharing of joy, and problems by which people of different opinions reached understanding and eventually fusion of ideas took place. Thus, tribal ecclesiology implies that the church is a community of fellowship (*koinonia*) to reflect the trinitarian fellowship. As a community home was a sign and instrument of a village community, the church has to be the sign and instrument of the Kingdom community. As the community home was a mirror in which people saw the true picture of the village community, today the church should also be a ling mirror to see the true picture of the Kingdom of God.

Christian life in the local congregation of tribal ecclesiology will be characterised by the absence of alienating structures, by direct relationship with God and with one another, by reciprocity, by the communion of believers (*koinonia*), by mutual trust and support, by equality and freedom. It is the visible body of God, the community, guided by the principle of *tlawmngaihna*, which motivates each member of the local congregation to put the interest of community before their own individual interest, and to labour together as a community to bring about social transformation.

The tribal ecclesiology is a call for a shift of emphasis from hierarchical institutionalised church to a grassroot community of believers, from a mystified concern for spiritual development to a realistic concern for genuine development of people, from ritualistic ministry to an involvement in the concrete situation of people's struggle. The shift of emphasis is not however an "either-or-approach", upholding one at the expense of the other. It is rather an attempt to rectify the lopsided emphasis in the history of the church so as to keep balance in the structure and mission of the church.

CHAPTER VIII

COMMUNITY OF GOD, HUMAN AND WORLD

The theological debate on the model of God has been swinging back and forth between the two poles of the transcendental and immamental models. My study of the tribal cosmology leads me to propse a communitarian model of God which I see reflecting most accurately the biblical understanding of God.

Since our perception of God is determined by our understanding of cosmology, the inter-relationship of God-Human-World, we will briefly discuss the meaning of cosmology. The term "cosmology" may be defined in many different ways. It is a combination of two Greek words - *cosmos* and *logia* (cosmology), it literally means the science of universe. It is a branch of philosophy or science that deals with the study of the universe as a whole and its form, nature, etc. David Tracy and Nicholas Lash define in various ways including a theological account of the world as God's creation, philosophical reflections on the categories of space and time, the observation and theoretical study of the structure and evolution of the physical universe; and then finally "world view".[1] The tribal cosmology is understood in this chapter as the way tribal people perceived the universe or their world view. Their perception of the relationship between God, Human and the World is at the core of their cosmology. Our concern in this chapter is to rediscover the tribal cosmology particularly their concept of this God-Human-World relationship as one of the transformational motifs to be theologically reconstructed.

It will be helpful to discuss briefly the centrality of God-Human-World relationship in Christian theology and how the gradual shift in the understanding of God-Human-World relationship has been taking place before discussing the actual tribal concept of God-Human-World relationship. This will help us to see the validity of the tribal understanding of God-Human-World relationship for Christian theology.

Since our world view or understanding of God-Human-World relationship affects our attitudes, the way we understand ourselves, the

---

1 David Tracy and Nicholash Lash (ed), *Cosmology and Theology*, (Edinburgh and New York: T & T Clark and Seabury Press, 1983), p. vii

way we relate to other people, and the way we relate to environment, the earth and all creatures, a proper articulation of Christian understanding of God-Human-World relationship is important. A right understanding of God-Human-World relationship will not only give us an appropriate vision of society, it will also inspire us to struggle to build a new social order.

Theology itself may also be defined as a systematic and coherent articulation of how the community of faith perceives God-Human-World relationships, to assist the community and individual believers to be more effectively engaged in the mission of Jesus Christ for the realisation of the Kingdom of God here and now.[2] For David Tracy "God-Human-World" is an analogical imagination of an ordered relationship, which expresses the inseparable inter-connection of these realities. It remains possible to distinguish them, to understand them distinctly but in order to unite these mutually reinforcing realities into their similarities-in-difference, their inter-connectedness must be emphasised and explained in the construction of theology.[3] Theology is concerned to explain how people have perceived and experienced the inter-relationship of these three realities.

A. Theological Debate on God-Human-World Relationship

In the history of Christian thought this relationship has been described basically in two models, the transcendental model (master-servant relationship) and the immanental model (organic relationship). These models have been used to classify the two types of "God-Human-World" relationship in the history of religions as indicated below :

Transcendental Model	**Immanental Model**
Kathenotheism	Animism
Henotheism	Fetism

2 Sallie McFague: "Theology, I believe, has special responsibility for the symbols, images, the language, used for expressing the relationship between God and the world in every age". Imaging a Theology of Nature: the World as God's Body", *Liberating Life*, edited by Charles Birch, William Eakin, Jay B. McDaniel, (New York: Maryknoll: Orbis Books, 1990), p. [illegible]

3 David Tracy, *The Analogical Imagination. Christian Theology and the Culture of Pluralism*, (London: SCM, 1981), pp. 429-430

Deism	Polytheism
Monotheism	Dualism
Absolute Monotheism	Pantheism

Though this distinction of two types is in some respects superficial, it reflects the basic trends of religious thought in general and in Christian theology in particular. The transcendental model insists that God is prior to, distinct from, and thus "beyond" the world, not to be confused with anything in the world but has its being and comes to the world from "beyond". Karl Barth summarises his early point of view as an emphasis on God as '*wholly other*' breaking in upon us 'perpendicularly from above', and on the "'infinite qualitative distinction' between God and man."[4] This concept of God "out there" or "up there" necessitates the "creator-creatures" or "master-servant" or monarchical model of the God-Human-World relationship.

Many theologians have questioned whether, strictly speaking, it is meaningful to think of God "out there" or "up there".[5] Bishop Robinson argued that the idea of God "up there" and "wholly other" was a concept based on the Ptolemaic cosmology. When this cosmology was overturned by the Copernican view, the spatial view of transcendence was interpreted by Christians in a symbolic sense. The idea of God "out there" for Robinson lost its significance. It is "a projection, an idol, that can and should be torn down".[6] Increasingly theologians have either made the shift from a traditional transcendental model to an immanental model, or are at least have sought to reconcile the two.

The emphasis on the *immanence* of God often uses the "Self-Body" relationship as an analogical tool to explain God-Human-World relationship. Charles Hartshorne suggests *Panentheism* as an authentic Christian concept of God-Human-World relationship to integrate the two models.[7] Macquarrie has defined his approach as follows :

---

4 K. Barth, *The Humanity of God*, (Atlanta: John Knox, 1960), p. 42

5 For example, G. Kaufman, "Two Models of Transcendence", *The Heritage of Christian Thought*, Essays in Honour of Robert L. Calhoun, ed. by R.E. Caushman and E. Grislis, (New York: Harper & Row, 1965) and "On the Meaning of "God": Transcendence without Mythology", *Harvard Theological Review*, Vol. 59 (1966), pp. 105-132

6 John A.T. Robinson, *Honest to God*, (London: SCM, 1963), pp. 17, 41, 54

7 C. Hartshorne, *The Divine Relativity*, (New Haven: Yale University Press, (1948) Sixth Printing, 1976), p. 89 ff

> Being in the *transcendence*, and this term indicates not only God's distinction from the world but in "wholly other" character as over against whatever is within the world. Yet at the same time, the acknowledgement that there "is" no being apart from beings, and that being "is" present-and-manifest in every being, guards against an exaggerated transcendence of God, such as has been common in recent theology, and seeks to do justice to his immanence.[8]

Macquarrie reacted to the idea of the otherness of God and said that some theologians have made it more difficult because they have assumed a concept of God which separates him so absolutely from the created order that the gulf between can never be bridged. If there is no affinity between God and the human race, if God is 'Wholly other' and separated from us by an 'infinite qualitative difference' then it seems to him that the incarnation of Jesus Christ is not only 'absolute paradox', but a sheer impossibility.[9] Between these two extreme poles of the immanence and transcendence of God, the tribal vision of God-Human-World relationship can also provide an integrating concept, and may be used to develop an authentic Christian doctrine of God-Human-World relationship.

B. The Tribal Voice in the Debate

The concept of God-World relationship is one aspect of cosmology or *world view.*[10] The tribal concept of God-Human-World relationship is another transformational motif to be theologically rediscovered. The overt forms of tribal religion may disappear in their encounter with modern

---

8 John Macquarrie, *Principles of Christian Theology*, (London: SCM, 1966), pp. 109-110

9 John Macquarrie, *Jesus Christ in Modern Thought*, p. 376

10 World View here is regarded as the pattern of thought, attitude, concept and how the people hold together their experiences based on their perception of God, Human and the World. It shows how things look and provides some coherence. On the other hand, it is the way people see themselves in relation to all else. Robert Redfield, *The Primitive World and Its Transformation*, (New York: Cornell University Press, 1953), p. 85 ff; Clyde Kluckhohn, "The World View of the Navaho", *Ideological Foundations of World Orders*, edited by F.S.C Northrop, (New York: Yale University Press, 1949), pp. 356-384

civilisation, modern technology and other religions, but their world view prevails and shapes their lives. This world view can and should become part of a theological basis for social transformation in North East India.

The tribal religion in general has been described as animism. But animism does not sufficiently explain the belief system of the tribal people. In the tribal traditional religious belief there was an implicit idea of a supreme being which anthropologists generally called "high God", as if they were worshipping a low god and a high god. Most of the tribals in India believed naturally in the existence of a supreme being, a God of all humanity and goodness.[11] That supreme God was known by different names to different tribes - *Ukpenuaffu* (Angami), *Lijaba* (Ao), *U Blei* (Khasi), *Tartara Robunga* (Garo), *Pathian* (Mizo, Kuki, Chin), *Dharmes* (Oraon), *Singbonga* (Mundas and Santals) and so on.[12] The observation of traditional anthropologists and missionaries seem to have been determined to a great or lesser extent by cultural imperialism.

Apart from the supreme being, they also believe in the existence of celestial beings who are more personal and more involved in human affairs than the supreme being, who is remote. They also believe the existence of both benevolent and malevolent spirits. As they regarded the malevolent spirits to be the cause of suffering, they used to offer sacrifice to evil spirits. When the missionaries saw the tribal people offering sacrifice to evil spirits for appeasement, they generally thought that they were *worshipping* evil spirits. As far as the North East Hill tribes are concerned, no tribe claims that their ancestors were worshippers of evil spirits. The idea of worshipping evil spirits seems to have been developed by observers, not the tribals themselves. This observation of anthropologists on tribal religion, which influenced the

---

11 Thanzauva, "Christianity and Tribal Culture in North East India: A Theological Perspective", A Paper presented in the Consultation held in Gauhati on Tribal World Views, 7-9, Jan. 1990. Both Shakespeare and A.G. McCall stated that the Mizo people believed in the existence of "one Supreme God, a God of all humanity and goodness," A.G. McCall, *Lushai Chrysalis*, (London: Luzac and Company, 1949), and J. Shakespeare, *Op cit*. 61 ff. Similarly Renthy Keitzar siad, "Most Nagas have a belief in a High God or Supreme Being", *In Search of A Relevant Gospel*, (Guwahati: CLC, 1995), p. 21

12 *Ibid*., pp. 8 & 9

missionaries, is what the native Americans have called the legacy of Colombus.[13]

They also believed that both the good and the evil spirits dwell in all the places and objects. They used to keep certain animated objects at home to bring blessings. At the same time, they were afraid of certain objects and places which they believed were inhabited by evil spirits. Some human beings were believed to be god-human beings and some were regarded as animal-human beings. In their relationship there is distinction but no separation. The diagram of the tribal cosmology may be formulated as follows :

Supreme Being
(Almost every tribe practised the worship of Supreme being in various names name)

Celestial Beings
(Number of celestial being differed from tribe to tribe, Mizos have three, Pu Vana, Vanhrika and Vanchungnula)

Benevolent spirits
Some of the benevolent spirits among the Mizos are Khua, Khuavang, Lasi, Khualtu, etc.

Malevolent spirits
Some of malevolent spirits Ramhuai, Chawm, Hmuithla, Khawhring, Phung, etc.

Human Beings
god-humans, animal-humans Spirit of human person, animated objects (fetish)

Based on their cosmology - the heaven above and the earth below - they belived that the abode of the supreme being and all other celestial beings and lived with them [14] Thus, human beings who live on earth see

---

[13] Bartholomew Mella, "Indigenous Culture and Evangelization. Challenge for a Liberating Mission", *International Review of Mission*, Vol. 81, (No. 324, Oct. 1992), pp. 551-561

[14] Wati Longchar narrated the story of the visit by *Lijaba*, the supreme being, to the village in disguise. He went door to door requesting for shelter but every one made excuses. Finally the two orphan sisters invited him to their humble hut. A similar story is found among the Mizos and other tribes. Indeed it has its equivalent in many other cultures. Wati Longchar, *The Traditional Tribal Worldview and Modernity*, (Jorhat: N. Limala Lkr. 1995), p. 33-34

their existence as living in the midst of spirits, and so they offer sacrifices to the spirits.

One may think that tribal people in reality do not worship the supreme being but the evil spirits, for they often offer sacrifice to them. In the light of a theological debate on theodicy, the offering of sacrifice to evil spirits may be explained as the tribal solution to the problem of evil. How is the existence of evil and suffering in the world consistent with the existence of a supreme God who is believed to be both omnipotent and good? Adherents of all religions faced this question and pondered on the possible origin of evil. The Hindus regard *karma* (the deeds of human being) as the root cause of evil. Christians regard sin as originating from Satan, Buddhists consider the origin to be in the desires of human beings. Tribals held malevolent spirits responsible for all evils. For the Hindus and Buddhists, it is the human person who is responsible, whereas the Christians and tribals found the root cause not merely as originating from human beings, but from a power beyond human control known as Satan or evil spirits. The traditional Christian idea of Satan and the tribal idea of malevolent spirits have certain affinities. The tribals, who experienced human limitations in their day-to-day encounter with nature, tried to protect themselves from misfortunes and blamed malevolent spirits instead of blaming either God or human beings. In this way they removed God from the picture. Ultimately, the supreme God becomes uninvolved in human affairs.

The seeming transcendence of God in tribal tradition is a product of the problem of evil. In other respects, however, they believe in the immanence of God. The supreme being is believed to be a compassionate and gracious God who acts not coercively, but persuasively and lovingly. The supreme being is not a silent spectator. The chant or invocation used by a Mizo priest during the sacrificial offering to the guardian spirit of the clan or family reflects that the supreme God is acting through a particular a guardian spirit who is believed to be everywhere :

Ah-h Arise from the village, Aw-w. And accept out sacrifice
Ah-h Arise from the open space in the village. Aw-w. And accpet our sacrifice.
Ah-h Arise from your dwelling places. Aw-w.
Ah-h Arise from the paths. Aw-w

Ah-h Arise from the gathering mists. Aw-w
Ah-h Arise from the yam plots. Aw-w
Ah-h Arise from Buhchuam hill. Aw-w
Ah-h Arise from above the road. Aw-w
Ah-h Arise from below the hill. Aw-w
Ah-h Arise from Vahlit hill. Aw-w
Ah-h Arise from Muchhip hill. Aw-w.[15]

Ah-h Arise from the new village site. Aw-wh
Ah-h Arise from the shelf over the hearth. Aw-a
Ah-h Arise from the village. Aw-w
Ah-h Arise from the earth. Aw-w
Ah-h Arise prayed to by our ancestors, Accept our sacrifice.[16]

Bless Luta's house (the householder's name).
Bless us with sons, bless us with daughters,
Bless us while in bed, bless us around the earth,
Make us to flourish like a sago palm,
Make us to flourish like a hai tree,
Bless us while the sun shines,
Bless us while the moon shines,
May those above us bless us, may those below us bless us.[17]

This invocation and an analysis of other cosmogonic myths of the tribes in North East revealed a belief that the indwelling spirit of God is all around them.[18] According to the Ao Naga tradition, *Lijaba*, the supreme being, enters into the earth with the seeds and rises again along with crops. He is the one who gives vegetation in the land and regenerates the earth by entering into the earth every year.[19] There is certainly distinction but no separation between the creator and creatures, the being and beings and all other entities. Distinction

---

15 J. Shakespeare, *The Lushei Kuki Clan*, *Op cit.*, pp. 70 & 71
16 *Ibid.*, p. 71
17 *Ibid.*, p. 71
18 In the story of Mauruangi, her mother became a fish and then a tree in order to feed her daughter Mauruangi. There are many more stories such as *Tualvungi, Nguhei, Lalruanga*, etc. which explicitly show that tribals had no distinction in the sense of dualism between nature and humanity. All creatures and realities are seen as inter-related.
19 A. Wati Longchar, *The Traditional Tribal World View and Modernity*, p. 37

is maintained only at the existential level. Baidyanath Saraswatti rightly observed that in the tribal perception, neither humanity nor god (spirit) is unique. Nobody reigns supreme *in the sense of transcendence, one is only different from one another*. Every creature performs the same paradigmatic act of creation, preservation and destruction. The cosmic order is maintained by a harmonious functioning of each one. The first principle of the cosmos is 'one-two and many', and what makes the cosmos one undifferentiated reality is its eternal law of non-duality.[20]

Referring to the African traditional religion, which is a tribal religion, Taylor argued that an essential feature of primal religion was the sense of cosmic oneness and said,

> Not only is there less separation between subject and object, between self and non-self, but fundamentally all things share the same nature and the same interaction one upon another - rocks and forest trees, beasts and serpents, the power of wind and waves upon a ship, the power of a drum over a dancer's body, the power in the mysterious cave of **kokola**, the living, the dead and the first ancestors, from the strone to divinities of hierarchy of power but not of being, for all are one, all are here, all are now.[21]

The apparent hierarchy in the relationship of beings is sacred order (hieros) rather than a social idea or the ideal of gradation. The spirits, humans and animals are differentiated at the existential level, but there is no real distinction in the tribal cosmology that may convey the ontological separateness between the Supreme being, spirits and human beings. Perhaps the best way to grasp the differentiation is to think of the functional aspects of interrelatedness of all existing things and beings in the larger context of the cosmic process.[22] In spite of functional differences, God-Human-World formed a community in which they are inter-related; it is, therefore, quire legitimate to describe this relationship as a "community model of relationship".

---

[20] B. Saraswati, "Introduction: Anthropology of Tribe", *Tribal Thought and Culture*, (New Delhi: Concept Publishing Company, 1991), p. 17

[21] John V. Taylor, *The Primal Vision: Christian Presence amid African Religion*, (London: SCM, 1977), p. 54

[22] B. Saraswati, *Op cit.*, pp. 17 & 18

C. Rediscovery of a Community Model of God-Human-World Relationship

It is quite clear from the preceding discussion that the tribal concept of God-Human-World relationship is derived neither from strict ideas of transcendence nor immanence, nor monotheism nor polytheism. None of these categories reflects adequately the tribal understanding of God-Human-World relationship. "A Community model" seems to be the most appropriate model to express the tribal concept of God-Human-World relationship. They believe that God is in all and all is in God. In the tribal understanding of God-Human-World relationship, God is never perceived as wholly other but as the one who become human and participates in the life of the world. Hesselgrave rightly notes that the tribal world-view transcends the sacred-secular dichotomy peculiar to Western thinking, and brings together in a single system, nature and supernature, space and time, this world and the other world. Thus unity is not that of monism or pantheism, however; it is rather a unity of continuance in which boundaries between deities, spirit, animals, humans and natural phenomena are more or less abscure and shifting.[23] If we are going to explain this complex relationship with help of a model, it is a community model of God-Human-World relationship which would certainly provide the best explanation.

A brief discussion of three different models may help to further clarify the meaning of a community model of God-Human-World relationship.

1. Monarchical or Transcendental Model : This model, as mentioned above, maintains a sharp distinction between God and all other creatures. The idea of extreme transcendence of God is developed from the monotheistic concept of God (one-God-ism) which is a belief that there is but one supreme Being, who is personal and moral and who seeks a total and unqualified response from his human creatures.[24] It was a great achievement on the part of the people of Israel to acknowledge God as distinct and different from all other creatures,

---

23 D.J. Hasselgrave, *Communicating Christ Cross Culturally*, (Michigan: Zondervan Publishing House, 1978), p. 149

24 John Hick, *Philosophy of Religion*, (Englewood Cliffs: Prentice Hall, (1963), (1973), p. 3

over against pantheism and polytheism which dominated the world of religion. This idea of transcendence was continued and developed by Christianity to the extent of making God "wholly other", living "out there". In the portrayal of God's relation to the world, the dominant Western historical model has been that of the absolute monarch ruling over his kingdom.[25] In this model, the relationship of God-Human-World is made possible by mediators such as prophets, priest and finally Jesus Christ. A group of theologians brought together by WCC to discuss the theme of *Justice, Peace and Integration of Creation* as a preparation for the Canberra Assembly expressed the problem of this model. "As we think about the way to express the relationship of God to the world in our time, we realise that metaphors such as king and lord limit God's activity to the human sphere; moreover, these metaphors suggest that God is external to the world and distant from it".[26] God was thought to be wordless and, accordingly, the world could be conceived as godless.[27] Since this concept of God is considered partly responsible for the ecological crisis today, Moltmann insisted that, "the first change we must make is to our image of God, because the way we think about God is also the way we think about ourselves and nature."[28]

2. Organic or Immanental Model : The organic model of "God-Human-World relationship" emphasises the inter-connectedness of all else and uses the self-body analogy to explain the nature of this relationship. The relationship of the 'body' and 'self' is transposed to the relationship of God as the self of the universe which is his body. From this perspective, an organic model seems to be the most appropriate to express both the immanence of God in the entire creation as well as God's transcendence of it. An organic model means that humans and other living creatures live together within the body; they are part of each other

---

[25] The monarchical model of God as King was developed systematically, both in Jewish thought (God as Lord and King of the Universe), in Medieval Christian thought (with its emphasis on divine omnipotence), and in the Reformation (especially in Calvin's insistence on God's soverignty) and the Conservative and Neo-Orthodox theologies together uphold this model. Ian. Barbour, *Myth, Models and Paradigms: A Comparative Study in Science and Religion*, (New York: Harper & Row, 1974), p. 156

[26] "Liberating Life: A Report to the WCC", *Liberating Life*, edited by Charles Birch, William Eakin and Jay B. McDaniel, (New York: Orbis Books, 1990), p. 276

[27] J. Moltmann, "Reconciliation with Nature", *Pacifica*, Vol. 5, (1992), p. 304

[28] *Ibid.*, p. 306

and can in no way exist separately.[29] While the inter-connectedness of all creatures and God is profoundly expressed, the model seems inadequate to explain the doctrine of sin, human freedom and uniqueness.[30] Some of these problems can be clearly seen in the WCC's convention in Seoul (1990) which made covenant with other creatures. It sounds to many observers that the relationship of human beings and fellow creatures is romanticised. Genuine covenant is possible only between partners who are capable of entering into reciprocal relationship.[31]

(c) Communitarian Model : Like the organic model, this model affirms the common origin and inter-connectedness of all creation, but maintains, unlike the organic model, the distinctive identities of all creation, and acknowledges the unique position of humans in the created order. The uniqueness of human beings is certainly not in ontological discontinuity, but by degree of development in the evolutionary process in which human become more capable, rational, free and powerful. This unique condition of human beings is expressed by the priestly writers, as endowed with the image of God. It is important for human beings to be constantly aware of the fact that we are a part of the larger living community and unable to exist in isolation from other creatures. The European Ecumenical Assembly speaks of integrity of creation as mutual inter-relation.[32] The concept of human community, the feeling of oneness, a sense of identity, an *esprit de corps*, is widened to include all creatures. The ecological community means the commonality of all creation in which diversity exists, but the human consciousness of inter-dependence and unity of all creation in the midst of diversity recognises and respects the intrinsic rights of nature. In this community, God is seen as the originator and ground of community. Thus, the act of creation

---

29 "Liberating Life: A Report to the WCC", *Op cit.*, p. 279

30 The Organic Model does not provde a proper explanation of the doctrine of sin and evil, human responsibility and freedom. Does God also become sinful along with human beings as a part of the body? How do we explain human responsibility and freedom within the same organ? These are the fundamental questions which cannot be convincingly explained by the organic model.

31 Rene Costa, "The Ecumenical Dynamics of 'Justice, Peace and Safeguarding of Creation'", *Concillium*, Vol. 4, 1991, pp. 19, 20, 25 ff

32 The European Ecumenical Assembly held at Basel from 15-21 May, 1991, jointly sponsored by the Conference of European Churches and the Catholic Council of European Bishops' Conferences issued a document *Peace with Justice*.

is regarded not as what a potter or an artist does, but as "bodying forth" as the mother does. This means that the universe, including our earth with all its creatures, "livs and moves and has its being" in God.[33] Creation is an event in time, a dynamic of becoming, from which human beings emerge and in which they find themselves involved. They are therefore creatures among other creatures in the community of creation. Many of these ideas have been helpfully developed in conjunction with feminist approaches to theology.[34]

D. Theological Validity of a Community Model of God-Human-World Relationship

God's relativity to all else is increasingly stressed in modern theology, particularly in the Process and the Ecological Theologies. We have seen that this idea is not new to tribals, indeed it was the way they viewed God-Human-World relationship. The theological trend today seems to be moving towards the tribal concept of God-Human-World relationship. H. Richard Niebuhr expressed this trend a generation ago :

> The counter to this secularisation, however, is the sanctification of all things. Now every day is the day that the Lord has made; every nation is a holy people called by him into existence in its place and time to his glory; every person is sacred, made in his image and likeness; every living thing, on earth, in the heavens, and in the waters is his creation and points in its existence towards him; the whole earth is filled with his glory; the infinity of space is his temple where all creation is summoned to silence before him.[35]

---

[33] Charles Birch, W. Eakin and J.B. McDaniel (ed), *Liberating Life, Op cit.*, p. 280

[34] Significant contribution is made by S. McFague, in *Models of God: Theology for an Ecological Nuclear Age*, (London: SCM, 1987).

[35] H. Richard Niebuhr, *Radical Monotheism and Western Culture*, (New York: Harper & Row Publisher, 1960), pp. 52-53. "There is increasing awareness not only among Christian theologians, but even more among ordinary believers that, if God is, in fact, the all encompassing reality that Christian faith proclaims, then that reality is to be experienced in and through our actual lives as a biological organism who are persons, part of nature and living in society," said A.R. Peacocke, *Creation and the World of Science*, (Oxford: Clarendon Press, 1979), p. 16-17

It is not merely secularisation which compelled theologians to reconsider the traditional concept of God-Human-World relationship. It is also a change of world view brought about by modern science. The 'Big Bang' theory of astrophysics, the denial of Newtonian simple location, the theory of relativity in physics and the emergence of evolutionary theory in biology have all made their impact on Christian theology. E.W. Shideler points out that the questions of interaction and relationship replaced the nature of entities as the central issues. Instead of 'substance' determining relationships, functional relationship became the clue to the nature of being and matter became energy.[36] For him the denial of simple location in physics means that the view of the world as a 'model of fixed parts associated mechanically' has to be given up for a 'model of mutually interdependent parts associated in *communion*.[37] In the context of a scientific world view, as well as the tribal world view, a community model of God-Human-World relationship becomes more meaningful.

The relationship of God-Human-World would not be rightly described in terms of "vertical and horizontal relationship'. It will be more appropriate to think of it in terms of a circle in which all are a part of the whole community. Whitehead, as process philosopher, argued that "Connectedness is the essence of all things and types... Abstraction from connectedness involves omission of an essential factor in the fact considered. No fact is merely itself."[38] We begin to see that the omnipresence of God more meaningful when the relationship is perceived in terms of radical or radial relationship.

For the tribal people, the analogy of community could be a meaningful one. God-Human-World might be understood as a community analogous to the divine community - of Father, Son and Holy Spirit. On this view, there is no meaningful existence outside significant in communion with human beings and other creatures, so much so that human beings become truly human in communion with God, with fellow human beings and other creatures. In this community, the value and significance of all creation is realised as they all are independent. In fact, a person exists

---

[36] E.W. Shideler, "Darwin and the Doctrine of Man", *Journal of Religion*, XL, July, 1960, p. 198

[37] *Ibid.*, p. 198

[38] A.N. Whitehead, *Modes of Thought*, (New York: Free Press, 1968), p. 9

only in relation - in relation to other human persons and to non-human realities. It is not possible for a person to come to be or to grow without relation to other persons and things.[39]

As noted earlier, the organic model does not sufficiently explain the ambiguity of relationships in the universe, nor adequately deal with such questions as the nature of sin and human freedom. The communitarian model or the doctrine of kinship is certainly more appropriate than an organic model to deal with these issues, for it maintains distinction, at the same time, inter-connectedness of God, Human and World in the relationship. This is what the tribal people called "kinship". William A. Browns points out that the doctrine of a kinship between God and man gives the standard for measuring the significance of sin.[40] The question arises, still, whether in this community model of God-Human-World, there is an implicit "all are equal partners in the community." We might draw inference logically but not theologically. Certainly, God is the originator and ground of community but God so loves the world and becomes one of the members of the community as parents are in a family. The relationship in this analogy is not pantheism, in which a created being is regarded as having a fragment of God. It is more like a kinship by which members of the community are bound together. All creatures belong to the one family of God.

In the community of all creation, the unique position of humanity cannot be denied, just as in human community, the members of community have different functions and responsibilities. Throughout the history of Christian thought a human being has been seen as a being in transcendence with the capacity to grow towards God.[41] When this "transcendence of humanity" is discussed, the writer is aware of the exaggeration of the uniqueness of the human person in Christian theology, to the point of cutting the link with the rest of cosmos, and ending up with dualism. So the concept should be used with much care. Human

---

39 Paulos Mar Gregorios, "New Testament Foundations for Understanding the Creation", *Liberating Life: Contemporary Approach to Ecological Theology*, *Op cit.*, p. 39

40 W.A. Browns, *Christian Theology in Outline*, p. 239. Alienation from God is perceived as sin.

41 John Macquarrie, *Jesus Christ in Modern Thought*, (London: SCM, 1990), p. 372

transcendence is the possibility to develop oneself or perhaps to go beyond oneself as God has created him to be with and be like him. The self-transcendence of human beings is the basis of their responsibility and freedom for others.

The community partners of "God-Human-World" are interconnected but distinct from one another. While God is distinct from the others as the originator and ground of community, human being is also distinct from nature as a responsible and free being endowed with a capacity for self transcendence. Macquarrie put this point as follows :

> On the one hand, I have wanted to stress man's continuity with nature, and thus his essential creatureliness; but on the other hand, such a leap is made with the emergence in man of rational, responsible being, that we cannot treat him as just a part of nature. One of the meanings intended when we say that man "exists" is just that he stands out from the background of nature. He has indeed been shaped by nature, yet in turn he proceeds to shape nature and to *look after it*.[42]

The concern in the search for an authentic model for God-Human-World relationship is how to maintain the distinction of various entities, the intrinsic rights of nature as well as the unity of all creation, without undermining the uniqueness of human being. The Communitarian model, as discussed above, seems to be the most appropriate model. Nonetheless, a model is only a tool to explain the reality. Perhaps no model perfectly and sufficiently explains the ambiguity and complexity of these relationships.

E. Theological Significance for Social Transformation

We now turn to consider what positive contribution this model may take as part of the theological basis for social transformation. Primarily the "Communitarian Model of God" means, for the tribal Christians in North East India, returning to their roots or original understanding of the God-Human-World relationship. The idea of the "other-worldliness of God" and the "dichotomistic concept of reality" were not original tribal concepts. They were inherited from Western

42 J. Macquarrie, *Principles of Christian Theology*, p. 209 Italics are mine.

missionaries. Christianity was introduced in North East India in the middle of 19th century by Western missionaries who were the products of the Evangelical Revival in Europe and North America. The theological seeds that they sowed in North East India was of the conservative evangelical theology which emphasized the transcendency of God, verbal inspiration of the Bible and salvation of souls for life after death. Eventually this has made Christians other-worldly, maintaining sharp distinction between soul and body, secular and religion. It is important to explain these problems briefly before exploring the theological significance of the community model of the God-Self-World relationship for social transformation.

The problem of a dichotomistic concept of reality, developed mainly among the educated or enlightened people, was that their religious conviction and moral teaching are meant only for the purpose of religion, they had nothing to do with their day-to-day life. This dualistic concept of reality, separation of secular and religion, body and soul, is partly responsible for the present rampant corruption and increasing social evils in the tribal society. This theology, although it was inherited from missionaries, gained momentum since 1960s and penetrated the whole Christian community in North East India. Since saving soul for life after death was the ultimate concern, they stressed the "born again" experience in order to be saved.[43]

There are a few tribal scholars who hold the view that dualistic concept of reality is not alien to tribals. It is found among certain tribes. For example, the Mizos, traditionally, perceived a human person as having *thlarau* (spirit) which after death roams around the village, then goes to either *mitthi khua* (village of the dead) or to *pialral* (paradise). Because of this concept, some scholars considered that Mizos had already developed a dualistic concept of reality before the coming of Christianity. But it is observed from the myths, songs, beliefs about 'spirit' and lycanthropy and other practices that they were not dualists. This is, rather, a typical tribal expression of the mystery of life as having

---

[43] In order to stress the necessity of being "born again", the total depravity of humanity was emphatically taught, and distinction of life before and after the "born again" event was maintained as "saved" and "unsaved". The primary concern of the "born again" movement was salvation of the soul for life after death.

spirit. They believed in the existence of spirits which indwelled nature as well as human beings. However, the traditional idea of indwelling spirit in all was modified and developed by the missionary theology into a belief about *human* spirit, which in turn was reinforced and developed by the "born again" movement into a dualistic concept of reality maintaining separation between body and soul, sacred and profane, secular and religion.

Unconsciously or consciously, Luther's "two-kingdoms" theory, developed from Augustine's ideas of "two cities", was adopted and has become a lasting, dominant social theology since the time of the missionaries till today.[44] This idea is reinforced by Indian secularism which advocates separation of religion and state. While this is a socio-political necessity, many Christians neither see the need nor make efforts to bring Christian values to bear upon the social system. They live with a dichotomistic view of reality.

While the imported theology, to certain extend, is responsible for the orientation of tribal Christians towards other worldliness, we have also to look into the history of tribal Christianity itself. It is quite probable that the hardship and frustration of the early Christians in North East India resulted in "other worldliness". It is interesting to note how the traditional celebration of life turned out to be a longing for eschatological celebration. The hypothesis established from the writer's extensive interviews with people in Mizoram is this: The Mizo communitarian society celebrated life together not only in the many festivals but also in their daily work and leisure time. When they were converted to Christian

---

[44] Luther wrote, "We must divide all the children of Adam into two classes; the first belong to the Kingdom of God, the second to the kingdom of the world. Those belong to the Kingdom of God are all true believers in Christ and are subjected to Christ and the Gospel of the kingdom ... All who are not Christians belong to the kingdom of the world and are under the law. Since few believe and fewer live a Christian life, do not resist evil, and themselves do no evil, God has provided for non-Christians a different government outside the Christian estate and God's Kingdom, and has subjected them to the sword ... For this reason the two kingdoms must be sharply distinguished, and both permitted to remain; the one to produce piety, the other to bring external peace and prevent evil deeds; neither is sufficient in the world without the other," Martin Luther, *Secular Authority: To What Extend It Ought to Be Obeyed*, (1523, WA II, pp. 249 f).

faith, they gave up drinking rice beer, abstained from participation in the festivals and became a lonely, isolated, marginalised minority group. When the revival came, the frustration and hardship turned into a hope for a greater and everlasting celebration in heaven. The gift of the Holy Spirit was perceived as a foretaste of a celebration to come, accordingly heaven was perceived as a place of endless congregation and celebration.[45] The problem with this hope is its 'other worldliness', a consequent mystification of life's problems and escapism from life's struggle among the common people.[46] The hope of heaven has, to a certain extent, made them irresponsible and escapists avoiding struggle for better society.

1. Significance of a Communitarian Model : The understanding of God-Human-World as belonging to one community helps the tribal Christians to rediscover a holistic concept of reality from their tradition. Such a concept would be in stark contrast to the dominant theology in North East India, with its sharp distinction between the secular and religious. It would provide a theological basis to inspire and orient the churches towards social involvement to bring about social change. A holistic concept of reality emphasises the inter-relatedness of all things, against dualism. The significance for social transformation is primarily a theological re-orientation of the churches to be more realistic and subsequently be inclusive in their ministry and mission. A holistic concept of reality is a call to Christians to be more sensitive to the needs of situation, and be more inclusive and balanced in their theological articulation and actual ministry.

This would lead us to broaden the circle of salvation, from salvation of individual souls for life after death to an understanding of cosmic salvation - the total salvation of human beings with their body, soul, spirit, society and all other creatures as well, here and now and in the future. Along this line, Gutierrez has written, "Salvation is not

---

45 This hypothesis is supported by many songs and hymns composed by the Mizo Christians in the early period.

46 With the education and guidance of missionaries, the Christians were comparatively more progressive and could cope with the social change better than non-Christians. However, the empirical research proved that 'other worldliness' is still common among the charismatic groups of common people.

something other worldly, in regard to which the present life is merely a test. Salvation is something which embraces all human reality, transforms it to its fullness in Christ."[47] Paulos Mar Gregorios said that human redeption of the whole creation.[48] Accordingly, history wil be regarded as "one". There is no separate history of salvation and profane history. There is only one human destiny, irreversibly assumed by Christ, the Lord of history. The history of salvation for Gregorios is the very heart of human history.[49] The idea of a singular history rejects the monopoly of historical process by the privileged groups of society, putting the vast majority of the people on the underside of history. The concern of Christian mission also has to be broadened, from conversion for saving souls to include liberation of the total human being, society and nature from the bondage of sin. Above all, it implies reconstruction of theology in order to re-orient the churches toward a holistic approach in mission and ministry.

2. Significance for Feminist Theology : The non-hierarchical structure of the community of God-Human-World is meaningful for feminist theology in the struggle against the social structure dominated by man. In the Christian tradition, God is pictured as male which affirms and reinforces the male domination. In some of the tribes, God is perceived as bi-sexual or female. For example, *Khuanu* in the Mizo religion is a female term used for the supreme being. It may be useful for the exploration of this feminist - communitarian perspective.

The term *Khuanu*, a feminine term for *Pathian* (God the holy father), has not been used in biblical and theological circles, but is commonly used in the Christian hymns and songs. *Pathian* literally means Holy Father ("Pa" = Father, "Thian or Thien" = Holy). *Khuanu* means the Mother of Nature ("khua" means nature, "nu" means mother). Since *Khuanu* was commonly used in poetry, Rev. Zairema was convinced that it could be the poetical name for *Pathian*.[50] For example, let us consider these lines from a hymn and a song :

[47] G. Gutierrez, *A Theology of Liberation*, p. 151

[48] Paulos Mar Gregorios, *Op cit.*, p. 30

[49] G. Gutierrez, *Op cit.*, p. 153

[50] Zairema, "The Mizos and Their Religion", *Towards A Tribal Theology: The Mizos Perspective*, edited by K. Thanzauva, (Aizawl: MTC, 1989), p. 39

Chung khuanu-leng ruat sain Inneihna a lo awm	According to the will of *Khuanu* Holy matrimony takes place.
Khuanu tuah remsa dam lai Tawite hi hmang thain	The life *Khuanu* has made and planned must be lived properly.

Khuanu is all pervading, the worship of which became *Sa-khua*.[51] Later on the combiation of *sa* and *khua* (*sakhua*) is used as a synonym for religion.

Khuanu would be a useful hermeneutical clue for the development of a feminist theology in the Mizo context. *Sakhua* is nothing but the worship of *Khuanu* by a family or a clan. Traditionally the Mizos seemed to understand the functions of the supreme being in terms of the motherly function. *Khuanu*, though it has divine connotations, is an expression of the divine love, compassion and care, above all an expression of the immanence of God who is involved in human affairs lovingly, affectionately and persuasively. It would not be quite right to call *Khuanu* the goddess of love as Zairema suggested, because the Mizos di not conceive of a duality of supreme beings. The spirit called *Khua-vang* is regarded as acting as helper and sustainer. While the idea of *Pathian* expresses the transcendental nature of God, *Khuanu* expresses the immanental nature. If the Supreme Being is perceived as *Pathian* (Holy Father) and, at the same time, as *Khuanu* (mother of nature), the Mizo concept of God is bi-sexual. This provides an appropriate model of God for faminist theology. This would eventually challange the patriarchal society and inspire the churches to work for equality of men and women.

3. Significance for Ecological Theology : The tribal concept of "God-Human-World relationship" is making a significant contribution to the emerging ecological theology. In the tribal concept of "God-Human-World relationship", there is no room for an arrogant approach to nature, to treat land and its creatures as mere objects for

---

51 *Sakhua* is the way by which the Supreme Being (*Khuanu or Pathian*) was worshipped by a clan or a family. Literally "Sa" means animal, the means (sacrifice) by which the Supreme Being was worshipped, "Khua" means nature or life principle. Zairema, "The Mizos and Their Religion", *Op cit.*, p. 35. The most important sacrifices a Mizo had to perform was the "Sakhaw Biak" for which castrated pigs must always be kept by every family and the biggest one was reserved for that purpose.

human use. The land with all its creatures is sacred, a holy temple, the self expression of God and above all it is part of their lives. Nirmal Minz rightly observed,

> Tribal life is based and built upon a vision of human existence in which they are aware that land, forest, and the country they occupy are the gifts of God. They are not the owners but custodians only ... Therefore, man-nature-spirit continue as the basic texture of existence, as what makes man truly human. Balance and harmony of man-nature-spirit are essential for man to continue to remain human. Any imbalance between and among these intitiates a dehumanising process and hence this harmony has to be protected and promoted from generation to generation.[52]

Seeing the urgency of the environmental crisis, it is important to rediscover and revitalise the traditional tribal concept of God-Human-World relationship and utilise it as a theological basis for the liberation of life as a whole. "We need a cosmology that attributes intrinsic values to life, mind, and the cosmos as a whole if we are to have an appropriate environmental ethic flowing out of it."[53]

Corresponding to the model discussed above, the tribal approach to ecological crisis is a communitarian approach. Denis Edwards typified various approaches to ecological crisis as the *Exploitative Anthropocentricism*, the *Conservationist Anthropocentricism*, the *Intrinsic Right of Animals,* the *Intrinsic Value of the Whole of Creation* and *the Theocentric Approach.*[54] While it is quite helpful to understand the differences of scholars in their approach to ecological crisis, it is superficial to categorise their responses so sharply. The rejection of the anthropocentric approach by most of the ecological theologians as exploitative and harmful to the harmony of the created order has to be considered carefully. Is there

---

[52] N. Minz, "Primal Religion's Perspective on Ecology", *Ecology and Development*, Edited by Daniel D. Chetti, Madras: United Evangelical Lutheran Church, Gurukul Lutheran Theological College & Research Institute and Board of Theological Education, Senate of Serampore College, (1991), p. 49

[53] Cited by Charles Birch, in "Christian Obligation for the Liberation of Nature", *Liberating Life, Op cit.*, p. 57

[54] Denis Edwards, "The Integrity of Creation: Catholic Social Teaching for an Ecological Age", *Pacifa*, Vol. 5, (No. 2, June, 1992), pp. 182-203

any approach which is not anthropocentric, including Denis Edwards' theocentric approach? In reality, the whole environment movement arose out of the concern for human survival and future generation. It is from this perspective (anthropocentric) that environmentalists and ecological theologians began to talk about the intrisic rights of nature and the rights of future generations.[55] Whether it is a biocentric or theocentric or an anthropocentric approach, whatever label may be used, the kernel issue is the option between "utilitarian approach" and "communitarian approach" to our fellow creatures.

The utilitarian approach does not recognise the intrinsic value of other creatures. Their existence is regarded for the purpose of human use. They are evaluated according to their usefulness for human being. Here human being is at the centre of the whole assessment of the utility of other creatures. Therefore, such an approach is rightly called an anthropocentric approach. The fundamental issue is condemnation of *destructive* utilitarianism. The communitarian approach regards our fellow creatures as co-members of the same community. Without them human beings alone cannot survive. Nature does not have to change its attitude, as it is not responsible for the present crisis. It is human beings who have to give up their utilitarian, exploitative and arrogant attitude to other creatures. We must realise that we are only a part of the same community. Moltmann rightly calls human beings to make a reconciliation with nature.[56] Then human beings will regard and respect other creatures as their fellow members and care for them.

Since the issue of land is so fundamental in tribal life, it will be dealt with separately in the next chapter rather than dealing with it under the "Ecological Theology". Clearly, the issue of land is one aspect of a communitarian theology.

---

[55] The Earth Summit 1992 held in Rio de Janeiro, June 1992, was concerned how to save this planet for the future of human beings. The Ecumenical Assembly at Basel 15-21 May 1991 was concerned about the rights of future generations. The Vancouver Assembly 1983, Seoul Convention 1990 and Canberra 1991 of WCC called human beings to recognise the integrity of creation and to change their attitude towards other creatures from utilitarianism to unitarianism. The primary motif behind this movement is the concern for human survival.

[56] J. Moltmann, "Reconciliation with Nature", *Pacifica*, Vol. 5, (1992), p. 30 ff

CHAPTER IX

COMMUNITY LAND

The tribal concept of land is essentially based on the tribal vision of God-Human-World relationship.[1] For tribals land is the source of life and is sacred, for there is no other temple except the land iself. Land is the gift of God who, at the same time, dwells in the land. Land owns the tribal community and gives them their identity. It is integral to their concept of history. It is by the land that they count their time, measure distance and understand their lives. It cannot be owned by legal menas except by living in it. Two citations of the testimony of aborigines may reflect the tribal concept of land in general :

> Whenever I have travelled in the Aboriginal World, there has been a common attachment to the land. This is not the land that can be speculated, bought, sold, mortgaged, claimed by one state, surrendered or counter claimed by any other ... The land from which our culture springs is like the water and the air, one and indivisible. The land is our Mother Earth. The animals who grow on that land are our spiritual brothers. We are a part of that creation that the Mother Earth brought forth. More complicated, more sophisticated than the other creatures, but no nearer to the creator who infused us with life.[2]

> The land is my backbone. I only stand straight, happy, proud and not ashame about my colour because I still have land. The land is the art. I can paint, dance, create and sing as my ancestors did before me. I think of land as the history

1 One of the common myths cited by Wati Longchar may reflect the integrity of God, Human and World. *The Traditional Tribal World View and Modernity*, p. 6

> A human, a tiger and God (some says spirit) live happily, eat together and lacked nothing when their mother (earth) was alive. In those days the human knew nothing of death or fear of death. God, human and animal spoke the same language. They did not have to work hard. Food was abundant within their reach.
>
> They did not have to worship God.

2 George Manuel and Michael Posluns, *The Fourth World: An Indian Reality*, Donald Mills, (Ontario: Collier-Macmillan Canada Ltd. 1974), p.6

> of my nation .... We will be the lowest people in the world, because you have broken down my backbone, took away my arts, history and foundation. You have left me with nothing. Without land, I am nothing.[3]

The above citations not only reflect the tribal concept of land, they also reflect the exploitation, alienation, struggle and cry of the tribals for their land. We have briefly discussed different approaches to creation. Before dealing with the tribal concept of land in detail, we will discuss in brief human attitudes to the land that may help us to understand the tribal concept of land.

A. Human Attitude Towards Land and Other Creatures

There are many ways of understanding the attitudes of human beings towards the land and other creatures. I would like to classify them into three different approaches : (a) the utilitarian, (b) the unitarian and (c) the communitarian approaches :

1. The Utilitarian Approach : This is a dominant attitude which places human beings at the top of pyramid in the order of creation with the right to explore and exploit the earth regardless of the consequences. In this view, land is to be tilled, the minerals in it are to be mined, rivers are to be dammed, fishes are to be caught, rain forests are to be cut down for human use. Some of the modern environmentalists accused the Judeo-Christian tradition of providing a theorical basis for utilitarian approach. The traditional doctrine of creation, in fact, propounds the view that God acts in and upon nature. It teaches that nature is both to be dominated and used by human beings for their own interests. Nature is under both the providence of God and the mastery of human beings. The accusation of contemporary environmentalists seems to true that the traditional Christian doctrine of creation contains "the historical roots of our ecological crisis today". It is partly due to this doctrine that human beings regard themselves as having intrinsic value in themselves alone, while they treat land and all other creatures as having no intrinsic value in themselves, but utilitarian value only. The value of land and all other creatures depend on their utility for human beings. In this view, land is

---

3 James Galarrwuy Yunupingu, "Letter from Black to White", *Land Rights News*, NLC, (December, 1976), p. 9

seen as a comodity which can be bought, sold and owned by human beings. Since human is made the centre of all creatures, and whose value is used as the criterion to determine the value of all other creatures, this view is also called anthropocentric approach. Here I prefer 'utilitarian approach' to 'anthropocentric approach' for the simple reason that none of the approaches are free from anthropocentricism. Even the present concern for protection of environment is anthropocentric in the sense that its fundamental concern is human survival.

2. Unitarian Approach : As a corrective measure to the traditional doctrine of creation, which is now regarded as one of factors responsible for ecological crisis today, the World Council of Churches Assembly in Vancouver 1983 adopted a new concept "integrity of creation" to express its concern for and commitment to the protection of environment. Though WCC has not concretely define the meaning of "integrity of creation", the concept seems to be developed from the insights gained from the modern science which affirms our common origin with all other creatures in the original fireball which was formed as a result of the "big bang", and we also shared with other creatures the common evolutionary history on Earth.[4] The fundamental argument of this view is that human beings are part of all creation, related to it all. We are interconnected with protons and pulsars, and with every living thing on our planet.

The World Council of Churches with many individual theologians and environmentalists call the churches to recognise the intrinsic values of all creatures and to consider the creation for its own sake, not merely

---

[4] Scientists traced the origin of our planet to the "big bang" which occured about 15 million years ago. For upto a million years the universe existed as ball of glowing plasma, dominated by radiation. Everything that has come into existence springs from this fireball. The formation of galaxies had begun, and the stars were born with their planets. One of the planets is our mother Earth. We not only do we share a common heritage with all other creatures in our original fireball, and in the furnaces of stars, but we also all share a common evolutionary history on earth. Our solar system took shape about five billion years ago, and the first signs of life appeared o Earth about three and half billion years ago. Human kind appeared about two million years ago. Denis Edward, "The Integrity of Creation: Catholic Social Teaching for an Ecological Age" *Pacifica*, Vol. 5, (1992), p. 196

for the sake of human mind. The shift here is from an utilitarian approach to the recognition of intrinsic value of other creatures. In this new approach, the importance of creation is reconized. There is even a sense in which the human creatures is a late and perhaps a reluctant participant in a creational glory which precedes and vastly transcends its own consciousness: "Creation came into being by the will and love of the Triune God, and as such it possesses an inner cohesion and goodness. Though human eyes may not always discern it, every creature and the whole creation in chorus bears witness to the glorious unity and harmony with which the creation is endowed. And when our human eyes are open and our tongues unloosed, we too learn how to praise and participate in the life, love, power and freedom that is God's continuing gift and grace."[5]

In this approach, land is regarded as a part of creation. It should not be treated as commodity nor as space to be exploited. In the history of human civilization, the land of tribals and aborigines was regarded by the invaders as *tera nullius* which rejects the intrinsic rights of land and the rights of its original inhabitants. As the churches together with all others are called to recognized the intrinsic rights of land and the purpose of God in his creation of land.

3. Communitarian Approach : A communitarian approach recognises land and all other creature as distinct entities, at the same time as fellow members of the same community. This is the tribal approach. While the WCC concept of "integrity of creation" has organic unity as the basis of integrity, a communitarian approach has the community of God, Human and Other Creatures as its basis of integrity. Like an unitarian approach, the communitarian approach maintains the inter-connectedness and inter-dependence of all creation including God and creator himself, and yet maintains their respective dinstinct identities. This concept will futher be explained when dealing with the tribal concept of land below.

---

5 A Statement of a Consultation in Granvollen, Norway, 1987, cited by Douglas John Hall, "Creation", *Ecumenical Dictionary*, (Geneva: WCC, 1991), p. 249

B. Tribal Concept of Land

The relationship between the tribals and their land is difficult to understand for modern people who look at the land from an utilitarian perspective and treat the land as an object to be explored and exploited. Therefore, we would briefly discuss the relationship between tribals and their land.

1. Land is a Temple : Land, for the tribals, is sacred because their religion does not centre around a temple or a church or a particular shrine, but the whole earth is sacred and holy, animated by spirits. For them the whole earth is the temple where they worship God. Most of the tribes performed purification rite for the soil at the beginning of jungle clearing for the jhum. The priest invokes the soil saying,

> O Earth, wherever it be my people dig, be kind to them. Be fertile when they give the little seeds to your keeping. Let there be rich harvest and until the paddy seeds are reaped, let no epidemics visit the village. Whatever seeds we sow in the field, let the crops be healthy as it could be.[6]

The tribal people performed several ceremonies such as purification of forest at the beginning of jungle clearing, purification of soil after burning of the jhums, dedication of seed just before sowing seeds, dedication of fields to the Supreme Being after showing seeds, dedication of paddy during the weeding, rededication of paddy, fruit testing and the thanksgiving or harvest festival.[7] Here most of the ceremonies are directed by the process of jhum cultivation, and therefore directly connected with the fields. Since the tribal life depends heavily upon the fertility of the soil, they develop respect for the earth. They invoke the soil to be kind, fertile and generous as they work and sow seeds on it.

According to the traditions of the Ao and Sangtam Nagas, God enters or indwells the earth as the seed to give fertility and help all other seeds to germinate and grow.[8] A religious rite was performed to please

---

6 L. Imti Aier, *Ao Naga Social and Customary Genealogy*, (Mokokchung; Author, 1969), Second Edition, p. 26

7 A. Wati Longchar, *Op cit.*, pp. 75-80

8 A. Wati Longchar, *Ibid.*, p. 65

God that the soil may become more fertile and fruitful. During the ceremony, at least for three days, no one was allowed to dig or break or poke the soil, nor may the mud be collected.[9] As the activities of worship were taking place on the ground, the earth for the tribals is a temple, the dwelling place of God.

2. Land is a Mother : According to the tribal myths as well as the biblical narrative, the earth is a mother from which human beings came forth. Most of the tribes have myths which say that they were born out of the earth. The Mizos, the Nagas and Garos traced their origin to a particular stone from which, according to their myths, their ancestors emerged from a big hole of the earth or from the bowel of the earth.[10] As a baby is sucking milk from the mother, human beings are sucking the milk of the earth in various ways.

The alienation of tribal land is an almost universal phenomenon. Enormous problems of the alienation of tribal land and conflicts over the land have developed in so many countries. This is fundamentally due to the different concepts of land between the tribals and non-tribals. This is a manifestation of the conflict between the unitarian and the utilitarian concept of land. While the tribals regard land as a part of their lives, the non-tribals see it as a property to be used and judge the value from its utility. Unfortunately, the utilitarian concept of land has become the dominant concept, so that the tribals are bound to be victims of the alienation of land. Mr. Ram Vidas Paswan, the Labour and Welfare Minister, Government of India, pointed out in the course of discussion on the subject "A Fair Deal For All".

> The biggest problem with the welfare of the Scheduled Tribes, 94 per cent of whom live in forests, is a basic difference in the perception of the land by them. They considered the forest their own property and many conflicts occur due to these differences of perception. Particularly so when the forest land is utilised for construction of different projects.[11]

---

9 A. Wati Longchar, *Ibid.*, p. 77

10 A. Wati Longchar, *Ibid.*, p. 64

11 Ram Vidas Paswan, "A Fair Deal For All", *Prabhat Khabar*, (August, 14, 1990), p. 5 cited by N. Minz, *Op cit.*, p. 41

There are, however, some tribes who did not, in the recent past, face the problem of land alienation by non-tribals. These are those who were a long time ago driven out of the fertile areas and pushed into the remote hill ares. As they took shelter in the hill ares, beyond the reach of the invaders, they have been keeping better integrity of their tribal identity. They did not suffer the same degree of alienation of land by non-tribals as those tribals who have been living together with more powerful groups.

In the tribal traditional tenure of land, land usually belongs to the community. Thus, the right of land is acquired only by becoming a member of the community. The shift of ownership from "community by living" to the "ownership of government by legal fiction" reduced a large number of simple tribals to the status of slaves. To lose their land and their place in the community made them utterly dependent on other persons, other communities, even on their own land. Many tribals who have been living in the forest for many generations were, without recognition of their right to land, evicted by an act of law and declared as forest encroachers.[12] As a result of the construction of infra-structure for development - such as dams, industry and mining - thousands of tribals were displaced.[13] Moreover, as mentioned in chapter III, the tribals have been alienated from their land by immigrans and their non-tribal neighbours. In India, despite government efforts to protect tribals from further alienation of land, beginning with an order of prohibition in 1946 prohibiting transfer of

---

12 The first National Forest Policy of Independent India was promulgated in 1952, which says, "Village communities in their neighbourhood of forest will naturally make greater use of its products for the satisfaction of their domestic and agricultural needs. Such use, however, should in no event be permitted at the cost of national interest." The national interest displaced the tribals all over India. Walter Fernandes, et. at, *Forest, Environment and Tribal Economy*, (New Delhi: India Social Institute, 1988 as more people oriented, it does not recognise the tribals' rights to the forests.

13 According to one estimate, during the first two decades of planned development (1951-1972), 127, 200 ha of forest land has been lost to industry alone. Walter Fernandes, "Forest Policy: A Solution to Tribal Deprivation", *The Indian Journal of Social Work*, Vol. 51, (No. 1, Jan., 1990, p. 44); 12,000 tribal familes faced displacement in the World Bank Project in Singbhum District in Bihar. *Tribal Voice*, Premier Issue, 15, (November, 1988), p. 17

tribal land to non-tribals, the studies conducted by government as well as non-government organisations show that the laws have been circumvented. Many tribals are marginalised labourers on their own land, serving the non-tribals who confiscated their land by force or fraud.[14] Thus, the struggle of tribals is primarily a struggle for land rights.[15]

The hill tribes in North East India are not facing the problem of alienation of land by outsiders or non-tribals as in other parts of India, but their problem is alienation of simple villagers from their traditional communal land in the process of privatization of land. An understanding of the traditional land system is necessary to rediscover the traditional concept of land. This will help us initially to see the impact of concept towards the purpose of liberating people from alienation of land. The following descriptions provide a brief comparison of the traditional land tenure of major hill tribes in North East India.

> **Mizo :** Community ownership under the stewardship of *Lal*, a village chief, was practised. Every member of a village community has right to use, hunt, live as long as they belong to the village community. Every year the chief in consultation with the village elders selected a particular range for *jhum* cultivation for the whole village community. After that, the land remained fallow until the cycle of about 8-12 years, was completed. In recognition to the chiefship, *fathang* (paddy) was given to the chief by every family of the village. The British administration recognised the chiefship and demarcated the village boundary. A land tax of two rupees for every family was introduced in addition to the traditional *fathang*.
>
> **Garo :** A *khing* land was owned by a clan under the stewardship of *Nokma* who was the leader of a clan. That was divided into several zones for each village. The zone was sub-divided into several sectors,

---

14 Reports, "Depriving Tribals of Land: Andra Move to Amend Land Transfer of Laws," by N. Subba Reddy, *Economic and Political Weekly*, (June, 16, 1988), p. 1458

15 Nancy Gibbs, "This Land is Their Land", *Time Magazine*, (Jan, 14, 1991), pp. 34-35; Bryan Keon-Cohen and Bradford Morse, "Indigenous land Rights in Australia and Canada", in Peter Hanks and Bryan Keon Cohen (ed) *Aborigines and the Law*, (Sydney: George Allen & Unwin, 1984); John D'Arcy Mary, "Human Rights as Land Rights in the Pacific," *Pacifica*, Vol. 6, (No. 1, 1993), pp. 61-80

each sector was cultivated for two or three years, and allowed to rest for 7-8 years. The cultivators were allowed to come to the same plot after the fallow period was over. The jhum cultivation did not require any rent. Legally a *Nokma*, selected by members of a clan, is the leader of a clan and owner of the land. But practically it was his wife who managed the land. The *Nokma* was not the owner of land, he was a manager. The system of *Nokma* was continued and legally empowered in the British period. Unlike Mizo *Lal*, the *Nokma* has several villages under his jurisdiction. Wet-permanent cultivation was owned individually and transferable.

Khasi and Jaintia : The land was broadly classified as *Ri-Kynti*, a land owned by a clan and *Ri-Jaid*, a land owned by a village community. If any member of a clan wanted to sell a plot of his or her share of the *Ri-Kynti*, the consent of all the co-sharers is necessary. A member of village community has the right to use the *Ri-Jaid* with the permission of the village council. The *Syiem* (chief), as he was elected by the people from certain hereditary families, did not control the land. The British owned the land by treaties or purchase in urban areas. A house tax was introduced on those who lived in British land. Apart from this, the land belonged to the community. The Raja received voluntary contributions from his subjects. The British introduced a house tax to all families and a land tax of 10 annas per *bigha* was introduced in the low land fit for wet cultivation.

Naga : In Nagaland, each tribe had a well demarcated territory within which the villages inhabited by that tribe were located, with well-defined boundaries. Though the practice of each tribe differed, the village land was generally classified as (a) common village land, (b) clan land, (c) individual land and (d) *morung* land. The village land included house site, public places and forest land. The village council was responsible for the management. Clan land was mostly *jhum* land owned by a particular clan. Certain areas, usually terraced land, were owned by individuals. Some portion of the village land and designated for *morung* where the young boys slept together.

Arunachalist : The villagers in Arunachal Pradesh claimed that the village community was the owner of all land. Permission of a village community should be obtained before clearing the jungles for *jhum*. The *jhum* land Regulation 1947 recognised permanent, heritable and transferable rights to individuals and communities over lands where shifting cultivation was done. Some villages of Adi tribe practised acquiring several well-demarcated plots of land by a family in which a family did *jhum* cultivation in rotation. Wet cultivation of low land was allowed to acquire individually.

Souce : *The Report of the Woking Group on Land System among Tribals in the North Eastern India - Planning Commission, May 1984.*

It is noted that despite the differences in the detailed land system, the fundamental principle is communal ownership. The chief of the village or the clan might be the theoretical owner of the land. Some plots or fields might be owned individually, but practically and fundamentally the land is owned by the community. Ownership is restricted to the privilege of use, but this right is so carefully recognised that if a person decides (in the case of Garos and Adis of Arunachal) that some of his/her fields will lie fallow, no other farmer may use them without the permission of the owner. They cannot sell or give it to others without the consent of the community or the chief. E. Adamson Hobel, who studied tribal life in Asia, noted that on the whole, tribal people overwhelmingly treat their land resources as a communal asset.[16]

In the absence of any alternative means of livelihood, the tribal people depended directly on the products of land and developed a deep sense of attachment to it. Land for them is a Mother-land, which feeds them and keeps them alive. They do not see land and all the things in it as dead objects but regard them as having life and power in themselves. The tribals believe that disharmony and imbalance in relation to the created order brings disorder and threatens the well-being of all.[17]

C. Rediscovery of Tribal Concept of Land for Theology

While the way trial people used their land, particularly the shifting (*jhum*) cultivation, is seen by the Central and the State Governments as a diabolical method of agriculture, dangerous for the environment, an attempt is made here to rediscover and evaluate theologically the traditional concept of land.[18]

---

[16] E. Adamson Hobel, *Man in the Primitive World: Introduction to Anthropology*, (New York: McGraw-Hill, Inc., 1958) (second edition), p. 441

[17] P.R.G Mathur, "Tribal Medicine: A Study in Rural Science and Superstition," in *Tribal Thought and Culture, Op cit.*, p. 151

[18] Planning Commission, *Report on Development of North Eastern Region*, 1981, p. iv, Government of Mizoram, *Annual Plan, 1991-1992*, p. ix

It is important to note that the shifting of ownership of tribal land from community to government and the process of privatization in recent years confused the tribals and changed their attitude towards their land. Here the shifting cultivation (*jhumming*) is not romantically defended. It is a traditional practiced for several centuries in the absence of alternative agricultural systems and technology. Certainly, *jhumming* is unable to cope with the increasing population and it is environmentally destructive, especially as the cycle or rotation of *jhumming* is decreasing. The idea of "rediscovery" here is that in the process of introducing an alternative system, the community must be made responsible for their own land in order to keep their traditional love of the land.

The major problem with tribal land today is that, as a result of frustration with the existing system,[19] there has been dangerous transition from constructive to destructive dependence on forests. Walter Fernandes, who did extensive research on "tribals and forest" in Orissa and Chhatisgarh, came to the same conclusion that, "Our studies in Orissa and Chhatisgarh, and of others elsewhere, lead us to the conclusion that there has been a transition to a destructive type of dependence during the last few decades."[20] The fundamental problem is that the government officials who, living in a distance place, have no knowledge and love of the village, are controlling the village land from their office table. The Village Council, mediator between the people and Government, is a political body which has become a destructive instrument, for it is no longer accountable to the community but to Government. In the context of these problems, the following elements seem essential in the process of social

---

19 The present system in Mizoram is this: All lands are now considered to be Government land. People enjoy those rights which are recognised by Government. Ownership of land is classified as Temporary Pass, Periodical *Patta*, Land Settlement Certificate. The temporary pass is a licence issued for a certain period of time and implies no right of transfer or sale. The periodic *patta* is a licence to use the land for the period of a lease. The land can be used in any manner the owner likes. If the land is required for public purpose, the Government may take it back without any compensation. The land settlement certificate confers on the owner of a permanent heritable land and transferable right of use. If the Government wants to get it back for public purpose, due compensation is required to be paid.

20 Walter Fernandex, "Forest Policy: A Solution to Tribal Deprivation," *The India Journal of Social Work*, Vol. 51, No.1, (Jan. 1990), p. 39

transformation: community ownership, recognition of land as the people's place and their life, and the recognition that land rights are human rights.

1. Community ownership of land : The tribal theology of land regards community as the only legitimate custodian of the land, because land is the gift of God. "The Earth is the Lord's and the fullness thereof, the world and those who dwell therein" (Ps. 24.1).[21] The exclusive ownership by God implies, for the tribal people, that land equally belongs to all with equal right and freedom to live in it, and that no human being can claim it exclusively for themselves nor can they sell it as though it is their own property. So even though tribal people 'own' land, they do so only within the greater recognition that all land belongs to God. People's perception of land as the gift of and owned by God is the basis of the community's claim of a legitimate ownership of land, because God is the God of the people. The resources of the earth are for the benefit of all. Private ownership may be an appropiate way of administering those resources for certain cultures, but private ownership means stewardship or trusteeship, not the right to exploit the land and deprive others from access to land. Private ownership has to be subordinate to common use.[22]

Thelogical affirmation of community ownership is made here not merely because it is a traditional practice of tribal people. It is, rather, an attempt to restore the sense of community ownership and to protect people from further alienation and exploitation. Albert Fritch's idea of land use endorsed the tribal communitarian use of land. He writes :

> People have a right to land, but this is a communal rather than an individual right. The local community has a right to

---

21 "Earth" and "land" are both legitimate translation of the Hebrew *erets*, but each is used in different contexts with different connotations. "Earth" is especially used in the context of the creation narratives, while "land" is at home in the historical narratives of Israel's struggle for national and religious identity. If "Earth" points to the physical basis and environment for life, "land" points to territory that is possessed, struggled over, used, and perhaps exploited. Geoffrey R. Liburne, *A Sense of Place: A Christian Theology of the Land*, (Nashville: Abingdon Press, 1989), p. 31

22 Leonard Weber, "Land Use Ethics: The Social Responsibility of Ownership," *Theology of the Land*, edited by Bernard F. Evan and Gregory D. Cusack, (Minnesota, Collegeville: The Liturgical Press, 1987), p. 30

> access to its land, and to be empowered to distribute that land in such a manner that the health and welfare of the community is best served. Corporate or "legal: persons do not enjoy a right to land as such, but exist at the pleasure of the people. When corporate lands are found to be excessive from the standpoint of community well-being, a redistribution program should be exacted. Small family holdings must be encouraged as better suited to land stewardship and conservation...
>
> Land use planning is a necessity for the integrity of the community. It must include citizen participation and decision-making and be decentralised in nature and structure as the local conditions allow ...
>
> While those who disturb land must be made to restore it to its original condition, it is the local community's responsibility to oversee the operation and to judge ultimate use of the land.[23]

2. Land is a place : Land is not merely a space, it is a *place* which gives identity to the community. "Space" means an arena of freedom, without coercion or accountability, free of pressure and void of authority, freedom from constraint and absence of responsibility. "Place", by contrast, connotes "home" and is bound up with a sense of belonging, a story which conveys an identity, a basis for participating in history.[24] As noted earlier, the Mizos until recently identified themselves with their village. A stranger, rather than telling his/her own name, tells the name of his/her village. Since the land holds the community together, there is no genuine community owns the land, individual personal identity is subordinated to community identity. But, as we have seen, a change of land system shattered the tribal sense of belonging and eventually created identity crisis. Alienation of tribal land means alienation of their culture, personhood and sense of place.

---

23 Albert Fritsch, *Green Space: A Citizen's Guide to Proper Land Use*, Lexington, Ky: Appalachia-Science in the Public Interest, (1982), pp. 155, 176 188

24 Walter Brueggeman, *The Land: Place as Gift, Promise and Challenge in Biblical Faith*, (Philadelphia: Fortress Press, 1977), p. 3; Geoffrey R. Liburne, *A Sense of Place: A Christian Theology of the Land*, (Nashville: Abingdon Press, 1989), p. 25

3. Land is life : For tribals, land is a living entiry endowed with spirits. For this concept of land tribals are known by outsiders as animists. From the tribal perspective, this attitude is a recognition of the value, power, and validity of the land for item is sacred, a temple in which they worship God, their ancestors and spirits. In a non-literate society, the land is their Scripture through which they read about the spirits and God and create myths and songs. The deceased village ancestors are buried in the soil, which contributes to the sacred feeling of intimacy of the group with its land. Thomas Sieger Derr has commented that, "It is also common to agree that the desacralization of nature, by removing the spirit from natural objects, rendered them harmless and made them subjects for man's objective inquiry."[25] To the tribal people, land is sacred, and therefore, desacralization of land has been profoundly alienating.

4. Land rights are human rights : Struggle for land rights in the context of the tribals means the tribal rights to land as well as the intrinsic rights *of* the land and all its creatures. In the Western context 'human rights' is understood in terms of individual freedom - freedom of speech, freedom of press, freedom of religion, freedom of franchise, freedom from arbitrary arrest and so on. In the tribal situaiton protection from the alienation of land, 'land right' is a concrete term, more conceivable than 'human right'. A human right in the tribal community is seen as the reponsibility of human beings to contribute to the common good. In other words, it is a community right, part of what it means to exist authentically. Thus, the tribals' struggle for land rights is a struggle for community rights of land. It is also a condemnation of an exploitative utilitarian approach to land which alienated them from their land. It is, futher, an affirmation that land is the gift of God to all. The tribals' demand for their land in recent years should also be seen as part of an attempt to reshape and redefine the invaders-tribals relationship through peaceful means, as compared to how their lands were confiscated by violence or fraud. J. D'Arcy rightly suggests that rights to land need to be supplemented by rights of the land, extending to the earth as the home of the one human community and nature as the matrix of all life.[26]

---

[25] Thomas Sieger Derr, *Ecology and Human Liberation: A Theological Critique of the Use and Abuse of Our Birthright*, (Geneva: WSCF Book, III, No. 1, 1973), Series No. 7, WCC, p. 98

[26] Joh D'Arcy May, "Human Rights as Land Rights in the Pacific," *Op cit.*, pp. 61-80.

D. Theological Validity of the Tribal Concept of Land

Land is one of the central themes of biblical faith, particularly of the Old Testament. It is a promise to the landless, uprooted, wandering Arameans that they might live with dignity in their own land. They confessed their faith :

> A wandering Aramean was my father; and he went down into Egypt and sojourned there, few in number; and there he become a nation, great, mighty, and populous. And the Egyptians treated us harshly, and afflicted us, and laid upon us hard bondage. Then we cried to the Lord the God of our fathers, and the Lord heard our voice, and saw our affliction, our toil, and out oppression; and the Lord brought us out of Egypt with a mighty hand and outstretched arm, with great terror, with signs and wonders; and he bought us into this place and gave us this land, a land flowing with milk and honey (RSV).[27]

The people of Israel perceived the land as God's gift, as the fulfilment of the promise. When the land was owned privately, depriving common people from access to land, they were reminded that "the land should not be sold in perpetuity, for the land is mine" (Lev. 25:23). Seeing the plight of the peasants in the process of *latifundialization*, the 8th century prophets condemned *latifundialization*.

> Woe to those who join house to house, who add field to field,
> until there is no more room,
> and you are made to dwell alone in the midst of the land.
> The Lord of hosts has sworn in my hearing;
> "Surely many houses shall be desolated,
> large and beautiful houses, without inhabitant.
> For ten acres of vineyard shall yield but one bath,
> and a homer of seed shall yield but an ephah.[28]

---

27 *Deut.*, 26:5-9

28 This is comparable with Micah 2:2-4, Isaiah, 5:8-10. Verses 8-24 of Isaiah 5 contain a series of woe oracles which are considered authentic to Isaiah. (R.E. Clements, *Isaiah 1-39, New Century Bible Commentary*, 1980; G. Fohrer, "The Origin, Composition and Tradition of Isaiah I-XXXIX", *Annual of the Leeds University Oriental Society*, (1962), Vol. 3, pp. 3-38). If these oracles are authentic, the prophets' struggle for land rights was codified in Holiness Code (Lev. 25:23) in the 6th century. (G. Forhrer suggested that the final redaction of the Holiness Code in 6th century B.C., *Introduction to Old Testament*, (1970), p. 142, and Martin Noth, *Leviticus. A Commentary* (Revised Translation, 1965), p. 128

The struggle of the 8th century prophets for land rights seems to have been codified in the later period by the priestly writers. It is quite evident that land is meant fundamentally for the community and that private ownership was subordinated to the community ownership. We will consider the question of what significance these insights - tribal and biblical - contribute toward the transformation of Mizo society.

E. Theological Significance for Social Transformation

It was observed from the analysis of tribal society in Chapter II that the society is in the initial stage of transition from subsistence economy to market economy. While this transition is an imperative result of development, the steady worsening of the situation of villagers and common people, which is directly related to the loss of easy access to their land, requires serious reconsideration of the land system.[29]

Under the subsistence economy labour is considered as a social duty to be performed. The bond of kinship which governed the social life within the community were also the bonds which governed the economic activities. With the rise of the market economy there is a complete change in the community and the structures of production.[30] The lands which were owned by the community and freely used by all members of the community have now gone into the hands of the rich and privileged people. The common people are landless, victimised by

---

[29] There has been no reliable survey on the process of privatization of land. However, it is quite evident from my interviews with the villagers and common people in the towns that much of the land traditionally owned by the community has been transferred to individual property. Many of the land owners are no longer the members of the community, they are living in the towns and Aizawl city. The gradual process of *latifundialization* in Mizoram began with Indian Independence, when community land was transferred to the Government, it was intensified with the dawn of development, particularly with the introduction of New Land Use Policy in 1990.

[30] D.N. Premnath made a general observation on the impact of the shift from subsistence economy to market economy which is also true to Mizo society. "The Process of *Latifundialization* mirrored in Isaiah 5:8-10: A test-case for the use of comparative and historical sociology as a methodological component in Old Testament Studies," a paper presented in the Faculty Seminar at United Theological College, Bangalore, (on 30th, Jan., 1985)

the system, and life becomes harder and harder for them. The surplus products of the land are no longer distributed within the community, they are transferred to rich people within the outside of the state. Because of this system people began to lose their sense of belonging to the land and developed dependent and destructive uses of land. Land which was traditionally never regarded as a commodity is increasingly treated as private property which can be owned by legal fiction and used as one likes.

To meet this challenge, the traditional concept of land must be theologically rediscovered and reclaimed to make the local community responsible for their land. Theology certainly does not provide an alternative system of land tenure but may enlighten the people to evaluate critically and challenge the evil system. It is also important to understand that the root cause of the present mindset that spawned and rationalised the existing system. While legal reform is necessary and important, it is not the whole solution to these problems. In a region where Christians formed 86% of the population. Christian theology has an important role to enlighten, orient, inspire and enable the people to understand, challenge and seek appropriate changes to the system.

While in this section we have not described precisely what these changes might be, it is clear what the fundamental principles are for these changes. Indeed from the preceding discussion of major motifs for social transformation, it is clear that what is needed is a comprehensive and integrated change, a wholesale re-orientation of life in Mizoram, towards the values of the Kingdom of God. Our purpose in this chapter has been to show that these values can be expressed through a rediscovery of central aspects of the tribal culture.

CHAPTER X

COMMUNITY OF MEN AND WOMEN : Co-humanity as vision and criterion

We have discussed in general the relationship of human beings in the tribal communitarian society and pointed out its significance for constructing a tribal Christian theology. Communitarianism is reconceived and reinterpreted to provide the tribal Christians an alternative doctrine of human to the modern concept of human which gives too much emphasis on individuality of human. We do not undermind the importance of individual personal freedom. We acknowledge the fact that the emphasis on reason and individual personal freedom in the Enlightenment philosophy did bring about the emancipation of individual person ushering in a new age of modern civilization, but it is this autonomous individual who has again turned the world into the wilderness again. While we are rediscovering the traditional tribal communitarian life, which in certain aspects reflects biblical concept of human better, we should also critically examine the tribal community rather than romanticizing it. This is a methodological imperative.

As in any other community, the relationship of men and women in the traditional tribal society is certainly not equal partnership. The weakness of tribal community lies in the relationship of men and women in which women being regarded as subordinate to men, women have been oppressed and deprived of opportunities. This should have been transformed by the power of the gospel when we embraced Christianity, but the relationship seems to be basically remaining unchanged. God's intended community, a Trinitarian community, which far transcends the tribal community becomes the ideal community for judging the tribal community. However, this is certainly not a denial of the significance of the tribal communitarian life as a whole, this chapter is an attempt to examine the relationship between men and women in order to rectify and transform the tribal communiatarian society to make it more liveable and effective. We would, therefore, examine the relationship of men and women in the tribal society. In this effort, the concept of **co-humanity** is used as the vision and criteria of a tribal community.

The concept of **co-humanity** is used here to express the relationship of men and women in which equal partnership is regarded as the fundamental nature of human relationship. According to the biblical creation story, God did not want man to be alone and said, "It is not good that the man should be alone; I will make him a helper fit for him," (Gen. 2:18). Here, we note that it is God's intention in his creation that man and woman should be together. God wills that men and women should live in partnership but opinion differed in the perception and practice of partnership. The phrase "a helper fit for him" (Gen. 2:18) has been used to justify subordianation of women. The English term "helper" connotes the role of servant or of the superior. However, the Hebrew word *ezer/ozer*, which is inaccurately translated in English as "helper", is consistently used in the Old Testament for Yahweh who is a helper par excellence. This means the word 'helper' does not denote subordination for Yahweh is never subordinate to the people of Israel. The feminist interpreters seem to be correct when they claim that it is the male bias which has influenced traditional interpretation of the text to imply subordination of women; the correct interpretation is that woman is the only competent person who can help man in as much as man is a helper for woman. Man and woman without each other is incomplete. Humanity is therefore **co-humanity** in which man and woman compliment one another in equal partnership. God's intended relationship for man and woman is best seen in the doctrine of Trinity.

A. Commonality and Diversity of the Women Issue in the Tribal Communities of North East India

The diversity of tribal traditions and practices in North East India makes the women issue, like any other issue, complex and difficult to comprehend. All those who studied the status and problems of women in this region recognized the problem. Prof. F.S. Downs expressed this problem very well.

> The historical study of the status of women obviously is a very complex undertaking. It involves the traditional evaluation of women as revealed in folk stories, saying and songs - and the determination of whether or not and to what extent such traditional attitudes have carried over into the present; it involves women's role in society - which is

> in itself very complex because there are many different levels ranging from that of the home to public polity and, in the North East, the study of the dynamics of both matrilineal and patrilineal societies, it involves an evaluation of the rights of women in relation to property, marriage and children both in theory and practice; it involves an investigation of the many ways in which women relate to men, including whether or not there is social legitimization of the abuse of women (e.g. beating of women by husband); and finally involves an evaluation of the contextual factors that have resulted in changes in the status over time. In the North East this is further complicated by the fact that one is not dealing with one cultural context but many. Because no two tribes have the same culture, no two tribes have the same history.[1]

F.S. Downs, who is regarded as one of the authorities in the history of Christianity in North East India, looks at the tribal issues from a historical perspective and recognizes the problems involved in the study of women issues. He has identified the diversity of cultures and languages of the tribes and the paucity of written materials as the primary problems for research scholars to understand North East India as a whole. It is extremely difficult for any scholar to comeout with any concrete principle applicable to all tribes. In spite of diversity, there is also commonality among the tribes, particularly in the status and problems of women. Since the approach in this paper is a theological approach, we are concerned to identify the commonality of women issues among the tribes, rather than dealing with particular problems of each tribe. Therefore, we cannot avoid generalization in certain cases. For this purpose, "the relationship of men and women" is used as an organizing principle. This approach is goal-orineted, it has "co-humanity" or "equal partnership" as its goal, therefore the approach is not purely objective and value free which some historians and sociologists try to do. Realization of "co-humanity" is regarded as its goal and criteria.

---

[1] F.S. Downs, "The Impact of Christianity on the Status of Women Among the Hill Tribes of North East India." A lecture delivered in the Professor H.K. Barpujari Endowment Lectures, organised by the Department of History, North Eastern Hill University, (1994), p. 2

The difference between the patriarchal and the matrilineal societies is quite obvious. The Khasi, the Jaintia and the Garo tribes come under the matrilineal system of society whereas all other tribes come under the patriarchal system of society. The status and condition of women in the matrilineal society is comparatively better than in those tribes belonging to the patriarchal society. The condition of women seems to be comparatively better in the Ao Naga society than in the Mizo society. Mary Mead Clark, a pioneer missionary who, with her husband, had worked among the Ao Nagas for some twenty years said that "There is no degradation of women among this rude, uncivilized people."[2]

B. Relationship of Men and Women in the Traditional Tribal Community

Lt. Colonel J. Shakespeare who subdued the Mizo people and later became the first superintendent of Mizoram expressed his observation on the condition of women that the Mizo women fetched the wood and water, cooked the food and did the greatest part of the weeding and harvesting; they also made all the clothing for the whole household from cotton grown in the *jhum*, which they themselves gathered, cleaned, spun, and wove into strong cloth.[3] He narrated how the Lushai women spent the day.

> A Lushai woman has to rise early, fill her basket with empty bamboo tubes, and trudge off before daylight down to the spring, which is generally some way down the hill, and the supply of water is frequently soscanty that it takes her some time to fill her bamboos. Having conveyed her basket full to the house, she has to set to work cleaning the rice for the day. The necessary amount of unhusked rice has been dried the previous day on the shelf over the hearth, and this she now proceeds to pound in a mortar in the front verandah, and winnow on an oval bamboo tray till it is clean enough for use. The breakfast of rice has then to be cooked, and by the time it is ready her husband is awake. After the meal the real work of the day begins. In the cold weather

2 Mary Mead Clark, *The Ao Naga Woman*, (Boston: 1896), p. 8

3 J. Shakespeare, *The Lushei Kuki Clan*, (Aizawl: Tribal Research Institute, 1988), p. 16

> the women settle themselves to some of the operations connected with cloth making, while the men prepare to pass a day of complete enjoyment, ... About noon there is a meal of rice and herbs, after which work is resumed and continued till the evening, when the housewife has to make another journey to the spring, and on her return the pig must be fed with a mixture of composed of rice husks and species of edible arum bulb, mashed and boiled together, the fowls enticed into their baskets, and finally the family collected for the evening meal, ... As soon as it is dark, all the female members of the family gather around the hearth, and carry on such work as can be carried on by what light they can get from the fire; ... The men either gather in the Zawlbuk or in some house where there is drink going. In the other season of the year, that is from March to December, the people are engaged in their jhums from the morning to the evening meal...[4]

A similar observation was made by J.H. Hutton on Angami women that "the position of women among the Angami would at first sight appear to be free but a low one."[5] Davis, one of the officers working in Assam expressed his observation on Naga women in the Assam Census Report of 1891 that after marriage they "became mere household drudges."[6] There were among the British administrators who did not think that tribal women in North East India were subordinate to men. N.E. Parry wrote about the Maras (Lakhers) in 1932 that, "social relations between the sexes are easy and natural, men and women meeting freely and on an equal basis."[7] J.P. Mills had a similar opinion about the Ao women and said, "an Ao woman is very far from being slave and drudge. Her position is no whit inferior to that of a man."[8] These contradicting views on women confused not only the non-tribals who studied the position of women, but also the tribal themselves. F.S. Downs,

---

4 J. Shakespeare, *Ibid.*, pp. 16-17

5 J.H. Hutton, *The Angami Nagas*, (London: 1921, 2th ed. 1969), p. 167

6 Cited in J.H. Hutton, *The Angami Nagas*, (London: 1921, 2nd ed. 1969), p. 167

7 N.E. Parry, *The Lakhers* (London: 1932), p. 276

8 J.P. Mills, *The Ao Nagas*, (London: 1925, ed. 1973), p. 211

along with the Christian feminists in the region, argued that what really matter was the criteria they used to judge and say "low" and "high" status of women. Some used the condition of women in the Hindu and Muslim plain societies of the nineteenth and early twentieth centuries as their comparative standard, other used the western societies during the same period.[9]

The new understanding of Khasi and Garo Societies is emerging. They are now lebelled as matrilineal society. The term "matrilineal" is a term that has become in common use only in recent years. The Garo, the Khasi and the Jaintia societies which were known as matriarchal societies in recent past are now known as matrilineal societies, because sociologists and anthropologists have proved that matriarchy in the sense of strict women's rule never existed with them. This new concept seems to be more accurate to describe the position of women in these societies. The relationship of me and women in the matrilineal society seems to be comparatively better, but not free from subordination of women. A missionary woman, Miriam Russell who spent many years of service among the Garos, expressed her observation.

> Unlike women of the plains, they (Garo women) appear to enjoy perfect freedom. They attend religious services, go to the weekly market, visit neighbouring villages and, in company with male relatives, often visit distant places. When speaking of a man and wife, the woman's name is mentioned first; this would seem to show respect to her ... The Garos say that the man and not the woman would be offended by inverting the expression. Owing to the fact that property descends through the female instead of the male line, the women seem to have great honour. A more intimate acquaintance with the people, however, shows that the women are not honoured by the men but are really held in contempt by them. A man may cruelly beat his wife, but if she so much as strike him once, he can cast her off. It degrades a man to have a woman sit in front of him. She must not eat before her husband has been helped ... the freedom of the Garo women differs from that of the purdah - woman of the plains in kind rather in degree. In both cases, the word of the man is the law that governs her action.[10]

[9] F.S. Down, *Op cit.*, p. 14

[10] Cited from F.S. Downs, *Op cit.*, p. 6

Her observation is quite right that the nature of subordination of women in matrilineal society is differed in kind, to a limited extent by degree as well, but there was not equal partnership in the relationship of men and women even in the matrilineal society.

The nature of relationship between men and women is to a certain extent revealed when we study some of the sayings and the traditional social practices. The Mizos have a few derogatory sayings concerning woman: "Crab's meet is not a meat, women's word is not a word", "The wisdom of a woman does not cross the brook", "a woman and a walnut tree, the more you beat them the better they become", "an old fencing and a wife should be changed", etc. Similar sayings are also found in other tribes. The Khasis have a traditional saying that "if a hen crows, the world is over". This means that women are not expected to make speeches or preach in the public though they rule at home. The Kukis have the following sayings, "the words of women and the horns of the female mithun are no use", "the speaking of women is like the chirping of birds at night". The Ao Nagas used expressions like *sungochung* (a bunch) and *tetsur tanur* (women-children) for women. These sayings reflect the attitude of men towards women.[11]

A woman in the traditional tribal society was bound by taboos. She was not allowed to participate in some of the religious rites and functions. Her menstruation and pregnancy made her in some cases taboo or unclean which prevented her from active participation in social functions and limited her freedom and activity. Though there were no uniform customs, in most of the tribal societies, the customary laws did not recognize the right of woman to own immovable properties like land and house. The right of ownership was granted to women to own only the things they brought along with them in the marriage from their parents home like cloths, garments, ornaments, implements, etc. While in some of the tribal societies, like in the Ao Naga and Khasi societies, love marriage was practiced, but in most of the societies women were sold as property. In the Garo society, a boy was captured for a girl by her relatives. As long as women were not allowed to own immovable

[11] For sayings see, R.L. Hnuni, "The Impact of Christianity on Hill Tribal Women." A paper presented in the Seminar on Christianity and Tribal Cultures in North and North East India, Serampore, (1996)

properties and were deprived of the right of inheritance in the patriarchal society; and as long as there were certain things the women were prohibited from doing in the society, we could not deny the fact that there was subordination of women in the traditional tribal society, though the degree of subordination might be different from tribe to tribe.

What could be the root cause of subordination of women in the traditional tribal society? Most of the feminists in North East India identified patriarchy or man's rule and selfish interest which looked at things from the men's perspective as the primary cause, but they did not ask "why did patriarchy exist in the tribal society?" I am convinced that it is the environment in which they lived that determined the relationship of men and women. I pointed out in 1989 the possibility of the traditional practice of head hunting to be one of the primary factors responsible for subordination women.[12] My assumption is that human beings have been living with war throughout history but the head hunting endangered the lives of men constantly; therefore the intensity of risk for men was much greater in the head hunting society than in the society where occasional war was practised. In such a head-hunting society, it was natural that women were subordinated to men because the role of men was risky. The role of men in the situation of head-hunting and constant inter-village feuds was to provide security to the villagers, but not to engage themselves or help women in the domestic work which was left to women. The tragedy is that even after the practice of head-hunting ceased to exist, subordination of women continues.

C. Relationship of Men and Women in the Tribal Christian Society

The conversion of tribal people in North East India into Christian faith brought about radical changes in the tribal society, but opinion about the change differed widely. A majority of the non-Christian writers, with a few British administrators, are critical about the change. They argue that Christianity is responsible for the erosion of tribal culture which consequently has culturally alienated the tribals and caused them

12 K. Thanzauva, "Women in Society: Traditional, Cultural and Anthropological Factors that Define and Influence Women in India." A paper presented in the North India Theological Students' Conference, Jorhat, (1989), p. 3

an identity crisis.[13] On the other hand, most of the tribal Christians, both theologians and sociologists, together with a few non-Christian anthropologists and sociologists, think thta Christianity has transformed tribal society in North East India without which they will never be what they are today.[14] Taking the middle course, a few scholars have admitted erosion of tribal culture but held the British administration and the process of modernization as the primary factors responsible for this. They regard Christianity as providing an alternative ideology to cope with this change.[15]

In spite of differences in the opinion of scholars about the change in general, most of them seem to acknowledge with appreciation the contribution of Christianity towards the upliftment of women. Of course there are exception among the administrators who were critical for some other reasons. C.L. Hminga expressed his observation,

> In the pre-Christian society divorce was easy and common because women had very little right if any at all. Husband and wife relationship was not cooperative. Every husband was afraid of being dubbed as "henpecked" and so would not lift his finger to help his wife in any domestic work. In fact, members of the family often would not speak to one another kindly! Christianity has transformed Mizo family life, divorce is rare, husbands are less bossy and more helpful to their wives, love and kindness are seen in the relation of the family members.[16]

---

[13] J.H. Hutton, *The Angami Nagas*, (London: 1921), J.P. Mills, *The Ao Nagas* (1925), Animesh Ray, *Mizoram Dynamics of Change* (1982), Vik Sarin, *India's North East Inflame* (1980).

[14] C.L. Hminga, *The Life of Witness of the Churches in Mizoram* (1987), J. Puthenpurukal, ed., *Impact of Christianity in North East India* (1996) in which several scholars strongly argued that Christianity has transformed tribal society in North East India. M. Kipgen, *Christianity and Mizo Culture*, (1996).

[15] F.S. Downs, *Christianity in India: North East India in the Nineteen and Twentieth Century* (1992).

[16] C.L. Hminga, *The Life and Witness of the Churches in Mizoram*, (Serkawn: 1987), pp. 293-4

Improvement of the relationship between men and women was mainly due to the prohibition of during *zu*[17] (local rice beer) and the emancipation of women. Most of the Protestant missionaries working in North East India came from an evangelical background and had a tradition of anti-alcoholism. Looking at the tribal practice of drinking *zu* from this perspective, they tried to stop the practice and imposed a prohibition of drinking *zu* for Christians.[18] In fact, drunkenness was greatly responsible for wife beating, family tension and disharmony, harassment of children, and constrain on the family economy. When drinking *zu* was given up, ill-treatment of women and dicord in the family were radically reduced. This could be the reasons why even a non-Christian girl preferred the Christian boy for her husband.

Education was one of the primary factors responsible for the emancipation of women. As a result of the emancipation of woman, the quality of human life in general, particularly the quality of woman's live was improved that in turn effected the relationship of men and women in Christian society. Most of the scholars whom I know, except a few British administrators who were critical of the mission education at the initial stage,[19] hold the view that the missionary education brought about

---

17 The term ***Zu*** is widely used among the tribes in NEI for local rice beer. It was very much a part and percel of their lives, without ***zu*** they could not think of any social gathering - festivals, feast and getting together.

18 The Catholic Missionaries were comparatively tolerant to the use of liquor. F.S. Downs suggested that Christians became sensitive to the social problem of alcoholism in the countries first effected by the Industrial Revolution. Since most of the protestant missionaries came from North America and England, where alcoholism became a social problem as a result of Industrial Revolution, they were more intolerant to the practice than the Roman Catholic missionaries who, mostly came from continental Europe. F.S. Downs, *Christianity in North East India*, p. 147

19 J.P. Mills said that some Ao Christians themselves complain to him that, girls who have had a Mission education find it hard to settle down to village life and are liable to go on the loose. I do not mean to imply that no girl educated by the missions keeps straight; far from it. But the concensus of opinion among respectable Aos undoubtedly is that there is grave risk a Mission trained girl getting "above herself", and so idle and immoral. And after all the Ao is likely to know more of his womenfolk than any outsider. *The Ao Nagas*, p. 213. A similar opinion was spread among the Mizos that educated girls used their education only for writing love letters to their boy friends.

the emancipation of women in the tribal society in North East India. Because the policy of mission education was different from that of the Government which aimed at educating only the chiefs' sons. By educating women and marginalized children, Christian mission revolutionized the tribal society changing the social structure and the status of women. Eventually the poor children became the leaders of society.[20] Comparatively the progress of girls education was slower than that of the boys, for girls were very useful at home and less favoured by their parents than boys.

It is interesting to note that at the formative stage of Christian church, there seemed to be no discrimination against women, they actively participated in the Church as evangelists, teachers and deacons. Active participation of women in the early Church could be due to lack of human resources and non-availability of competent male leaders. Though the society in general was critical about the educated women, they were more competent than their fellow uneducated girls and given respect and important responsibilities in the church and society; their contribution and leadership were eventually accepted. The Church not only provided education, also a new avenue for women to interest with their male counter part, and freedom to preach and to teach which they had never done in the traditional society. The formation of a separate women department of organization in the church provided enormous opportunity for women to develop their leadership quality. The Church through its educational activities and woman organization empowered

---

[20] In reference to Mizoram, as early as 1900, there were 11 girls out of 66 students in Aizawl, and later on three of them were appointed to be the teachers. There were 12 girls out of 77 students in 1903, 20 girls out of 225 students, 81 girls out of 77 students in 1910. K. Thanzauva, (compiled), *Report of the Foreign Mission of the Presbyterian Church of Wales on Mizoram 1894-1957*, (Aizawl: Synod Literature and Publication Board, 1997), pp. 19 ff. P.K. Bhattacharya, without referring to mission education, attributes the changes that hve taken place in the status of women in the Naga society to education - "a new age of womanhood is just ushering in as an inevitable sequel to modern education ... the tide of changes in social order and outlook set in with the advent of Christianity gradually gained intensity and towards the late thirties of the present century a few Naga women of celebrate zeal venture to go outside the hills for further studies" Cited by F.S. Downs, "Impact of Christianity on the Status of Women Among the Hill Tribes of North East India," p. 11

women and eventually brought about the emancipation of women. This certainly contributed towards the improvement of women's quality and the relationship of man and woman in the Christian society, but equal partnership was still far from realization. There were certain traditional practices which remained unchanged even after the community had embraced Christianity.

1. Right of ownership was not changed : In the patriarchal society men continued to be the sole owner of immovable properties and inheritor of ancestral property. In the matrilineal society, the youngest daughter inherited ancestral properties but she was not the owner. She could not sale or dispose inherited properties, it was the paternal uncle who decided. She was acting as a steward of the properties.

2. Exclusion of women from decision making bodies : Whether it was in the church or society at large, women's role was limited to assisting role in implement the planning and decisions made by men. Women were excluded from the planning and decision making. This indicates that the Christian tribal community was still greatly influenced by the traditional saying of "the wisdom of woman does no cross the brook". In the case of Garo, the *nokma*, the male chief, was the nominal head in the administration of the clan or village, it was the maternal uncle of the *nokma's* family who acted as the manager executing all matters pertaining to the clan's or village's land, but the final decision was with the *nokma*. The power of *nokma* is certainly different from that of the Mizo *lal*, the Khasi *syiem*, and the Konyak *ang*. Although the institution of chief was either abolished with the independence of India or getting very weak even where it continues to exist, its impact is quite significant. The chieftainhood, with a few exceptional cases of women who became chiefs for a short period of interval, was exclusively for men. This tradition continues up to the present time

3. The attitude of men towards women remain unchanged : As the quality of woman was improved, men certainly have shown more respect to women than before, but the fundamental concept of womanhood as inferior to manhood was not changed by Christianity. This is clearly reflected in the structure of the Church in which women were given low positions such as leadership in their own women department, responsibility of teaching in Sunday School, cleaning and decoration of the church and the responsibility of fund raising. They were excluded from decision making. Feminist theologians keep on attacking the institution of the church for maintaining patriarchy. Despite the significant contribution of Christianity towards the improvement of women's status, it is in the church that women are excluded from the decision making bodies.

The basic problems of women remain unchanged. In what way is the Christian community different from the traditional tribal community in the relationship of men and women if the basic problems of women remained unchanged? The most significant change in the status of woman was the improvement of women's quality through the mission education. The improvement of woman's quality through education changed the relationship of men and women and brought about the emancipation of women in the tribal society. The change, of course, is far from adequacy judging from women's vision of full emancipation today.

D. Relationship of Men and Women in the Modern Tribal Community

Women's movements all over the world have gathered momentum and moved the United Nations, Governments and Churches to re-examine and reform their legislations, to increase resources allocations to enhance the status of women and try to mainstream them in all aspects of social life. The UN's concern for women has been expressed through its "World Conference on Women" starting with the Mexico 1975, Copenhagen, Nairobi and Beijing, 1995. This has inspired Governments and NGOs including churches to work for women. However, the feminist consciousness among the tribals in North East India is originated from the theological colleges influenced by the ecumenical theology. Most of the women who are struggling for women cause in NEI are theologians who have, of course, the same agenda with the secular feminists. Their struggle today is for gender equity. Though they have the same agenda and goal in their struggle, the root problem they identified is different. While the tribal Christian feminists in North East India accuse of the church of maintaining patriarchy and advocating subordination of women; their secular counterparts in India hold the institution of family as upholding traditional value system which deprives of and suppresses women.

1. Women Situation Today : It is necessary to look into the actual problems and demands of women movement today, and examined the steps that have been taken by the Central and State Government and the churches. The statistics given below may partially reflect the condition of women today.

Basic Statistical Record of Women as 1991 Census

Particulars	Meghalaya	Manipur	Mizoram	Nagaland	All India
Tribal	15,18,000	6,32,000	6,54,000	10,61,000	6,77,58,000
Population	85.53%	34.41%	95.75%	87.70%	8.08%
Female	997	959	982	946	972, 1000 males
Literacy Rate					
Female	43.63%	44.48%	78.74%	54.51%	18.19%
Male	49.78%	62.39%	86.67%	66.27%	40.65%
Rural and Urban Population					
Urban	13.56%	8.42%	45.25%	12.04%	7.39%
Rural	86.44%	91.58%	54.75%	87.96%	92.61%
Work participation					
Female	37.78%	45.97%	43.98%	40.15%	43.71%
Male	48.63%	47.38%	51.05%	43.68%	54.74%
Life Expectancy					
Female					58 years
Male					61.1 years

When we think of the change in the status of women from that of in the primitive society, the women movement has come along way and achieved so much. We do not find in the statistical records of 1991 Census much disparity between men and women in the literacy rate, work participation and life expectancy. The emancipation of women is obvious in the field of education, particularly in the result of High School Leaving Certificate Examination; more than 50% of the top tens are always captured by women in recent years.

A case study was conducted at Aizawl in Mizoram.[21] The statistical records of Mizoram 1992 shows a significant difference between men and women in the public sector employment. In category of the group A, the number of male is 1,800, Female 311; in Group B Male 3,485, Female 1,249; in Group C Male 15,608, Female 5,055; in Group D Male 9,504, Female 1,191, in the total there are 30,397 male and 7,806 female. In the whole state of Mizoram there is significant difference between male and female in the public sector employment, but the situation in Aizawl town is quite different. In the civil secretariat, the largest office in Mizoram, there are 179 male and 341 women in the category of group 'B' and 'C'. In Aizawl town, female employees are much more than male, but in the whole of Mizoram, male employees are still far more. The disparity of men and women in the category of group A and D is much greater.

In the Aizawl main market, the daily average of persons going for marketing is 1,600, of which 100 are male and 1,500 are female. In the main commercial centre of Aizawl, there are 217 male shopkeepers and 168 female shopkeepers. In the Solomon's cave, the supper marketing complex of Aizawl, out of 106 shops, there are 28 male shopkeepers and 78 female shopkeepers. Women are emerging very fast. A similar situation is also seen in other state as well. In many aspects, men and women have shared equal opportunity and lived in mutual respect. The relationship of men and women is comparatively better than in the past.

2. Efforts of the Government and the Church : Credit is given to the Christian Mission particularly to its education for the emancipation of tribal women in North East India. It was the missionaries who challenged the traditional tribal social structure and value system which suppressed women and made significant contributions through its education for the improvement of the quality of women. After independence, the Government of India has made sincere effort to develop women. The Constitution of India guarantees Fundamental Rights to all Indian citizens without any distinction of male and female.

---

[21] Mr. Vanengliana, a field director of CASA working Mizoram did extensive survey in 1992 which was published by Synod Social Front. *Khawiah Nge Mizo Mipate*, (Aizawl: Synod Social Front, 1992)

Article 14 confers equal rights and opportunities on men and women in the political, economic and social spheres. While Article 15 prohibits discrimination on the ground of religion, race, caste, sex, etc., a provision under Article 15 (3) enables the State to allow affirmative discrimination in favour of women. Articles 16 guarantees equality of opportunity in public employment. The States also impose a fundamental duty on every citizens to renounce practices derogatory to the dignity of women.[22]

Concern for women is also seen in the Five Year Plan. The report of Indian Government says, "In order to meet the needs of women and children, there has been a progressive increase in the Plan outlays over the last four developmental decades. The outlays of Rs. 4 crores in the First Plan (1951-56) has gone up to Rs. 2,000 crores in the Eight Five Year Plan (1992-97)."[23] Several policies were adopted to protect and empower women, some of those are : (a) Nation Perspective Plan for Women (1988) which aims at mainstreaming of women, (b) The National Plan of Action for the Girl Child (1991-2000) to protect and develop children particularly the girls, (c) Reservation of Women in Grass-root Level Democratic Institution (1993) for the enhancement of women leadership, (d) Mahila Samriddhi Yojana (MSY) (1993) to empower women by raising their economic status, (e) National Credit Fund for Women (1993) to improvement the income of rural women, (f) National Commission on Women (1992) was set up to review the Constitutional and legal safeguards for women.[24]

The States are responsible for the implementation of the provisions of the Constitution, policies and programmes of the central Government in their respective areas. In this way women are given opportunity and empowered throughout the country. The effort of the Government certainly plays important role for the rapid emergence or irruption of women in North East India.

The World Council of Churches, the largest ecumenical body, is deeply committed to the cause of women liberation. From the inception of Ecumenical Movement, the concern for equal participation

---

[22] *Fourth World Conference on Women, Beijing 1995: Country Report Government of India*, Department of Women and Child Development Ministry of Human Resource Development, p. 24

[23] *Fourth World Conference on Women*, *Ibid.*, p. 25

[24] *Fourth World Conference on Women*, *Ibid.*, p. 25 ff

was expressed. At the 1910 International Missionary Conference, the issue of women's work came on the agenda; and a study on "The Place of Women in the Church in the Mission Field" published in 1923 carried the recommendation: "What we askis that the church to keep pace with other agencies that are accoding to women a new status and a new opportunities for development and an achievement. The church, because of her own conservatism and lack of vision, is allowing trained, talented women to slip away from her into other lines of activity."[25] Though concern for women was expressed it did not draw the attention of majority members until 1970s. As a preparation of the ecumenical churches to participate fully in the International Year of Women, designated by UN in 1975, WCC organized an international consultation on Sexism in Berlin 1974 which gave a dynamic impetus to the women who later attended the WCC assembly in Nairobi (1975). The Nairobi Assembly had "seeking Community" as one of the sub-themes in which the need for equal partnership of men and women in the society and church was strongly expressed. A study project on "The Community of Women and Men in the Church" was proposed and undertaken by the joint venture of Faith and Order and the Sub-unit on Women in the Church and Society. The sixth assembly held in Vancouver took up the women issue and resolved as proposed by the Central Committee of 1987 that there should be a special decade during which the churches would demonstrate their solidarity with women. The decade was launched on Easter day 1988 in order to empower women at all levels to participate more fully in the decision that effect their destiny, to be partner with men in shaping the lives of their families and their socieites and to be equipped for ministry in the churches in the full fellowship of the people of God.[26]

The WCC's policy on women impacted upon the ecumenical churches in India, particularly the Church of South India and the Church of North India which eventually decided to reserve 25% of seats in the Executive Committee for women. However, this has not been realized up to this time. Since the churches in North East India are not member of WCC and do not participate in the debate, they are not influenced by the decisions and theology of WCC except a few theological student

---

[25] Cited by Paulien Webb, "Women in the Church and Society" *Dictionary of Ecumenical Movement, Op cit.*, p. 1069

[26] Paulien Webb, *Op cit.*, p. 1072

who did their theological training in the ecumenical theological colleges. This is the reason why the church became the target of feminist movement in North East India.

3. The Agenda for Women in NEI : "Co-humanity" or equal partnership of men and women in all spheres of life is the core agenda for women today. In spite of significant achievement that was made, there are many areas in which equal partnership has not been achieved.

(a) Equal Partnership in the Church : R.L. Hnuni rightly said that, "Discrimination is more common in the Church than in secular circles. There are high ranking women officers, M.L.A. and even a woman Minister in the secular sector. It is in the Church circle that leadership of women is not fully accepted whereas it should be the other way around."[27] She also pointed out that, "women contribute a lion's share for the betterment of the church, but they are debarred and marginalized in ecclesiastical employment. Fully trained women are denied their ordination, and with respect to leadership, administration, policy making and so on, they are expected to play assisting roles only."[28] Though women are actively involved in the Church, there is no equal partnership in the leadership and decision making.

(b) Equal Partnership in Ownership : Right of ownership of properties is still a problem for women in the patriarchal society. In the tribal society of North East India, the customary laws have not been codified and changed. Even in a society where it was codified with certain amendments, it has not been put into practice. The customary laws, in most the patriarchal societies grant the right of inheritance to sons only. According to the Inheritance of Property Act, 1956 of Mizoram, a person can make a will and nominate the inheritor, "Every person of sound mind not below the age of 18 may dispose of by will his/her property which he or she alienates during his or her life. Where there is no will, such property may devolve in accordance with the customary law for the time being in force."[29] In the absence of male

---

27 R.L. Hnuni, "Women in the Context of the Bible and North East India." A paper read at a faculty-student seminar at ETC, Jorhat on 13th March, 1987, p. 3

28 R.L. Hnuni, *Ibid.*, p. 3

29 *Mizoram Hnam Thurochhiah Dan 1956* (Inheritance of Property Act, 1956), p. 13

offsping, daughters can inherit the property of the parents. Properties which a woman brought to her husband at the time of marriage shall be returned to her in the event of divorce. The new customary laws seem to protect women's right of ownership and permit women to inherit ancestral properties, but laws alone cannot bring about abiding changes in the tribal society unless the culture itself is changed. Moreover, legislation may not be quite effective, as long as the enforcing agencies and institutions often remain predominantly gender-biased.

(c) Equal Partnership in the Hearts : The main problem lies in the attitude of men towards women. Men still think that women are inferior and they must be subordinated to men. Certainly there are areas in which women are inferior and less capable, so also there are areas in human life in which men are inferior and less capable than women. What really prevents human beings from living together in equal partnership is the attitude of men towards women. This has to be changed. When we think of women liberation, we should know this fact that men have to be liberated first from traditional ideas which have been enslaving women.

E. Vision for a New Tribal Community: "Co-humanity" is a New Human Community We are Seeking.

"Co-humanity" is used by Karl Barth to define his concept of "image of God". For Barth, image of God is to be found in the relationship of God and human being, and man and woman rather than in the quality of human being. He said,

> Man has plurality like God, who is plural. Being man means being in togetherness: man and wife ... Image has double meaning: God lives in togetherness with himself, then God lives in togetherness with man, then men live in togetherness with one another.[30]

The purpose of God in his creation of human being in his own image is co-humanity to live together in mutual love, trust and friendship as seen in the triune God. As seen in the creation story, the first man,

---

[30] J.D. Godsey (Recorded and Ed.), *Karl Barth's Table Talk*, (Richmond Virginia: John Knox Press, 1962), p. 57

Adam, had to learn how to live with Eve, other human being, like but unlike himself, without whom he could not survive in one household of diversity and unity.[31] Equal partnership of men and women is therefore regarded as God's intention which again provides women a vision of society.

A tribal feminist theology may be explained as a theology that seeks for a new community in which the traditional relationship of men and women is tranformed by the power of the Gospel into a new relationship of equal partnership of men and women. The tribal feminist theology is committed to transform the traditional tribal community transcending the old pattern of the relationship of men and women, and to build a new, just, participatory and harmonious society free from discrimination of human beings by fellow human beings on the ground of sex, colour and race. In other words, tribal feminist theology is making the traditional communitarian life effective and relevant in today's situation. It means to let the tribal communitarianism pervade the relationship of men and women which, in the traditional community, was patterned on the relationship of master and servant.

Tribal community, like any other community, become irrelevant in the changing world. It was pointed out that in the communitarian society, women were subjugated and oppressed. That was the weakness of tribal communitarian society. To build a truly communitarian society, the traditional communitarian society has to be transformed which is the task of tribal feminist theology. The task of building a harmonious society finds its biblical basis in the affirmation of scripture that both male and female are created in the image of God and that in Christ both are incorporated into the one body, the church. Women's vision for society is drawn from the biblical teaching and their own experience of suffering of exclusion, being underestimated, silenced or unheard.

1. Women envision a just society : A society in which we live is not just. Discrimination and suppression of human beings by fellow human beings is against God's will for human beings. A seminar on Women in Dialogue: Wholeness of Vision towards the 21st Century in Geneva [illegible] their vision, "We have gathered as women to envision

---

[31] Pauline Webb, *Op cit.*, p. 1069

a just future in church and society, for women, for children and for men. Much threatens such as future. To create it will be hard work. For majority of women on earth, this first of all is the hard work of survival."

2. Women envision a participatory society : They are not only looking for equal partnership, they want to participate and make significant contributions to the church and society, but they have been asked to play only assisting roles. Women have been in the fore front in the church and in the production of food particularly in the jhum cultivation, but their voice has not been heard in the planning and decision making both in the church and society. They must be encouraged to participate in all aspects of the church and society.

3. Women envision a harmonious society : They are envisioning a peaceful, harmonious society; a society without war and conflict, a violence-free society. A society without racism, sexism, casteism and no xenophobia, with no discrimination, no alienation, no exclusion and no homophobia.

To realise the vision of society, the SAARC Workshop on the Girl Child and Coopertion for the 4th World Conference on Women suggest mainstreaming, empowerment of women and some other strategies. "Mainstreaming of gender perspective should be reorganized as a critical process requiring changes in attitudes and behaviour. These changes are required at the levels of the individual, family, community, policy and decision makers and Government. For this, innovative communication methodologies, appropriate gender training and networking between Government and non-Government systems are important pre-requisites. Since effective mainstreaming is an important statement of commitment to women's empowerment and requires consideration and action at the levels mentioned above, higher echelons of decision making system should display strong commitment and political will to recognize and give priority to mainstreaming in all development sector."[32] There shall be many more suggestions and strategies for empowerment of women, it is the context that decides the methods. What really matter is commitment to the cause of building a society envisioned by women. It is our theological task to struggle for the realization of a **co-humanity**.

---

[32] Cited in *Fourth World Conference on Women, Beijing 1995, Report of Government of India*, p. 41

CHAPTER XI

SINGING THEOLOGY

In this chapter we are not going to deal with 'theology of singing' but we will be discussing how the tribal Christians sing their theology. Singing is a way of life for the tribal people. It is difficult to comprehend for non-tribals how much the churches in North East India are singing. In certain occasions such as Christmas, Good Friday, particularly during the revival movement, some of the Christian communities in Mizoram, Manipur, Nagaland go on singing many days and nights. It is no wonder for those who know their culture that tribal people worked with singing, had fellowship in singing and conversed through songs and singing. Their feeling of joy and sorrow, aspirations and religious beliefs and experiences are expressed through songs. The tribal Christians sing their theology.

Since it is not possible to deal with various tribal songs in North East India, I have to limit my study to the tribal communities in Mizoram which I know best. In fact, among the tribes in North East India, the Mizos seem to singing more, ultimately compose more Christian songs than any other tribal groups.[1] The number of indigenous Christians songs

---

[1] Before the coming of Christianity the Mizos had developed various folk songs: Tthe *Thuthmun Zai* and *Salulam Hla* are the most primitive ones. The *Thuthmun Zai* literally means sitting song, it is a mourning song comparable to the psalms of lamentation in the Old Testament. *Salulam Hla* literally means 'songs of dancing' with the animal heads. It is a song of celebration of the success in the hunting of wild animals. The dancers acted as if they were chasing a barking deer. In the later period, various types of song were developed: (1) ***Dar Hla*** (songs of lament) was sung to mourn the dead, (2) ***Hlado and Bawh Hla*** (songs of the heroes). *Hlado* was sung and chanted by a hunter immediately after an animal was killed and repeated just before entering into the village. *Bawh Hla* was chanted by a successful worrier in the war (3) ***Chal Hla*** (festival songs) was mainly sung during the festivals such as the *Chanchar Kut* (Summer Festival) and other festivals. There were eight different types bearing the name of one who made the tune, e.g. *Thailungi Zai, Lianchhiari Zai, Mangkhaia Zai, Darlungi Zai, Lera Zai, Lalthiri Zai, Lianchhluri Zai, Durlung Zai, Dharmani Zai, Darpawngi Zai, Vatzawi Zai, Saikuti Zai, Aikhlungi Zai, Thanzara Zai, Chengmaluaia Zai* and *Aawithangpa Zai*. (4) ***Chawngchen Zai*** (dancing song for celebration) was sung during the *Thangchhuah*

composed by the Mizos is estimated around 2,000 it could be more than this figure.

A. Songs: The Sources of Theology

In the absence of written materials, myths, folklores, sermons and songs become the primary sources for constructing tribal theology. Because the faith and experiences of the tribal Christian community are often explicitly expressed through songs. If we are serious about doing theology with the people, it is our theological task to listen to songs and stories of the people. Any one who looks for a systematic, logical, coherent and profound theology from the tribal Christian communities at this stage will be disappointed, but this does not mean that the faith communities in the tribal areas do not have theology of their own. Their theology has been articulated mainly through their songs composed by the tribal Christian themselves. Therefore, in the process of theologizing in the tribal context, we should not neglect the songs composed by the tribal themselves.

B. Origin and Development of Indigenous Christian Songs

The first two missionaries, J.H. Lorrain and F.W. Savidge, who landed in Mizoram 1894 translated seven Western Christian hymns into Mizo language and made available a hand written hymn

---

Feast. There were a number of such types. e.g. *Luntui Zai, Tlangkhaw Zai, Bungkhaw Zai, Zailam Hla, Tlangphei Zai, Nilen Zai* and *Dawn Zai*. (5) ***Naupang Hla*** (children songs) was sung by children calling their parents to come home soon from the *jhum*. (6) ***Nauawih Hla*** (lullabies) sung to the babies to make them sleep. (7) ***Tlanglam Zai*** (communal dancing songs), originally known as ***Puma Zai***. This was usually sang by the community and accompanied by a communal dance. It continued to be popular among the non-Christians till 1945. This is also classified in various types: *Awithangpa Zai, Hrangchawni Zai, Lelthang Zai, Ruah Zai, Chalmar Zai, Rel Zai,, German Zai, Tualphei Zai, Labour Zai, Chheih Zai, Aizawl Zai*. (8) ***Lengzem Zai*** (love song) was sung or chanted mainly by young people expressing their feeling for their love ones, loneliness and hope, sometimes used as conversation. This has been modified according to the change of time. It may be classified as trational *Lengzem Zai*, *Kaih Lek* (composed using tunes of Christian hymns) and modern love song which is a synthesis of Western and Mizo original tunes.

book in 1897. The first printed Mizo hymn book entitled *Kohhran Hla Bu* (Church Hymn Book) was released in 1899. As the new converts were taught Christian songs, they were prohibited to sing the traditional folk songs. Though they love singing and were happy with and even proud of the translated Christian songs they had learned, they were not satisfied. It was the coming of **Revival** to Mizoram in 1906 and the subsequent waves in 1913-14, 1919-23 and 1930 which had brought about radical changes in the Mizo Christianity particularly in the Christians music and songs, first in the tune and then in the actual content of the songs.

Originally a number of hymns and songs were translated by the missionaries and the Mizo Christians themselves from English which were compiled and published as the Mizo Christian Hymnal. The table below may reflect development of Christian hymns and songs :

PARTICULARS	**1899**	**1903**	**1908**
Number of Hymns and Songs	18	125	273
Contributors			
Missionary Contribution	11	88	184
Khasi Contribution	7	21	29
Mizo Contribution	Nil	16	56

These hymns and songs were basically translated from English, a few of them were composed using the tune of certain familiar English or Welsh hymns and songs, only a very limited numbers were written with the tune of their own.[7] But the immense interest of the people in singing compelled the church to enlarge and publish the Mizo Christian Hymnal almost every three years. The first publication was in 1899 which contained 18 hymns, 1903 publication was only the first part and had 81 hymns, the second part published in 1904 contained 125 hymns. The 1906

[7] In the first Mizo Christian Hymnal, Savidge and Lorrain contributed 7 hymns, D.E. Jones 4, Rai Bhadur 7. In the 1908 edition, Edwin Rowlands contributed 61 hymns. D.E. Jones 54, J.H. Lorrain 38, F.W. Savidge 31, among the Mizo Christians Thanga made the larges contribution. He contributed 23 hymns. Thanga was the one who first translated an English hymn "We Shall Stand Before the King" into Mizo.

publication contained 195, and it was subsequently published in 1908, 1910, 1913, 1915, 1919 which had 558 hymns, 1922, 1942, 1955 with tonic solfa, 1983, 1985, 1990 and in 1992.[3] We may note that within twenty years the number of hymns increased from 81 in 1899 to 556 in 1919.

1. Indigenous Tune : The tunes of Western Christian hymns, in comparison with the Mizo traditional tune, were high pitch, rough, militant, not melodious for the Mizos. They did not satisfy the Mizo Christians could not express themselves and dance with the Western tune, spontaneously the tunes of translated hymns were softened and made melodious. The tune was neither the Mizo traditional tune nor the Western tune, from the interaction of the two different tunes, a new synthetic tune developed that really satisfied the Mizo Christians. I wish the same thing had happened in theology, but that did not take place. The theology we learned in the seminaries which we taught to the churches remain alien. Unless the fusion of horizons, the Judeo-Western Christian and the Mizo horizons, takes place and produces a new synthetic theology, Christianity will not take root deep into the Mizo culture.

2. Indigenous Christian Songs : The emergence of indigenous tune was followed by the composition of indigenous songs. Mizo Christians started composing songs of their own. Some of the first songs are mentioned below :

Title of the Songs	Composer	Year of Composition
Ka Ropuina Tur leh Ka Himna Hmun Where I shall be Honoured and Happy	Patea	1920
Lei Lal Puan Ropui Chu a Tlawm ang The Earthly Royal Gown Shall Fade Away	C.Z. Huala	1922
Tunah a Thar Hmangaihna Eng Nuamah Now in the New Blissful Light of Love	R.L. Kamlala	1922
Hunte an Kiam Zel a Time is Passing	Puna	1929

---

3 Tlanghmingthanga, "An Appraisal of the Eschatological Content of Selected Mizo Christian Songs with Special Reference to their Significance for the Church in Mizoram." A M.Th Thesis submitted to the Senate of Serampore, (1993), p. 86

Kan Nghak reng che Kan Lalber Lord, We have been Waiting for You	Suakliana	1930
Ka va ngai em Lalram ropui Oh, How I long for the Great Kingdom	Rianghleia	1934
Ni tla ngai lo Zion Khawpui City of Zion Where the Sun Never Set	Rev. Lianruma	1940

As mentioned above, the first indigenous Mizo Christian song entitled *Ka Ropuina Tur leh Ka Himna Hmun* was composed by Patea in 1919 followed by C.Z. Huala's song *Lei Lal Puan Ropui chu a Tlawm ang* composed in 1922 and Kamlala's song *Rinin Thlir Thiam ila*, composed in 1922.[4] Here we have observed that the composition of indigenous songs was the fruit of the third wave of revival movement. The third wave of revival which occured during 1919-1923 made remarkable impact on the life of the churches in Mizoram. The fruits of the third wave of revival movement, which later became the distinctive marks of Mizo Christianity, were the composition of indigenous Christian songs with a synthetic tune as described above and the introduction of the traditional drum, which was once rejected by missionaries, in the worship service. More and more indigenous songs, known as community songs (*lenkhawm zai)*,[5] were composed. Since new songs were being composed, several blank pages were included in the early publications of the Mizo Christian Hymnal for writing the new songs. As the number of new songs was rapidly increased, they were collected and published separately under the title *Hla Thar Bu* (The New Hymn Book). They were usually used in the community fellowship of singing known as *Lenkhawm*.[6] The contribution of revival movement towards

---

4 B. Lalthangliana, *Ka Lungkham (Introduction to Mizo Literature)*, pp. 1-12; C.Z. Huala, "Hla Phuah Thiam R.L. Kamlala," *MZP Chanchinbu*, (July, 1965), p. 5

5 *Lenkhawm Zai* is a community singing resulting from the Revival Movement. People gather together in a particular house appointed by the Church and have fellowship in singing. They keep on singing together with drums, a small and a big ones are rhythmically beaten. The singing is prolonged depending on the inspiration of the Holy Spirit, and whoever feels like dancing he/she dances as an expression of their joy. Sometimes the singing go on throughout night and day.

6 *Lenkhawm* literally means "visiting to get together". (*Leng* means visit, *khawm* means gathering). Gathering together is a common practice in the

indigenization of Christian songs is like a staircase, indigenization of the tune followed by the composition of Christian songs and re-introduction of the traditional drum in the church.

C. Singing Theology

When I consider whether songs should be used as one of the sources of theology or theology should be sung through the songs, the relationship seems to be dialectical. In the tribal context it is more common and effective to sing theology, that is the reason why for the heading of this chapter I put "Singing Theology". Christians sing their theological conviction which inspires the churches to act. Without singing no mass movement will occur. In the context of North East India, singing is an important instrument not only to communicate the gospel message and also to inspire the churches. Today we see a similar phenomena in the black movement in South Africa. The black movement has been inspired by and accompanied with singing and dancing without which they find difficult to express their political conviction. Any movement in Mizoram, whether religious or political movement, was always accompanied and inspired by appropriate songs and singing. For instance, the first political movement was poor people's movement against their tyrant chiefs, which eventually turned the table up side down ending the traditional system of chieftainhood and ushering a new era of democracy in Mizoram. The movement was supported and inspired by songs they themselves composed and sang. One verse is cited below :-

Mizo

Zalen Union pawla tang ve turin,
Tangka ro thangpui tel lo chuan,
Kan phal nem maw
Rairah riang kan tawnah.

---

communitarian society. They used to gather together in the occasion of festivals, community feasts, celebration, in the event of sickness, accident and death, and even just for drinking *zu*. What makes the Christian community gathering (*lenkhawm*) difference from the traditional gathering is its purpose and nature. They gathered without rice beer to praise the Lord and to have fellowship mainly through singing.

English

To join the party of Mizo Union,
We the oppressed people,
Do not welcome the ruling class;
Unless they pay gold and silver.

The poor people asserted themselves which was expressed in the verse cited above. In fact, the conversion movement in Mizoram could be described as poor people's movement, inspired by the songs of hope (eschatological songs) as discussed below. That "hope" became the energizing power for the early Christians not only to be able to survive in the midst of persecution, but to change their wretched condition.

1. Singing Hope : If we analyze the theological teaching of the first seven songs composed by the Mizo Christians, in spite of their differences in the expressions, we can say without any hesitation that "hope" is the central theme. All of them are eschatological songs in which the writers expressed explicitly their hope for heaven. "Hope for heaven" is not new to the Mizos. Before they embraced Christianity they had a similar concept called "pialral", a paradise for the warrior and the rich people who could perform *thangchhuah*. (Thangchhuah is a title conferred to those who either killed the required wild animals and enemies or provided public feasts four times giving away their possessions to the poor villagers). The first group of the songs composed in 1920s and 1930s tell much about the hope of "heaven" which is similar to the Mizo traditional concept of *Pialral*, and present Christianity as a better alternative way to go to heaven (Pialral). Most of them compare and contrast this "world" and "heaven" depicting the world as dark, full of troubles and boring; heaven as a joyful place free from suffering and sorrow. They also express their eagerness to go there.

If we put "heaven" in the existential language, it means hope for better life. This is quite evident when we study the socio-historical context of the songs. The early Christian community, the matrix of the songs, was a small, insignificant and marginalized community. The new converts, who in the non-Christian Mizo religion had not hope of going to "pialral", were not only hoping to go to heaven life after death when they embraced Christianity but also to finding a new identity and better means of living here on earth. Though they had hope for heaven (the new pialral) as well as a better living condition here on earth, they were still longing for their old way of life, particularly the fellowship they had in drinking *zu* (rice beer) together with friends, singing and dancing together. Though they had new hopes, but they were also frustrated. We will read the first stanza and chorus of the first song *Ka Ropuina Tur leh Ka Himna Hmun* composed by Patea :

Ka ropuina tur leh ka himna hmun
Ral hlauhawm leh thih, nat awm lo chu
Thlaler atang hian ka hmu rinin
Chu hmun hlun chuan min tuam vel vangin.

Ka thlir ni tin ang, ka thlen hma loh chuan
A hmangaihna eng leh lawmawm chu
Miten chu hmun chu hluiin ring mahse
Ka sawi thei dawn lo tharin a lang

English Translation

Where I shall be safe and honoured,
Where there is no more fear for enemy, pain and death,
I see it from this wilderness
For the shadow of eternal home encompasses me.

Till I reach there I gave everyday
The blissful and shining of his love,
Others may think that it has grown old,
I cannot tell why it ever new to me.

Though there were no more headhunting and inter village feuds when this song was composed, Patea might have remembered the condition of the old Mizo society and reflected on that situation from the Christian perspective. If we read Patea's song bearing in mind the social context he had in mind, the tribal inter village feuds and head hunting, his lines, "Where I will be safe and honoured, Where there is no more fear for enemy, pain and death", become meaningful. It is no wonder that the tribal people living in the steep hills of Mizoram, stricken by poverty and hardship, were deeply longing for heaven. In fact, hope for properity and comfortable life was prominent even in the Mizo traditional concept of *Pialral* (heaven). Moreover, life became much harder for the early Christian community which was not only small in number but also poor and marginalized in their own society; such experience could intensify their longing for heaven. The song is comparable with the Psalm composed during Babylonian captivity.

By the waters' of Babylon,
there we sat down and wept,
When we remembered Zion.

The early Christian community in Mizoram longed so much for heaven as the captive Israelites longed for Jerusalem. "If I forget, O Jerusalem, Let my tongue cleave to the roof of my mouth" (Ps. 137:1). With the same spirit, one Mizo composer, Mr. Thanchianga used this psalm with modification. "Who will sing the praise of God in Babylon, the land of graves." When we approach the song from sociological perspective, we realize that it is a cry for liberation.

Unless they are read with an understanding of the social context in which they were composed, they can be branded merely as songs of desperation and dream. This is the reason why some scholars think that the songs do not affirm this world, they rather denounce the world and encourage Christians to escape from life struggle. In fact, Prof. Siamkima commented on R.L. Kamlala's songs, "We see in his songs a thick dark cloud and trouble all the time hanging over him. The cloud of grief and trouble which envelops him is too thick. Like a mithun bears a heavy rain, he quietly bear the raining misfortune."[7] However, darkness is not the end, there is light and promise which gives hope to believers. R.L. Kamlala himself expressed :

Hmanah kan Pi-Pu ten,	Through the blood of love,
An hloh hnu van Pialral	We have regained the Pialral,
Hmangaih thisenah	Lost by our fore fathers,
Keinin kan lo hmu e	Long long time ago.
Angel varte awmna,	Where the white angels live,
Ni tla-senglo ram khi,	Where the sun never set
Aw I thisen zarah,	By the blood of Jesus Christ
Engtiknge ka thlen ang?	When shall I be there?

7 S. Khawlhring, *Zalenna Ram*, p. 78

He does not only hope for heaven, he also tells his conviction why he should be there. "By the blood of Jesus Christ, When shall I be there." It is because of the atoning blood of Jesus Christ that he will go to heaven (Pialral). While missionaries and church leaders rejected the term "Pialral" Kamlala, without hesitation, used it several times as synonym with heaven. The poet who has no hope of reaching the *pialral* (heaven) by means of heroic deeds or prosperity could express with assurance that because of Jesus Christ, he will go to heaven. C.Z. Huala is more symbolical in his expression and christological in content. The centrality of Christ in his thought is clearly reflected in his song, particularly in the chorus and the second and the third stanzas.

Lili par mawi Lal Isua ka nei
Ka tana par chatuan ram mawiah
Hrehawmah pawh Aman min awmpui fovang
Lili par mawi Lal Isua ka nei.

A hmangaihna ram eng mawiah chuan
Amah chu chatuan Varparh a ni,
Hrehawm tuar mah ila he mi khawvelah hian,
A ramah min la hruai dawn si.

Tunah tapin rum rih mah ila,
Thihnain ka mit a chhin hunin
Ka hlau lo vang thlan thim ata min tho ang a,
Ka mittui te chu hrufai turin.

English Translation

Jesus Christ the beautiful lily I possess,
It blooms for me in the ever beautiful land,
He will always abide with me in time of trouble
Jesus Christ the beautiful lily I possess.

In the bright and beautiful land of love,
He is the eternal shining star,
Though I suffer harship in this world,
He will lead me to his Kingdom.

Crying and groaning now I may be,
When death comes and closes my eyes,

I shall not be afraid, for he shall raise me from the dark grave
To wipe all my tears away.

The christological metaphors used by C.Z. Huala are not common in the New Testament. For him Jesus is the lily and the eternal shining star. It was the *Ramthing par* which, he saw on his way to *Biate* village, inspired him to use the lily flower to describe the beauty of Jesus. He could have used "Jesus Christ and beautiful *ramthing par* I possess" rather using "lily" which is not found in Mizoram. "The eternal shining star" is my own translation of Huala's Varparh arsi (Jupiter) which brightly shines before the dawn. The Varparh arsi is certainly a meaningful metaphor for the Mizos to describe the function of Jesus Christ, because Mizos regards *Varparh arsi* (Jupiter) as a sign of "dawn" and end of darkness. It signifies victory over the dark night and the dawn of new day. For C.Z. Huala, the function of Jesus is to liberate those who are suffering from discrimination and exploitation usheing in a new era of hope and freedom. Like John, he understand Jesus Christ as the way to heaven. Jesus is also the source of hope which gives him courage to face death. He said, "I will not fear the dark grave for Jesus shall rise me from the death."

There are many more contemporary songs commonly sang in the church and in the *lenkhawm*.[8] Out of 14 most popular songs listed in the footnote, 80% can be categorized as eschatological songs. The

---

8 Some of the most popular ones are : *A Ral Mek Lei Ninawm Hi* (The Troublesome-World is passing away), *Buaina Lo Kiang La* (When Trouble Will Disappear), *Damlai Tuipui Fawn Piah Lamah* (Beyond the Waves of the Sea of Life), *Hun leh Kumte an Ral Zel* (Time and Years passing away), *Ka Awm Khawhar Changin* (When I am lonely), *Ka Damlai Thlipui A Ral Hunin* (When the Storm of My Life Pass Away), *Tunah Buaina Tlang Chhip a Dingin* (Now Standing at the Mountain Peak of Trouble), *Nitin Ka Hnenah Awm Reng Ang Che* (Be with me Everyday), *Ka Hmaah Lui ral Khawmawi Chu a Awm* (Yonder the River There is a Beautiful City), *Min Hnem Ang Che* (Comfort Me), *Kan Nghak Reng Che Kan Lalber* (Lord, we are waiting for you), *Aw Ka Chhandamtu* (Oh, My Saviour), *En R'u Pathian Beramno Sual Phurtu* (Behold the Lamb of God Who Takes Away Our Sins), *Aw Khawiahnge Chhandamtu Chuan Lungngaih Hrehawm a tuar* (Where the Saviour has Suffered Passion).

theological content of these songs may be described as (a) "Hope" which gave the early Christians strength to overcome persecution and hardship, (b) "Cry for liberation" which is implicitly expressed and (c) Christology.

The problem of the theology of these eschatological songs is that, in some case as Prof. Siamkima commented, they advocate escapism rather than affirming the world. They do not inspire believers to struggle for change. We will not do justice if we treat the eschatological songs merely as "hope of desperation". But a careful study reveals the fact that desperation and suffering for the Mizo poets are the basis of hope. In fact, Patea is quite optimistic. He often used "flower or flowering" in his other songs and saw Jesus, human life and heaven as flower.[9] "Optimism" in Patea songs will certainly inspire Christians to work persuasively for transformation of individual and social life rather than waiting for heaven in desperation. However, their idea of hope has to be reinterpreted according to the change of context. The Christian hope has certainly transcended the traditional hope only for life after death. Christian faith should not only be concerned vitally with the future - indeed it must be characterized by a concern for future - but has also taken seriously how the future has to be here and now. Hope sets out from a definite reality in history and announces the future of that reality, its future possibilities and its power over the future.[10] Moltmann rightly said, "This is why faith, whenever it develops into hope, no rest but unrest, no patience but impatience. It does not calm the unquiet heart, but is itself this unquiet heart in man. Those who in Christ can no longer put up with reality as it is, but begin to suffer under it, to contradict it. Peace with God means conflicting with the world."[11]

2. Singing "Born Again" : Until 1960s there was no real change in the theological teaching, the theology of missionaries who came from pietistic theological background continued to be the dominant theology. This theology was highly ethical and pietistic. It emphasized personal piety based on the principle of abstention which went very

---

9 Patea composed 55 songs in which he used 40 times "flower or blooming". Siamkima Khawlhring, *Op cit.*, p. 70

10 J. Moltmann, "Meditation on Hope," *A Reader in Political Theology*, p. 25

11 J. Moltmann, *Theology of Hope*, p. 21

well with the tribal taboos based on “dos” and “don’ts”. The shift of emphasis in theology from “ethical emphasis” to “personal faith” occured in 1960s when some evangelical conservative missionaries taught tribal students in Shillong the necessity of born again for salvation of soul for life after death. The importance of “born again” as a result of individual personal faith and decision was emphasized. While this was not new for the Western churches, it was new for the tribal Christians in North East India. Although “justification by faith” was the fundamental, teaching of Protestant faith since the time of Martin Luther, but that was not understood by the tribal new converts in North East India. It was in the “born again movement” that the tribal Christians who had no concept of sin, began to learn the idea of original sin and redefined faith as inner conviction. As Schleiermacher internalized religion, the tribal Christians did the same in their own way. In the tribal Christianity, this was a significant shift from an emphasis on good deeds and pious living to internal faith. In other words, it was a shift from the tribal taboo oriented ethical teaching to personal faith based on feeling or from a religion of action to a religion of belief. The “born again movement” can be interpreted as the first successful attempt to internalize religion which in many ways over emphasized “faith” at the expense of good deeds. It spread like a wild fire.

The “born again movement” was like any other movement supported by songs. In fact, one of the factors responsible for the rapid spread was the songs. Hundreds of song were composed. One verse is cited below to show the nature of songs composed during the born again movement.

I Pianglhar tur a ni,	You must be born again
Hun lawmawm i neih lai hian	When you have opportunity.
Chhandamtu in a nghak reng che	The Saviour is waiting for you
I awm angin amah chu pan mai la	As you are, come to him now
I sual zawng zawng a lo ngaidam ang che	He will forgive all your sins

Mr. Lalthanliana, when he had born again experience, spontaneously compose the song given below to express his personal testimony :

Mizo Version	**English Translation**
Lal Isuan misual a lawm	Lord Jesus welcome sinners
Tupawh inchhira sim chu	Whoever repent,
Lal Isuan a hnenah a hruai lut zel ang,	To him, Lord Jesus will lead them

Khawvel parmawina lawma Ka vahbosan hnu pawhin Lal Isuan misual a lawm	Though I wandered away Enjoying the pleasure of this world Jesus welcome sinner
A makin a ropui e, Hrilh zo seng an awm lo'ng e Kei mi sual ber min lawm	It is wonderful and great, No one else can tell why he welcomes A sinful man like me.

It is quite common among the Mizo Christians to express their conversion experience through songs. Most of these songs tell the seriousness of sin, repentance, importance of faith, forgiveness, salvation and the new life and the experience of joy. The tunes are indigenous but the content is not different from typical evangelical songs and choruses.

3. Singing Mission : As the movement of "born again" quickly resulted in a missionary movement, the tribal Christians started singing Christian mission. Though there are many songs of mission, I have chosen a song composed by my own teacher, Mr. H. Lianmanga, for the study of tribal concepts of Christian mission.

ZORAM HMANGAIHTU LALPA	**LORD, LOVER OF MIZORAM**
Zoram hmangaihtu Lalpa A thlawnin Chanchin Tha min pe Hei leh chen hi kan tawmpui, Lalpa min ngaidam ang che.	Lord, lover of Mizoram Freely you have given us Gospel So long we kept it to ourselves We beseech you, forgive us.
Kan tih tur Chanchin Tha puandarh A thlawna pe chhuak turin Khawvel zawng zawng hi Lalpa ram a nih hma chuan.	Our duty to proclaim Gospel To give it out freely Till the whole wide world Become the Kingdom of God
Dak ula lote en r'u Seng turin an hmin zo ta e, In favah kengin tunah Lalpa tan thawk chhuak nghal r'u.	Rise and look around the fields They are ripe for the harvest Set out now with your sickles Start harvesting for the Lord.
Khawvel zawng zawng Lalpa tan, Kan bei zel ang kan hneh hma chuan Mahni, tawngtai, thilpekin Lalram kan din zel ang.	The whole wide world for the Lord We shall press on till we conquer By self sacrifice, prayer, giving We shall establish the Kingdom.

Harh r'u Zofate harh r'u
Hnehna ropui kan chang thuai ang;
Kan Pathian hmingin puanzar,
Kan zar ngei ang khawvelah.

Wake up, children of Mizoram
The great victory will soon be ours
In the name of God, the banner
We will unfold in the world.

This song is one of the missionary songs composed in recent year which has quickly swept through the length and breadth of Mizoram. From this song, we observed that the Mizo concept of Christian mission is quite traditional and triumphalistic. In the last stanza the poet says,

> "The great victory will soon be ours,
> In the name of God the banner,
> We will unfold in the world."

I am certainly critical about harmful triumphalism which undermined God's revelation in other cultures, but I have to think realistically that unless Jesus Christ is victorious over sin and death, what else have we to celebrate in our Christian faith?

In the song we also note that the motif of Christian mission is "thanksgiving" which seems to be the right motif. Not only Mr. Lianmanga, many others hold a similar view. In fact, the whole missionary movement in Mizoram is thanksgiving. For the Mizo churches, mission is tranksgiving. Mission work for them is an expression of their gratitude for what they have received. As such, when they don't do it sufficiently they feel guilty. This is the reason Mr. H. Lianmanga said,

> Lord, lover of Mizoram,
> Freely you have given us Gospel,
> So long we kept it to ourselves,
> We beseech you, forgive us.

Christians around the world should regard mission as thanksgiving. The Committee on World Mission and Evangelism (WCC) in its conference in Melbourne 1980 had a theme "Thy Kingdom Come" and "Thy Will Be Done" in San Antonio 1989. I wish the WCC should also explore the perspective of thanksgiving in Christian mission and has "Hollow be Thy Name" for its conference theme. It is through the service of love and gratitude that liberation shall be achieved, certainly not with the spirit of anger and revenge. We have to learn the joy of serving God and others.

The zeal for Christian mission ultimately inspired individual Christians to give generously. The importance of giving for Christian mission was expressed very well by Rev. H. Lengluta in his song, "Pe rawh u Tichuan Pekin in Awm Ang" (Give and You Will be Given).

PE RAWH U PEKIN IN AWM ANG

Khawvel suala bo hnu tlan chhuak leh turin
Pathianin a fapa mal neih chhun min pe
A tlansa suala bo ten nunna kawng an hriat theih nan
Thilpeka rawngbawl turin Lalpan min ko.

Pe rawh u ti chuan pekin in awm ang
Pekah Pathian in hneh ban thei lovang
Pathianin mihring lei a ba ngai lo
Malsawmna hnar a lo ni si.

Ka lo hre ta, Lalpa i sawmna aw hi
Kristian tin missionary atan min ko
Ka hlan che ka neih zawng leh ka taksa, ka nunna nen
I ta ka ni thisenin min lei tawh si.

GIVE, THEN YOU WILL BE GIVEN

To save those who have perished in this sinful world,
God gave us his begotten son,
For the redeemed but lost in sin may find the way of life,
He calls us to do the ministry of giving.

Give, then you will be given,
You cannot outdo God in giving,
God never owe human beings,
He is the source of blessing.

Lord, I come to undertand your calling
That all Christians are called to be missionaries.
I offered all that I have, my body and my soul,
I am yours for you have bought me by the blood.

It is clear with the background explained above why so much of money has been collected and spent for Christian mission. From the following facts and figure one can easily imagine what could be the impact of this type of songs and how the people in Mizoram would sing Christian mission.

Church/Mission Society	No. of Missionaries 1991	Local Workers 1991	Budget/PC of Total Income 1991-92
Presbyterian Mission Board of Mizoram	438	147	15477589 (1993) (32%)
Mizoram Baptist Mission	210	190	14,28,2500 (1194) (51%)
Total	648	337	2,97,60,089

It will be quite rare to find a regional mission board which spend more than 50% of the total income of the church for mission and evangelism. The zeal for mission and evangelism has been nurtured and inspired by the type of songs mentioned above. They sing their missionary conviction.

4. Singing Liberation : Struggle for liberation has been an integral part of the Christian missions operating in North East India. One of the concrete examples in the history Christianity in the region is the struggle for the abolition of slavery in Mizoram in 1920s. Dr. P. Fraser, a missionary of the Wales Presbyterian Church, was engaged himself in the struggle against the *bawi* (slave) system in Mizoram. He was influenced and inspired by the evangelical social teaching of anti-slavery in Europe and committed to the cause of the abolition of slavery. The British administrators and the chiefs wanted to retain the *bawih* system, but all the missionaries regarded it as a form of slavery which should be abolished. However, missionaries themselves did not evolve uniform approach. While Fraser regarded the system as incompatible with biblical teaching and the British laws which should be immediately abolished, senior missionaries Lorrain, Savidge and Jones thought that the system was on the way out and would wither away naturally. Fraser entered into serious confrontation with the British administration and the chiefs. He was expelled from Mizoram and dismissed by the Mission Board from service. He finally won victory and got the order of abolition of the *bawih* system in Mizoram. Though opinion in the approach to *bawih* system differed among the missionaries themselves, the view of the people was expressed by Upa (elder) Thanga in his hymn :

Aw Lalpa Chungnung ber kan fak hle a che
Pathian Nung leh Engkimtithei i ni e,
Hnehchhiahte, Bawih, Riangvai te, Misual te thian
Fahrahte, Retheite Lal, Pa leh Pathian.

Tawngtaina chhangtu Pathian i nih vangin
I miten an mamawh an dil i pe fo,
I fate tap leh rum i lo ngaithla thin,
Thudik tan, thil tha ti, i ensan ngai lo.

Hnam tin thim chhuahsan leh bawih chhuak lo lawm se
Chungnung berah Pathian ropui ber rawh se
Lei chunga a lawmte chungah rem leng se,
"Hosana, Hosana", tiin zai rawh se.

English Translation

Oh Lord, most high we honour and praise you
For you are God almighty and living God.
Friend of the oppressed, slaves, marginalisd and sinners
The Lord, Father and God of the orphans and the poor.

For you are the God who answered pryers,
You granted whatever your people ask their needs,
You hear the cry and groaning of your children,
Your never forsake those who stand for truth and do justice

Let all nations celebrate freedom from slavery and darkness,
To God be the glory in the highest,
Peace on earth among those whom he loved,
Hosanna, Hosanna let them sing.

This song was composed when Mr. Thanga heard the news of abolition of slavery. Quite a few songs of this type were composed. This song reflects the power and victory of the poor. Here we see the nature of God who takes the side of the poor, who hear their cry and answer their prayer.

Identity crisis is a common problem among the tribals in North East India. Mr. Rokunga responded to this problem with songs through which he tried to develop self-esteem among the Mizo people. One of his songs is cited below to study how self consciouness and self-esteems has been inculculated among the Mizos through songs.

MIZO KAN NI KAN LAWM E

Mizo kan ni kan lawm e
Kan tlang a thiang bawk si;
Kan rilru pawh a sang e,
Kan hming a thang bawk si,
Kan ram kan hnam din chhuah nan
Thinlung tihthianghlimin
Kan huai kan fel, kan finnate,
Thiamin i hmang ang.

Kan pi, kan pu mihuaiten
Dan tha kha mawi an ti,
Thian chhan thih an ngam fo thin,
An hming a thang bawk si.
Keini'n chu dan chu zawmin
Huai taka din kan tum;
Mizo kan ni kan hmel a tha
Kan tum a sang bawk si.

Chanchin Thain kan ramah,
Rambuai a tum bo ta,
Kan hnam din chhuahna bul chu,
Hei ngel hi a lo ni.
Huam dang hmusit hauh lovin,
Thianah i siam ang u;
Chutin kan hming than mawina chuan
Khawvel a deng chhuak ang.

English Translation
WE ARE HAPPY FOR WE ARE MIZOS

We are happy for we are Mizos
Our hills are pure and green
Our thinking is high,
Our fame spread wide.
Let us keep our mind pure
To build our land and nation.
Our bravery, efficiency and intelligence
Let us use them properly.

Our courageous ancestors
Admired the golden rules,
They were every ready to give their lives for friends;
They were famous as well.
Following the golden rules,
We courageously try to stand firm.
We are Mizos, we are beautiful,
Our aim of life is high.

Gospel has driven away
Evil spirits from our land,
This is the foundation and beginning,
For our nation to grow.
Without despising others,
Let us make friendship with them.
Then our fame will penetrate,
Through the whole wide world.

For tribals who are facing crisis in their identity, it is important to be able to say sincerely that "we are beautiful". The concept of beauty is often conditioned by the concept of dominant group set the criteria and imposed their value system on others through mass media and many other means. The problem with many tribes living in the plain is that they have lost self-esteem and confident which could be one of the primary factors for complacency. The black movement in Africa and USA is based on the new concept of beauty that "black is beautiful". Similarly, it is important for any marginalized community struggling for liberation to be able to say that "we are beautiful". Unless the community accept itself and be confident, it will be extremely difficult to struggle for their own liberation.

While Mr. Rokunga primarily drew inspiration from the Mizo traditions, particulars from the warriors who set examples in the heroic deeds and the Christian teaching. The two streams of his inspiration are synthesized in which the gospel is upheld as the foundation of development. This is how theology also should be done in North East India. There should be fusion of the gospel and our culture.

If we think that the praxis of thc church is important, people must sing a theology of praxis. I have been teaching liberation theology, several times I presented papers in seminars and consultations, now it is quite evident for me that in order to move the churches to engage themselves in the liberation actions, people have to sing liberation. This is quite evident from the past experiences. Unless people sing the liberation of the poor and oppressed, they will not be liberated. Unless they sing justice, justice will not be done. People must sing theology of liberation.

CHAPTER XII

THEOLOGY OF DEVELOPMENT

The history of Christian Mission has been interpreted differently by different people, for some people it is an instrument of colonization, deculturalization, Westernization and for others it is a means of social transformation. From the experience of tribal community of North East India in the last century, it was proved that Christianity has brought about radical social change but that change was a transformational change. A primitive society in the beginning of 20th century has now become a fairly modern society. Although missionary era is now over, their educational institutions and hospitals are still maintained and they make significant contribution for the improvement of society. In this postcolonial era, the churches in a predominantly Christian State, are confronting two fundamental issues- the task of evangelization and social transformation. The risen Lord, who called and sent us to evangelize the world, also called us to transform the world as the light to the nations and to be the salt of the earth (Matt 5:13&14). At the very outset, I should affirm that Christian Approach to Development is goal oriented-orientated toward and struggle for the Realization of the **Kingdom of God**[1] in which the name of the Lord is hallowed, the will of God is done here on earth as in heaven.

1. CHRISTIAN PRINCIPLE OF DEVELOPMENT: Social transformation or Development[2] has been the concern of people of all

---

[1] WCC- Assembly Melbourne, 1980 defined as follow, "The Kingdom of God which was inaugurated in Jesus Christ brings justice, love, peace and joy, and freedom from the grasp of principalities and power, those demonic forces which place human lives and institutions in bondage and infiltrate their very textures. God's judgment is revealed as an over turning of the values and structures of this world. In this perspective of the Kingdom, God has a preference for the poor" Section I, Good News to the Poor, No.1 appeared as ***Thy Kingdom Come***.

[2] **Development** is derived from France word "de-envelop" which means tearing off which envelopes the people. It may be perceived as liberation. Development should, therefore, be perceived as a multidimensional process involving the reorganization and reorientation of entire economic and social system. Michael P.Todaro, ***Economic Development in the Third Word*** (Fourth Edition),

faiths, particularly in the third world countries, but how the Christian approach is distinct from other approaches. I would like to reaffirm that its distinctiveness is in its motif and goal. The motif is God as Mother Teresa said that "we do it for Jesus". It is a *theocentric approach* and the goal of which is the Reign of God and its action has to be love in action.

We will briefly survey the different approaches of Christian church: The church has been responding to human need in different time and in different context from its inception.[3] I made an attempt to streamline varied development efforts in history:

> ***(1) Missiological Approach***: The first task and concern of the early Church was to proclaim the Gospel without ignoring the problem of the poor among themselves. When they proclaimed the gospel, it was not their intension to transform their social-political life of the people. But that very gospel is the power of God for salvation of total human life. Paul said, "For I am not ashamed of the gospel, because it is the power of God that brings salvation to everyone who believes: first to the Jew, then to the Gentile. For in the gospel the

---

Longman, New York, 1989. Paul P.Streeten, Director World Development Institute rightly said, " Development must be redefined as an attach on the chief evil of the world today: malnutrition, diseases, illiteracy, slums, unemployment and inequality. Measured in terms of aggregated growth rates, development had been a great success. But measured in term of job, justice and elimination of poverty, it has been a failure or only a partial success" ***The Frontiers of Development Studies***, New York; John Wiley, 1972.

[3] In those days when the number of disciples was increasing, the Hellenistic Jews among them complained against the Hebraic Jews because their widows were being overlooked in the daily distribution of food.(Acts 6.1). Paul encourages the early church by holding up the Macedonians as an example of a Christian community that, despite its own extreme poverty, was a living example of Christ-like living. They had almost nothing, but were extraordinarily generous with what little they did have. "Moroover, brethren, we make known to you the grace of God bestowed on the churches of Macedonia; And now, brothers and sisters, we want you to know about the grace that God has given the Macedonian churches. In the midst of a very severe trial, their overflowing joy and their extreme poverty welled up in rich generosity and even beyond their ability." 2 Cor 8:1-3

righteousness of God is revealed —a righteousness that is by faith from first to last, just as it is written: "The righteous will live by faith." Marx Weber, who was working on sociology of religion, argued in his article *The Protestant Ethic and the Spirit of Capitalism* which eventually became a book that the Protestant ethics, particularly Calvinism, was responsible for the development of capitalism[4]. Along this line, Billy Graham expressed his view that , "change the mind with the Gospel, everything will be changed". The experience of my own community- the Mizo community in north East India- would without hesitation affirm the view of Max Weber.

(2) ***Charitable Approach***: Charity might be derived from Latin *caritas* which means coastlines, esteem, affection. In Vulgate it is often used to translate Greek *agape*. In Christian Theology it means the love of God for man or of man for his fellow men, an act of good will or affection leniency in judging others, a voluntary giving of money or other help to those in need. It is not profit oriented, but helping those who are in need with love and compassion.

Charity is an integral part of Christianity from its inception. The work of charity is the traditional fruit of faith, it is regarded

---

[4] Weber's essay ***The Protestant Ethic and the Spirit of Capitalism*** is his most famous work. It is argued that this work should not be viewed as a detailed study of Protestantism, but rather as an introduction into Weber's later works, especially his studies of interaction between various religious ideas and economic behaviour as part of the rationalisation of the economic system. In *The Protestant Ethic and the Spirit of Capitalism*, Weber put forward the thesis that Calvinist ethic influenced the development of capitalism. He noted the post-Reformation shift of Europe's economic centre away from Catholic countries such as France, Spain and Italy, and toward Protestant countries such as the Netherlands, England, Scotland and Germany. Weber also noted that societies having more Protestants were those with a more highly developed capitalist economy. Similarly, in societies with different religions, most successful business leaders were Protestant. Weber thus argued that Roman Catholicism impeded the development of the capitalist economy in the West, as did other religions such as Confucianism and Buddhism elsewhere in the world.

as a classical expression of Christian. Act of charity was intensified in response to the suffering of people resulting from industrial revolution and increasing population in Europe. To help the working labourers, the Christians inspired by the Evangelical Awakening of various denominations engaged themselves in acts of charity, and promoted training for adults, schooling for children, worked for prison reform and involved in the anti-slavery movement. Numerous charitable organizations and institutions sprang up.[5] The work of charity continues, it will not be given up. Mather Teresa, the Nobel Prize winner and universal symbol of charity explained:

> *People have often told me that I should not offer people fish but offer them fishing rods. But many times they don't even have enough strength to hold the rods! By giving them the fish I help them to recover their strength for tomorrow's fishing. Our mission is to face the problem individually, not collectively, treat the person, not the crowd.*
>
> *I don't admire hunger, or homelessness, or cold, but I do admire the disposition of the poor to face all this, the courage they have to smile because of their love for life, to keep on living in spite of all this. I admire their capacity to discover treasures in the smallest things- like a piece of bread I once gave to a boy in India, and which he ate, crumb by crumb, thinking it would be more satisfying.*
>
> *Poverty exists because of selfishness. We don't have the generosity to share what we have with others. The rich are getting richer and the poor are getting poorer. We want to be a bridge between the rich and the poor, a bridge between these two worlds. We don't want a confrontation of classes, but a meeting, a*

---

[5] The Sunday School Society (1785), Hannah More's schools (1789), Protestant Benevolent Association of Evangelical Mission (1822), The Young Men's Christian Association (1844), The Young Women Association (1855, The Salvation Army (1865),

brotherliness, so that the rich save the poor and the poor save the rich.[6]

(3) *Relief Approach*: The emergency relief is an area where Christians often expressed concern for and love of those who are suffering. In recent years tsunami occurred several times in Asia.[7] In this kind of situation, both government and NGOs are drawn together to do relief work. Relief of this kind is very different from Mother Teresa's approach, it deals with crowd. One concrete example in India is the formation of **Church's Auxiliary for Social Action**. In respond to the request of Pandit Jawaharlal Nehru , the first prime minister of India, in the event of India's independence in which millions of Muslims and Hindus lost their property and lives, **Church's Auxiliary for Social Action** (CASA) was formed to do relief work that continued and emerged as one of the most significant Christian NGOs in India.[8] In the deserter management, we have to join hands with people of other faith without distinction of caste, creed, colour and race. It is important to participate as Christians.

---

[6] Cited by Frances O'Gorman, ***Charity and Change: From Bandaid to Beacon***, World Vision Australia: Melbourne, 1992, p.10

[7] Several Tsunami occurred in Asia in recent years (7.1 2004: Indian Ocean; 7.2 2006: South of Java Island; 7.3 2006: Kuril Islands; 7.4 2007: Solomon Islands; 7.5 2007: Niigata, Japan; 7.6 2009: Samoa; 7.8 2011: New Zealand, 7.9 2011: Pacific coast of Japan). The deadliest tsunami in recorded history was the **2004 Asian tsunami**, which killed almost 230,000 people in eleven countries across the Indian Ocean.

[8] At the stroke of midnight, on 15th August 1947 India awoke to freedom. The cost of this freedom was phenomenal in terms of loss of property and human lives as a consequence of partition. The exchange of population across borders forced millions to live in alien surroundings and subhuman conditions. In this hour of agony and grief, Pandit Jawaharlal Nehru requested his very close friend Bishop Picket to initiate a response from the Indian Protestant and Orthodox Churches. On his request, the National Council of Churches in India responded by forming the 'NCC Relief Committee' for immediate response as an expression of solidarity with the suffering masses, which later went on to become the **Church's Auxiliary for Social Action (CASA)**.

(4) Educational Approach: Education is regarded as the process of training and developing the knowledge, skill, mind, character, etc, especially by formal schooling, teaching and training. In brief it is often defined as "all round development of total human person." Education is an integral part of Christian Mission. The missionaries and to be more specific, the Protestant missionaries often exalted the bible as the ultimate source of authority and thus made it compulsory for Christian that they must be able to read it.[9] In Khasi Hill, one must be able to read in order to become a full member of the church. Thus, ability to read was so important and was the first concern for missionaries when they started school.[10] This is how some scholars termed education as means of or preparation for evangelism (*prepaeration evangelica*). To certain extent this might true, if this is the case the missionaries would not engaged themselves in the development of higher education which they do in some places, particularly in cosmopolitan cities. A.T. Embree's explanation of why education was so important to the nineteenth century evangelicals is worth repeating:

> *Their basic concept was that the character of man was a product, not of his physical, but of his moral environment, and that salvation could be achieved and the individual could be totally transformed by a direct assault on the mind. Education followed by personal conversion would change the whole nature of society.*[11]

Missionary education was certainly one of the primary factors responsible for both conversion and social transformation in North East. The people themselves explicitly said that it led them out from darkness into the light. However, in some

---

[9] Laird, M.A., ***Missionaries and Education in Bengal***, 1793-1837 (Oxford, 1971), pp 3-4.

[10] F.S. Downs, ***History of Christianity In India, Vol. IV Part 5, North East India in the Nineteenth and Twentieth Centuries***, The Church Hisotry Association of India, Bangalore: 1992 ,pp 196-207

[11] Cited by F.S. Downs, ***ibid***, p. 197

part of India, it was not at all an effective means of conversion. C. Ingleby studied Christian Missionary Education in India and made observation that missionary education had considerable impact on the culture in which it took place, but that it was not always the impact that the missionaries had intended. Similarly the culture affected the choices which the missionaries made. Missionaries' strategies changed as they experienced failure and success in achieving their aims.[12] Education is a traditional Christian development practice which has brought about significant change. In India alone there are 271 Christian Colleges in which 353,683 student are enrolled.[13] Some of the institutions have emerged as one the best in the country[14]

(5) ***Medical Approach***: Healing is an integral part in the ministry of Jesus Christ which drew the crowd. Jesus did healing out of love, not for fame. When missionaries first arrived in the region, disease was widespread. Sickness was regarded caused by evil spirit, and in the absence of modern medical facility it was the village priest who offered sacrifice to demon for healing. Infant mortality was very high, people short live. Faced with human suffering, the early missionaries often picked up an elementary knowledge of first aid and medicine, treating the simplest diseases as best they could. The native people quickly found out that a simple tablet was more effective than expensive sacrifice offered to the demons, that is the reason why many people came to missionaries for

---

[12] Jonathan C. Ingleby, A Study in Christian Missionary Education by English Protestant Missionaries in India with Special Reference to Culture Change" Ph.D Thesis submitted to The Oxford Centre for Mission Studies and The Open University, 1998, abstract.

[13] ***Directory of Church-Related Colleges in India*** published by AIACHE (All India Association for Christian Higher Education) New Delhi in 2001, the number will now more than this.

[14] Christian Medical College, Vellore; St. John Medical College, Bangalore, are regarded as the best medical college in the country, Christ College is regarded the best college for Bachelor of Business Course, other colleges like St. Xavier, Madras Christian College, Loyola etc are always in top ranking.

treatment. Despite the great need for medical care, the Protestant mission board were initially reluctant to establish regular medical programmes with qualified personnel, for they felt that this would divert their limited resources from their primary work of evangelism.[15] The need of the context compelled to do more and more, now the best hospitals in India happened to be some of the Christian hospitals.

In recent years HIV/AID has created havoc all over the world.[16] Government, NGOs and Churches are engaged in the fight against HIV/AIDS. WHO and UNAIDS jointly reported that at 33.4 million, [31.1 million–35.8 million] there are more people living with HIV than ever before as people are living longer due to the beneficial effects of antiretroviral therapy and population growth. However the number of AIDS-related deaths has declined by over 10% over the past five years as more people gained to access to the life saving treatment. They estimate that since the availability of effective treatment in 1996, some 2.9 million lives have been saved. It is good news to hear that New HIV infections reduced by 17% over the past eight years, and efforts towards universal access to HIV prevention, treatment, care and support are bringing AIDS out of isolation. The church is now facing the task of preventing, caring and integrating people living with HIV/AIDS.

(6) Reformation Approach: There were a few enlightened Christian who realised the limitation of charity, that it did not touch many of the causes of the social problem. They began to struggle for the reformation of State laws and for the emancipation of the oppressed groups. One of the remarkable struggles for reformation was initiated by William Wilberforce,

[15] F.E. Downs, ***Op cit***, p. 178

[16] **Human immunodeficiency virus infection / Acquired immunodeficiency syndrome (HIV/AIDS)** is a disease of the human immune system caused by the human immunodeficiency virus (HIV).[1] HIV is transmitted primarily via unprotected sexual intercourse (including anal and even oral sex), contaminated blood transfusions and hypodermic needles, and from mother to child during pregnancy, delivery, or breastfeeding.

who sought to abolish the slave trade. He had founded the Society for the Reformation of Mánners in 1784, and in a work published in 1797 he presented *A Practical View of the Prevailing System of the Professed Christian in the Higher and Middle Classes in the Country Contrasted with real Christianity*. After the formation of the ***Committee for the Abolition of the Slave Trade*** in 1787, ***William Wilberforce*** led the cause of abolition through the parliamentary campaign. It finally abolished the ***slave trade*** in the British Empire with the ***Slave Trade Act 1807.*** He continued to campaign for the abolition of slavery in the British Empire, which he lived to see in the ***Slavery Abolition Act 1833.***[17]

(a) ***Racism*:** Although slavery was legally abolished which was a great achievement, but racism continued. Racism might be defined as a belief or doctrine that inherent differences among the various human races determine cultural or individual achievement, usually involving the idea that one's own race is superior and has the right to rule others. It is also a policy, system of government, etc., based upon or fostering such a doctrine and discrimination, or hatred or intolerance of another race or other races. The World Council of Churches took

[17] The Antislavery Movement was the outcome several efforts made by several people. The movement began in 1783 among the British public. That year a group of Quakers founded the first British abolitionist organization. The Quakers continued to be influential throughout the lifetime of the movement, in many ways leading the campaign. On 17 June 1783, Sir Cecil Wray (Member of Parliament for Westminster) presented the Quaker petition to parliament. Also in 1783, Dr Beilby Porteus issued a call to the Church of England to cease its involvement in the slave trade and to formulate a policy to improve the conditions of Afro-Caribbean slaves. The exploration of the African continent, by such British groups as the African Association (1788), promoted the abolitionists' cause. Such expeditions highlighted the legitimate, complex cultures of Africans; before the Europeans had considered them "other" and uncivilized. The African Association had close ties with William Wilberforce, who became known as a prominent figure in the battle for abolition in the British Empire.

up the issue of racism more seriously from the Uppsala 1968 in which it was stated that, "racism is linked with economic and political exploitation" and went to define racism as "ethnocentric pride in one own racial group and preference for the distinctive characteristic of that group; belief that these characteristics are fundamentally biological in nature…strong negative feeling towards other groups who do not share these characteristics, coupled with the thrust to discriminate against and exclude the group from full participation in the life of community.[18] In the 1970s and 1980s, the WCC Programme to Combat Racism coordinated churches' response against apartheid in South Africa, as well as challenging racism elsewhere. In his sermon at the chapel of Ecumenical Centre in Geneva on 9 January, the World Council of Churches (WCC) general secretary Rev. Dr Olav Fykse Tveit paid respect to the anti–apartheid movement in South Africa, which was born in a church, one hundred years ago.

Despite the claim that in many nations a "post-racial" reality has been achieved, racism and similar instruments of discrimination continue to plague many populations throughout the world. People of African descent, the Dalits in South Asia, the indigenous peoples or triblas, the ethnic, linguistic and religious minorities in many places in the world continue to be more marginalized than before on account of the changing economic, political and social conditions that the present world has entailed. This is true even though human rights activism and liberation movements have made gains in highlighting these problems and some legislation has been enacted in an attempt to provide solutions. The legacy of discrimination and exclusionary practices persists, though sometimes in forms less obvious than in the past. The presence of these insidious forms of

[18] N. Barney Pityana, "Racism" In ***Dictionary of Ecumenical Movement***, Genevba, WCC, 1991, p.841-42

economic, social, cultural, and political exclusion reflects that the struggle against dehumanizing discriminatory practices continues and that our churches must assume a greater leadership role in challenging them in their old and new forms and guises. [19]

(b) ***Castism*** (Caste System): Similar to racism, caste system exists in southeast Asia, particularly in India. Caste is a social grouping that is peculiar to India society. *Varna* and *jati* are two Sanskrit terms, both translated in English as "caste", that are used for this phenomenon. *Verna* literally means colour refers to class four fold division of traditional society in Brahmin(priests), Khasatriyas (rulers and warrior), Vaisyas (merchant and peasants) and Sutras (workers and servants). This does not explain the complexities of thousand of groups belonging to *jatis* (lit.born). The system is religiously sanctioned by Hinduism. Gandhi used the term "Harijan" meaning children of God which many people of this community reject it as paternalistic, and preferred to call themselves *Dalits*.[20] It means torn apart, oppressed, broken which better reflect the reality of their lives.

Theoretically there is no *Dalits* nor *Brahmin* as it was no distinction of Jews and Gentiles in Christianity, the

---

[19] A Theological Challenge to the Persistence of Racism, Caste-Based Discrimination, and other Exclusionary Practices. Statement from the WCC Conference on Racism Today and the Rationale for Continued Ecumenical Engagement, Cleveland, Ohio, 26-29 August 2010

[20] In the late 1880s the Marathi word 'Dalit' was used by Mahatma Jotiba Phule for the outcasts and Untouchables who were oppressed and broken by Hindu society. The term **Dalit Christian** (sometimes **Christian Dalit**) is used to describe those low-caste who have converted to Christianity from Hinduism or Islam and are still categorized as Dalits in Hindu, Christian and Islamic societies in India, Pakistan and other countries. Hindu Dalits are referred to as "Harijans" while the Islamic Dalits are categorised as "Muhajir" or "Arzal".

church should be free from racial discrimination. But the reality is that Dalits who were converted to Christianity did not escape the caste system which has a strongly ingrained presence in Indian society that is not limited to Hindu religious ideals. The different branches of Christianity in India still engage in these societal practices with regards to the caste system, along with all its customs and norms. The Roman Catholic Church treated the caste system as part of the Indian social structure and, for much of its history in India, it chose to work within the established social system; similarly the Syrian Orthodox Churches responded in like fashion, except it has tended to collectively act as one caste within the caste system instead of maintaining different castes within their churches.[21]

To combat this problem, the Dalits Christians developed Dalit Theology and created numerous organizations fighting against caste based discrimination and oppression.

(c) ***Sexism:*** The term sexism was introduced into the ecumenical debate mainly through the 1974 consultation in West Berlin on "Sexism in the 1970s: Discrimination against Women". It is like racism, it is discrimination on the ground of gender. This is an out come of a larger feminist movement. The **feminist movement** (also known as the **Women's Movement**, **Women's Liberation**, or **Women's Lib**) refers to a series of campaigns for reforms on issues such as reproductive rights, domestic violence, maternity leave, equal pay, women's suffrage, sexual harassment and sexual violence. The movement's priorities vary among nations and communities and range from opposition to female genital mutilation in one country or to the glass ceiling in another.

---

[21] http://en.wikipedia.org/wiki/Dalit Christian dated 12/Aug/2012 .

The churches cannot ignore half of their members who are women. Thus, on Easter Sunday 1988, the World Council of Churches (WCC) launched "An Ecumenical Decade of Churches in Solidarity with Women" from 1988-1998 to give churches the opportunity to respond to God's call to inclusiveness, solidarity with the oppressed, and the sharing of power and resources within communities. So much have achieved but the women issue in the church remain a very crucial issue. They are called by the same God who also calls men, but their calling have been ignored and debarred from certain ministry; inequality and discrimination persist in the Church.

(7) ***Development Approach*****:** The idea of development became prominent after the second world war. The term, originally synonymous with "growth", often has been criticized as inadequate to express fully the reality of promoting human wellbeing- through societal transformation. Various factors contributed to the increasing use of the notion of development after 1945. One prominent factor was emergence, between 1946-1970, of new nations about 50 in Africa and Asia. Their expectation from political independence would automatically bring about social transformation which actually did not happened as expected.

Knowing the aspiration of people in the developing countries and persistence of abject poverty, the churches particularly in the west, which already had a long tradition of mission and social service among the poor people, become involved in the development effort. The church, which was reluctant to involve in the development effort for fearing diversion from its primary task of evangelization, is no longer discuss whether they should be engaged in the development, but how to do it. As a result of the WCC Assembly in Uppsala 1968, in 1970, the Commission on the Churches' Participation in Development (CCPD) was created. Similarly the International Congress on World Evangelization in Lausanne in 1974 became the beginning of a new era for the

Evangelicals. Though it affirmed the primacy of proclamation on social action, the Congress defined the Gospel of Jesus Christ as the Good News of liberation, of restoration, of wholeness and of salvation that is personal, social, global and cosmic. This provided a theological basis for holistic mission.[22]

(8) ***Liberation Approach*:** The euphoria of political independence which was expected to uplift their socio-economic condition died down. Their hope and aspiration was not realized. Rather the situation of the Third World was:

- On the economic level, technical backwardness, unequal distribution of wealth, foreign debt, dependency and unhealthy commercial relationship with the first world countries;
- On the social level, massive and absolute poverty, big gap between few privileged rich people and the poor masses, high infant mortality rate and over population,
- On the political level, weakness of political institutions, corruption, authoritarianism and outside influence;
- On the cultural level, pluralism, alienation and illiteracy,
- On religious level, pluralism, conservatism and proliferation of charismatic groups.

Some of the intellectuals are become critical with the global as well as internal system and structure which in their opinion is responsible for the problem in third world countries. They felt that developmental approach failed to deal with the root cause of the problem. They perceived globalization as a new form of colonization. In this process they are made to depend[23] on their old masters.

---

[22] ***Let the Earth Hear His Voice. International Congress on World Evangelization***, Lausanne World Wide Publications, 1975, p 3

[23] Theotonio Dos Santos forcefully said, "Underdevelopment, far from constituting a state of backwardness prior to capitalism, is rather a consequence and a particular form of capitalist development known as

In respond to this situation, a theology of liberation was developed. The concept of development is gradually being replaced by the more dynamic and humanistic concept of liberation. The pattern of economic growth and the international aid and trade system have made the poorer nations increasingly dependent on the rich countries. Liberation from the domination of economically powerful countries is a prerequisite for the development of countries in the third world.[24]

Paulo Freire introduced ***conscientization*** to make people conscious of their situation and wake them up to struggle for their liberation. Conscientization, for him, is a process of decoding reality, "stripping it down so as to get to know the myths that deceive and perpetuate the dominating structure," so that people are disposed to change that reality in the direction of humanization.[25] Some of the development agencies and members of some churches are involved in public education and analysed the situation and organized people. Some participated in the struggle of people for their rights.

2. INCARNATIONAL APPRAOCH FOR THE CHURCHES: After having a quick review of different approaches, we come to conclusion that it was the context which has determined the actual action. Whatever may be the action of different period of the time and situation, Christian development work should be principle based or value based. For that reason I hereby suggest an ***Incarnational Approach*** which implies that:-

(1) Theocentric Approach: It is God who incarnates in the form of human. As mentioned in the beginning that Christian Approach to development has to be a theocentric approach based on Mather Teresa's statement that, "We do it for Jesus". She is quite certain of the purpose and cause of what she was doing. Developmental activities are often done

---

dependent capitalism…dependence is a conditioning situation in which the economies of one group of countries are conditioned by the development and expansion of others.

[24] K.C. Abraham, "Liberation" ***Dictionary of the Ecumenical Movement***, Op.cit, p.605

[25] P.Friere, "Conscientization as a Way of Liberating" in ***Liberation Theology: A Documentary History, Maryknoll, Orbis Book, New York, 1990,p.9***

with selfish motif to get the benefit. Incarnation demands denial oneself or living for others. For Jesus is a man for others.

(2) *Love in Action*: Incarnation happened because God so love the world. The love of God does not end in the pronouncement, but the word become flesh. Sometimes development workers are so much concern for result, without really knowing for whom they are doing. They love the project, but not the people. Love endures all the difficulty that may come on the way.

(3) *Contextual Development*: As God himself become human, as development workers we have to work with the people for the people. We often do development for the poor, it is important that we have to do it with the poor and for the poor. It is easy to imposed alien ideology and practice, incarnational development require culture based development. The question raised from my context could be different from some other context:

- How shall the tribal people be protected from further alienation and erosion of their culture?
- How to protect from the exploitation of tribals by non-tribal and invasion of globalization.
- How could we emancipate and be transformed without losing our identity and dignity?
- How to do when we shift our struggle from 'armed struggle' to 'transformation struggle?
- How to carry out the task of transformational struggle without neglecting economically vulnerable and deprived?
- How could they become economically self sufficient or self reliant?

(4) ***The Reign of God as the Vision and Criterion of Development***: The Purpose of Incarnation is to establish the Kingdom of God where God's name is praised, and his will is done, where justice is done and shalom is realized. As

mentioned before the Christian's approach to development is goal oriented striving toward its goal. Economic development in itself is not the goal, it is merely a means of realizing the reign of God. I am aware of the many different ways of interpreting the reign of God. I am content, for the purpose of this paper, to define the Reign of God as 'where God's will is done'. We often recite the Lord's prayer: 'Our Father who art in heaven, hallowed be thy name, thy Kingdom come, thy will be done on earth as it is in heaven.' The Kingdom of God is a Kingdom where God's name is truly hallowed, his will is done on earth, men will have everything in abundance, all sin will be forgiven and all evil will be overcome. It will be a kingdom where in accordance with Jesus ' promise, the poor, the hungry, those who weep and those who are downtrodden will finally come into their own; where pain suffering and death will have an end. This kingdom is being realized, though the final realization of absolute righteousness of unsurpassable freedom of dauntless love of universal reconciliation of everlasting peace is yet to come. While we are waiting for the final consummation, our task is to struggle for the realization of God's Kingdom here and now.

Having the Reign of God as the goal and criterion, I would define development as growing together (Symbiosis) towards the promise of perfection in mutual love and care of sharing resources together. In the light of the Kingdom's values, the goal of development is ***shalom*** or common good for all. The effort for development is meant for growing together in tune with the tribal communitarian life. In this approach to development, resources should never be treated as a pie in heaven which can be owned and exploited by individuals for the satisfaction of endless desire. They are meant for God's people to be used as per their need and shared with one another.

(5) ***Human as the Subject of Development*:** Development is conceived not only in term of economic development, but also as a social, cultural and political one, for the goal of

development is not just maximization of capital but shalom (well- being). Genuine development is human development, because human being is the subject of development, not merely the object. Human development requires a global search for the well –being of all humans, together with a universal acceptance of the diversity inherent in nature and in all human cultures, an openness to learn from and identify with what other peoples can offer to improve the human condition on earth. Human development means sustainable development, for we are concerned for the survival of human race in future. Hope for survival of human race lies in our conscious choice to abandon our aggressive attitude towards nature. Sustainable approach to development calls for a shift in development from self-interest to common social concern for the well-being of all.

(a) ***Created in Image of God as the Basis of Development*:** Image of God is regarded as one of the best explanations of the Christian concept of human. There are two dimensions in the doctrine of image of God – the dimension of human responsibility and freedom which are dialectically related. Human being is free but responsible to God and his fellow human beings, because he is free for others. Having read the biblical text in its historical context of Babylonian exile, I perceive the meaning of created in the " image of God" as an expression of human struggle for dignity and liberation. If the 'P' tradition was written during the exilic period when the Israelites were captivated and enslaved by the Babylonians 'created in image of God' could be interpreted as an affirmation of human dignity and cry for liberation. God's intention in his creation of human beings is not for enslavement, but to be like him. If this is so, image of God is an affirmation of human dignity and protest against human oppression by fellow human beings. What does an affirmation of human dignity mean? What is to our task to affirm human dignity? Affirmation of human dignity in the context of tribals in the North East India is liberation from all forms of alienation, and empowerment of the people.

(b) *Development as Empowering the people*: When we accept human being as the subject of development, the question that confronts us today is how to empower the people. UNO, Government and Churches often made constitutional provision and legal protections for the poor and the marginalized people, which is of course necessary and should be appreciated. This is certainly one level of empowerment. But the constitutional provision and legal protections can remain as an ideal, unless they are translated into reality. A mere legal document without implementation is useless. It cannot by itself protect the people unless those who are in authority enforce it. The 'protection and promotion' policy of tribal development is a historical necessity. In fact, genuine development of any weaker section of society would require both 'Protection and Promotion', but how that actually functions is important. Today the towns and villages in the tribal areas in North East India are filled with non-tribal traders and business people. I asked those leaders of the states which require the 'Inner Line Permit" to enter into their states, whether any one of the Indian citizens who wanted to come to Mizoram and Nagaland are ever deprived of entry? What is the meaning of protection? Is it a legal fiction or the reality? While protection is necessary, it is evident from our experience that we have to move beyond protection. The idea of protecting someone from the intrusion of someone else or promotes someone by some body contradicts the very idea of people becoming the subject of development. My preference here is empowerment. Empowerment means empowering the people to protect or promote themselves. The means and method of empowerment could be different from place to place. It could be political, economic or educational empowerment, depending upon the need of the people. Concern for empowerment should remain as the core of development in the tribal Development.

(c) ***People Participation***: Since the subject and goal of development is the people with whom and for whom we do development, it should be their project in which they participate from the beginning to the end in the selection of the project, in the planning, in the process of implementation and in the evaluation.

3. ROLE OF THE CHURCH IN SOCIAL TRANSFORMATION: As we come from different context, our need may be different and it could be similar as well. I come from Mizoram where 90% of the population are Christians, very good in Christian giving and deeply committed to cause of mission. We have inherited from pietistic missionaries a very conservative evangelical theology which is good and helpful in many ways, but it has its own limitations.

(1) ***The task of Theological Reorientation for Development***: Before we move on to program and action plan, it is important to do theological re-orientation. Whenever we seriously consider changing society as a whole through theology, sometimes we cannot think of how change would be brought about, and we find no meaning of doing theology. But theology,like ideology, shapes the mind and change the attitude, and directs even the course of action. Re-orientation of churches in some places a necessity to let them participate in the task of social transformation. Therefore, doing theology in this context is certainly significant. Unfortunately, the dominant theology today in North East India lacks concern for social transformation. The task of theological re-orientation is therefore necessary and urgent to bring about change in North East India. Unless we change theology itself Christian community will not make significant contribution to bring about change. As an example, I would briefly discuss the need and possibility of re-conceptualizing Ministry and Mission.

(2) ***Holistic Ministry and Mission*** : I was a pastor, and eventually look after more than a hundred pastors as the leader of the Baptist Church of Mizoram. The ministry of the church is fundamentally conceived as evangelization and doing rituals. Definitions of holistic are abound, for the purpose of this paper it may be defined as a ministry/mission

is motivated by God and neighbours, mobilized to be engaged in multi-dimensional services to God by serving others inclusively caring for the spiritual, psychological, social, physical, etc. well beings of others, with multi-facet (religious & charity, public & private, etc.) services and at multi-levels (personal and institutional, local and global), in the framework of reconciliation vertically with God, horizontally with humanity and hierarchically with the created order.[26]

In the evangelical constituency, the theological debate took for some times to accept holistic ministry. We see the development from Lausanne first congress in 1974 to Lausanne II in Manila 1989 in which it is expressed in the manifesto: "We affirm that we must demonstrate God's love visibly by caring for those who are deprived of justice, dignity, food and shelter" (A-8) and "We affirm the proclamation of God's Kingdom of justice and oppression, both personal and structural: we will not shrink from this prophetic witness)(A-9).[27]

Christian leaders, mainly from the evangelical circle, developed the concept of integral mission which is in reality an abstraction of what the church has been doing throughout the history. The definition taken from Oxford Consultation as follow:

> Our definition of **integral mission** is taken from a consultation held in Oxford, United Kingdom, in September 2001, which resulted in **The Micah Declaration on Integral Mission** being produced. The introductory extract outlines the summarised definition of integral mission as follows:
>
> *Integral mission or holistic transformation is the proclamation and demonstration of the gospel. It is*

[26] Enoch Wan, ***holistic ministry/missions: reflections & resource material***, *www.enochwan.com/English, dated 14/Aug/ 2012*

[27] ***Lausanne II Manila:Proclaim Christ Untill He Comes: International Congress on World Evangelization***, (Minneapolis: Worldwide Publication, 1990)

> *not simply that evangelism and social involvement are to be done alongside each other. Rather, in integral mission our proclamation has social consequences as we call people to love and repentance in all areas of life. And our social involvement has evangelistic consequences as we bear witness to the transforming grace of Jesus Christ.*
>
> *If we ignore the world we betray the word of God, which sends us out to serve the world. If we ignore the word of God we have nothing to bring to the world. Justice and justification by faith, worship and political action, the spiritual and the material, personal change and structural change belong together. As in the life of Jesus, being, doing and saying are at the heart of our integral task.*[28]

It is not at all a new thing, it is rather recapturing and reaffirmation of what the church has been doing in its mission. Sometimes in recent past, some of the churches are prevented for fear of diverting from the primary task of evangelization. The debate took quite for sometimes particularly among the evangelicals, now the ministry and mission is perceived as holistic or integral.

(2) Recapturing Education: I see education from the perspective of tribal people. The tribal people all over the world are the ones who needed most the modern formal education. With reference to Mizoram Lal Dena perceived education as a legitimizing process of colonial rule and means of evangelization for the missionaries. Missionary education has its own limitations. It concerned character building, reading, writing, evangelization and training leaders for the church and society. It was extremely useful for their purpose in its contemporary world.

[28] ***Integral Mission***: www.micahnetwork.org/integral-mission, dated 14/Aug/2012

The management of school education in Mizoram was handed over to the District Council. That was the beginning of political intervention in the school education of Mizoram. Today, people lost confidence in Government education and now 80% of students in the urban area are opting for private schools. The private schools are basically business oriented schools whose primary aim is commercial purpose. It is time for the Church to recapture educational mission. Unless the Mizos are enlightened and trained to compete with the rest of the world, they will remain at the bottom of the social ladder even in India, they would never own and control their resources and land. It is a tragedy that Government will continue to fail in education particularly in the tribal area, for they have no real concern developing tribal people to be compatible for modern world. They are content with providing education for name shake, not for quality education.[29]

I am very happy that under my leadership as the General Secretary of the Baptist Church of Mizoram, we could start the Higher and Technical College of Mizoram, the first Christian College in Mizoram, and several Baptist English School to provide quality and value based education. This has proved to be a very significant step, but which is only a token. The Baptist Church of Mizoram which has the budget of Rs 11,460 lakhs, has 410 lakhs for education which is 3.5% of its total budget, whereas as 22% is used for mission. The Church should re-capture its educational mission to meet the demand of today.

(3) **Prophetic Ministry**: Prophets certainly see visions and announce oracle to whom God asked them to tell. At the same time they also fight for justice. Amos sees God as demanding justice from the people rather than worship. "I hate, I despise your festivals. But let justice roll down like waters, and righteousness like a mighty river" (Amos 5:21-24). Similarly Isaiah condemned the greedy rich people who grabbed the land. "Woe unto them that **join house to house**, that lay field to field, till there be no place, that they may be placed alone in the midst of the earth! In mine ears said the

LORD of hosts, Of a truth many **houses** shall be desolate, even great and fair, without inhabitant (**Isaiah** 5:8-9).

The basic **message** of 8th century prophets stresses the divine demand for **social justice** and concern for the oppressed. Many among Israel's wealthy members of the society at the time of **Amos** chose to be unjust and treat the disadvantaged as they wished.

Prophetic ministry today means struggle for justice. Seeing the situation today in Mizoram and other parts of Christian dominated states, we have to engage ourselves in the struggle for justice. Politics is an area where we have to fight for justice in order to fulfil our mission to be the salt of the earth. People keep on asking me why do you I enter into politics? I often replied, that the priestly ministry for me is over, it is time for me to seek peace and justice, not power that may become the salt of the earth. As responsible citizens, should we get involved the politics to transform the wrong system or escape from the struggle for fear of the criticism of others? There are so many ways and means to combat injustice, if we listen to the voice of God, we will come to know what we should do.

Thy kingdom come, Thy will be done as on earth as in heaven.

CONCLUSION

In conclusion, I would like to recaptulate what has been discussed in the preceeding eleven chapters. Contextual theology is an affirmation of the fact that cultural diversity is so intrinsic to humanity and therefore diversity of understanding and articulation of Christian faith is inevitable. No one denies the fact that the way people of different cultures confess Christ has never been uniform, it differed from one culture to another. It is the culture that shapes the voice that confess Christ. That is clearly reflected in the history of Christianity itself. As Christianity was born and brought up in the cradle of Judaism and nurtured in the Greco-Roman world, it took the form of Hebrew, Greek and Latin. It was wrapped and shaped by the Hebrew culture. As it grew up it was expressed with the language and thought form of the Greeks. When it was spread to Rome and to the rest of Europe, it became under the influenced of Latin culture and took the Latin form. With the Protestant reformation, it was again further modified and expressed with the thoughtform of different European nations.

When Christianity came to Asia and Africa which were culturally quiet different from Europe, real incarnation did not take place. Although it took the local colour in certain places, fundamentally Christianity did not take the Asian and African form. It remains alien to Africans and Asians. Contextualization is therefore a theological task for those who are doing theology in Asia and Africa. It is a missiological imperative.

One may argue that the need for contextualizing theology is the task of every theologian irrespective of nationality, culture and colour. Obviously, contextualization is the way theology has been done in the history of Christian thought. However, the issue that confronts the Asian and African theologians is different from that of Europe and North America. In Asia and Africa, the question is how Christianity shall be incarnated to take the form of Asia and Africa, not mere adaptation as in Europe and North America. In the Asian and African context, inculturation or indigenization has to be the kernel of contextual theology. The task of contextualization is Europe and North America is to reinterpret Christian message for every new generation, but not necessarily inculturation of the gospel which is the primary concern in Asia and Africa.

The diversity within Asia itself is far beyond, what a singular theology can deal with. There can be no end of contextualization if we are really concerned for constructing a relevant theology. This is the reality as well as the need that has to be accepted. We must not only allow but rather encourage and support theological reflection in the local context, otherwise Christianity will never take root deep into the local soil. But the question that confront those who are engaged in the contextual theology is the limit of diversity, to what extend should a contextual theology be allowed to be different? Here "diversity of theological reflection" should not be seen as contradicting the universality of Christian faith. Diversity has not been so much a problem for theology, rather giving universal validity to a particular theology constructed in a particular place and time seems to be more a problem. Diversity should be seen as enriching and complementing to the existing theology. No one denies the fact that in the midst of diversity there is commonality which transcends all other theologies. Though we are aware of the problems involved in the task of constructing a contextual theology, we cannot avoid doing it, because contextualization is the way how theology has been done. It is the very nature of theology. This is the reason why some of us are engaged in the construction of tribal theology.

Tribal theology is concerned how to articulate the faith of the community in Christ in the way understandable and meaningful to the tribal Christians in North East India. Here we are primarily concerned with the question of *how to confess* Christ in the context of North East India. The question of "how" is a methodological question which has, in fact, led us to engage ourselves in the construction of tribal theology. Tribal theology is therefore an attempt to answer the question of how to confess Christ in the context of North East India. The concerns in the construction of tribal Christian theology is to help :- (a) the tribal Christians understand and confess Christ that he may become a part of their own identity (incarnation), and (b) to help them realize the significance of Christ for them by which they may bring about transformation of society. The goal of tribal theology is not merely "understanding" as in the traditional theology though understanding is taken seriously, but to bring about change. Here we note the shift of emphasis that has bought about by tribal theology from "faith seeking understanding" to "faith seeking social transformation". The task of tribal theology is to achieve this goal. Tribal theology is therefore goal oriented.

Having these objectives in mind, we are asking certain fundamental questions such as "is tribal theology a suitable name because of pejorative conotations of the term tribal?" and what could be the most suitable methodology for constructing a contextual Christian tribal theology? Having discussed the pros and cons of the term "tribal" in chapter one, we come to the conclusion that "Tribal Theology" should be used for a time being. Various models of contextual theology are discussed in chapter III to identify the most suitable model for tribal theology. We have come to realization that no model can be consistently followed and therefore we have suggested a Synthetic - Praxis model which is a combination of a synthetic and a praxis models. The reasons and necessity of combining the two models to create a synthetic-praxis model are given in chapter III.

Construction of a relevant contextual theology, requires an analysis of the context for which a theology going to be constructed. This is the reason why one chapter is devoted to the analysis of tribal situation in North East India. To address the theological agenda identified in the analysis, we have to reinterpret the Bible. Such attempt is labelled in this book as tribal hermeneutics. Some of the hermeneutical clues are identified as *Promise Land, Pentecost, Exodus* and the *Aliens*. The problems and protections of the aliens in the Old Testament are used as the hermeneutical paradigm of tribal theology to describe the problems and aspirations of the tribals in North East India.

When we think of indigenization of theology land, at the same time, of providing a theological basis to bring about social transformation, we are wandering what exactly to be done. We are aware of the fact that indigenization is necessary in the situation where tribal people are facing crisis in their identity. At the same time, social transformation is necessary for the same people who are trying to catch up other in certain areas, particularly in the economic development. In our analysis of tribal situation we have identified the problem of the present development system. We have noted that culture happened to be a forgotten dimension in the present development effort in North East

India, which is greatly responsible for the existing problems of our economic development system. Considering all these factors, rediscovery of transformational motifs from the tribal culture is another methodological imperative. However, in the process of rediscovering tribal traditional values, the method of *reflection, adoption* and *transformation* has been applied. We have rediscovered some of the traditional values such as **communitarianism, tlawmngaihna** (tribal altruism), **traditional community home, traditional cosmology, communitarian land holding system** and **singing**. None of these are directly adopted, they are critically examined and transformed. The traditional attitude of men towards women is critically examined and more or less rejected.

Finally I have to explain why the title of the book THEOLOGY OF COMMUNITY was chosen. Communitarianism is an organising principle of tribal theology. It is a key to understand the tribal society. Human for the tribals is a communitarian being, *Zawlbuk* is a community home, *Tlawmngaihna* is a communitarian ethics. God is communitarian God who formed a community of God-Human-World, Land is a community land and Singing is a communitarian singing (*lengkhawm*). This is the reason why we are critical about the traditional attitude of men towards women and trying to provide a theological basis to build a community of men and women free from discrimination and oppression.

It is our hope and prayer that tribal theology will contribute towards the realization of the Kingdom of God.

BIBLIOGRAPHY

Agarwal, A.K., 1987 — Economic Problems and Planning in North East India, New Delhi: Sterling Publishers Pvt. Ltd.

Aier, Wati, — *Future Nagaland: A Socio-Politico-Theologial Vision for 1988 the Nagas,* Mokokchung: Arthur.

Allen, B.C. and et al, (ed), 1975 Reprinted — *Gazetteer of Bengal and North East India,* Delhi: Mittal Publication

Alem, O., 1994 — Tsungremology: Ao Naga Christian Theology, Mokokchung: Clark Theological College.

Allison, J., 1966 — Recent Empirical Studies in Religious Conversion Experiences," *Pastoral Psychology*, Vol. 7, pp. 21-34

Altner, Gunther, 1991 — "The Community of Creation as a Community in LawL: The New Contract Between the Generations," *Concilium*, Vol. 4, pp. 53-64

Ambroise, Yvon, 1989 — "Christianity, Religious Ideology and Social Change in India," *Social Action,* Vol. 39, April-June, pp. 151-161

Anderson, Gerald H, (ed) 1976 — *Asian Voices in Christian Theology,* Maryknoll, Orbis Books, 1976

Arnold, Adiss (ed), 1981 — *Crisis in North East India,* Madras: Gurukul Lutheran Theological College and Research Institute

Ariarajha, S. Wesley, 1995 — Gospel and Culture: An Ongoing Discussion With the Ecumenical Movement, Geneva: WCC

Arokiasamy, S and Podimattom, F. (ed) — *Social Sin: Its Challenges to Christian Life* Bangalore: Claretian Publications

Arya S.P., 1987 — "Social Movement - A Conceptual View," in *Social Movement of Development,* edited by S.K. Srinavas and A.L. Srinavas, Allahabad: Chugh Publications.

Assmann, Hugo, 1974 — *Practical Theology of Liberation,* (Trans by Paul Bums), London: Search Press

Astour, M.C., 1976 — "Habiru" *Interpreter's Dictionary of the Bible,* Suppl. Volume, Nashville: Abingdon Press

Augustine, John S., 1989 — *Issues in Development: Strategies for Third World Development,* New Delhi: Sage Publications

Bandhyopadhyay, B., 1991 — "Education for Enlightened Society," *Economic and Political Weekly*, Vol. XXVI, No. 7, Feb. 16, pp. 359-379

Banana, Canaan, 1979 — "Biblical Basis for Liberation Struggle," *International Review of Mission,* Vol. 68, pp. 417-423

Baptist Missionary — *Printed Report of the Baptist Missionary,* Society 1904-1935, London

Bardoloi, B.N., 1990 — *Constraints of Tribal Development in North East India,* Guwahati: Tribal Research Institute, Assam

Barkataki, M.S., 1985 — *British Administration in North East India (1826-1874)*: A Study of Their Social Policy, New Delhi: National Book Trust of India

Barpujari, H.K., — *Problems of Hill Tribes North East Frontier Vol. I: A Critical Analysis of the Problems and Policies of the British Government Toward the Hill Tribes of the North East Frontier from 1822-1842 based on Original Sources - both Published and Unpublished,* Guwahati: Lawyer's Book Stall

1976 — *Problems of the Hill Tribes. North East Frontier (1843-1872)*, Vol II, Guwahati:

United Publishers

1981 *Problems of the Hill Tribes North East Frontier, Vol III, (1873-1962),* Guwahati: Spectrum Publication

Barpujari, H.K., *The American Missionaries and North East India (1836-1900),* Guwahati: Spectrum Publication

Bas, Wielengal, 1985 *History of the Worker Movement,* Bangalore: Indian Social Institute

Bakshi, P.M. (ed), 1991 *The Constitution of India,* Delhi: Universal Book Trader

Barbour, Ian., 1974 *Myth, Models and Paradigms: A Comparative Study in Science and Religion,* New York: Harper and Row

Barr, William R., 1987 "Debated Issues in Liberation Theology," *Theology Today,* Vol. 43, pp 520-523

Barreto, Duarte, 1976 *India's Search for Development and Social Justice: Analysis of Indian Society,* Bangalore: GSA Publications

Barret, David B. (ed), 1982 *World Christian Encyclopaedia: A Comparative Study of Churches and Religions in the Modern World AD 1900-2000,* New York: Oxford

Barth, Frederick, 1969 *Ethnic Groups and Boundaries: The Social Organisation of Cultural Differences* Boston: Little Brown and Co.

Barth, Karl, 1960 *The Humanity of God,* Atlanta: John Knox Press

Bassham, Roger C., 1979 *Mission Theology: 1948-1975 Years of World Creative Tension Ecumenical, Evangelical and Roman Catholic,*Pasadena, California: William Carey Library

Battomore, T.B., *Sociology: A Guide to Problems and*

1971 (2nd edition) — *Literature,* Bombay: Blackie & Son Ltd.

Baum, Gregory, 1975 — *Religion and Alienation,* New York: Paulist Press

Becker, Christopher, 1980 — *History of the Catholic Mission in North East India,* Shillong: Vendrame Missiological Institute

Berger, Peter L., 1968 — *The Sacred Canopy: Elements of A Sociological Theory of Religion,* New York: Doubleday

1979 — "The False Consciousness of 'Consciousness of Consciousness Raising'," Mission Trends, No. 4, edited by Gerald H. Anderson and Thomas F.S. New York and Toronto: Paulist Press

Bernard, Jessie 1968 — "Community: Community Disorganization," in *International Encyclopaedia of Social Sciences*, Vol. 3&4, edited by David L. Sills, New York: Macmillan and Free Press, pp. 163-168

Bevans, Stephen, 1985 — "Models of Contextual Theology," *Missiology,* Vol. 13, April, pp. 185-202

1992 — *Models of Contextual Theology,* Maryknoll: Orbis Books

Bhat, H.K., 1991 — "Hinduization of Tribes: Critique and Perspective," in *Tribal Thought and Culture,* B. Saraswati, (ed), New Delhi: Concept Publishing House

Bieler, Andre, 1978 — "Gradual Awareness of Social Economic Problem 1750-1900," *Sepration Without Hope,* edited by Julia de Santa, Geneva, WCC

Birch, Charles, 1990 — "Christian Obligation for Liberation fo Nature," *Liberating Life: Contemporary*

	Approaches to Eccological Theology edited by Chalres Birch, William Eakin and Jay B. McDaniel, Maryknoll: Orbis Books
Bird, Phyllis A., 1981	"'Male and Female He Created Them': Gen. 1:27b in the Context of the Priestly Account of Creation," *Harvard Theological Review,* Vol. 74, No. 2, pp. 129-159
Blumental, David, 1989	"Ontological and Liberation Theology: Two modes of Religious Reflection, *Religious Studies Review* Vol. 15, pp. 122-125
Bosch, Davis, 1991	*Transforming Mission: Paradigm Shift in Theology of Mission,* Maryknoll: Orbis Books
Boff, Leonardo, 1978	*Jesus Christ Liberator,* Maryknoll: Orbis Books
1986	*Ecclesio Genesis: The Base Communities, Reinvent the Church,* Maryknoll: Orbis Books
Boff, Clodovis, 1987	*Theology and Praxis: Epistemological Foundation,* Maryknoll: Orbis Books
Boff, Leonardo and Boff, Clodovis, 1983 (1979)	*Salvation and Liberation: In search of a Balance between Faith and Politics,* Melbourne: Dove Communication
1991	*New Evangelization: Good News to the Poor* Maryknoll: Orbis Books
Bonhoeffer, Dietrich, 1959	*The Cost of Discipleship,* London: SCM
Bonino, Jose Miguez, 1975	*Doing Theology in a Revolutionary Situation,* Philadelphia: Fortress Press
1981	"Wesley's Doctrine of Sanctification from a Liberation Perspective," in *Sanctification and Liberation: Liberation Theologies in*

the *Light of Wesleyan Tradition,* Theodore Rynyon, (ed), Nashville: Abingdon Press

Bopegamage, A., 1979 — "Status Seekers in India: A Sociological Study of the neo-Buddhist movement," *Archives Europennes de Sociologie,* Vol. 20, pp. 19-39

Bose, A, Tiplut Nongbri and Kumar N. (ed)., 1990 — *Tribal Demography and Development in North East India,* Delhi: B.R. Publishing Corporation

Boy, R.H.S., 1977 — *Kristadvaita: A Theology for India,* Madras, CLS

Brown, A.R. Radcliffe., 1979 (10th edition) — *Structure and Function in Primitive Society,* London: Routledge & Kegan Paul

Brown, Robert Mcfee, 1978 — *Theology in a New Key,* Philadelphia: Westminster Press

Brueggeman, Walter, 1977 — *The Land: Place as Gift, Promise and Challenge in Biblical Fatih,* Philadelphia: Fortress Press

Buber, Martin., 1961 — *Two Types of Fatih,* New York: Harper and Row

Bultmann, R., 1966 — *Jesus Christ and Mythology,* London: SCM

Cadorette, Curt M.M., 1987 — "Basic Christian Communities: Their Social Role and Missiological Promise," *Missiology,* Vol. 15, No. 2, pp. 17-29

Ceresko, Anthony R., 1993 — *The Old Testament: A Liberation Perspective,* Bangalore: St. Paul

Chandran, Russell J., 1983 — "A Methodological Approach to Third World Theology," in *Irruption of the Third World,* edited by Virginia Fabella and Sergio Torres, Maryknoll: Orbis Books

Chapman, E., and M. Clark, 1969 — *Mizo Miracles,* edited by Majorie Sykes, Madras: Christian Literature

Chatterji, Saral K., 1988 — "Why Dalit Theology?" in *Towards A Dalit Theology,* New Delhi: ISPCK

Chaterjee, Suhas, 1985 — *Mizoram Under British Rule* New Delhi: Mittal Publications

Chattopadhay, S.K, (ed), 1985 — *Tribal Institution of Meghalaya,* Guwahati: Spectrum Publication

Chaudhuri, J.G., 1980 — *Tripura: The Land and Its People,* Delhi: Lee Adevi Publications

CHI Kwan, Myong, 1985 — "Theological Development in Korea," *International Review of Mission,* Vol. 74, Jan. pp. 73-79

Chib, Sukhdev Singh., 1984 — *North Eastern India:* Caste, Tribes and Culture of India, New Delhi: Ess Publication

Chouinard, Larry, — "Gospel Christology: A Study of 1987 Methodology" *A Journal for the Study of New Testament,* Vol. 30, pp. 21-37

Chube, Shibanikinkar, 1973 — *Hill Politics in North East India,* New Delhi, Orient Longman Limited

Clark, Mary Mead, — *The Ao Naga Women,* Boston: 1896

Cleary, E., 1984 — *Crisis and Challenge: The Church in Latin America Today,* Maryknoll: Orbis Books

Comte, Auguste, 1877 — *System of Positive Polity,* London: Longmans, Green and Co.

Cone, James H., 1969 — *Black Theology and Black Power,* San Francisco, Harper and Row

Cone, James H., 1973 — "Asian Theology Today: Searching for Definition: Liberation is Emerging as Its Chief Motif," *Christian Century,* Vol. 96, May 23, pp. 589-591

Costa, Ruy O., 1988 — "Inculturation, Indigenization and Contextualization," *One Faith Many Cultures: Inculturation,Indegenization and*

Contextualization, Maryknoll: Orbis Books

Coste, Rene, 1991 — "The Ecumenical Dynamics of Justice, Peace and Safeguarding of Creation," *Concilium,* Vol. 4, pp. (19-31)

1978 — "A Black American Perspective on the Future of African Theology, *Asian Theological Journal,* Vol. 7, No. 2, 9-19, 1978

Conn, Walter E. (ed), 1978 — *Conversion: Perspectives on Personal and Social Transformation,* New York: Alba House

Cook, G., 1985 — *The Expectation of the Poor: Latin America Base Ecclesial Communities in Protestant Perspective,* Maryknoll: Orbis Books, 1985

Corrie, M. Bruce, 1992 — "The Indigenous People of South America," *International Review of Mission,* Vol. 81, No. 324, pp. 551-555

Dalton, E.T., 1985 — *Tribal History of Eastern India,* Delhi: Cosmos Publication

Das, Rajat K., 1985 — *Manipur Tribal Scene,* New Delhi: Inter-Indian Publications (T-113)

Das S.T., 1986 — *Tribal Life of North Eastern India,* New Delhi: Gian Publishing House

Datta Ray, B., 1989 — *Tribal Identity and Tension in North East India,* New Delhi: Omson Publication

Davis, Charles, 1980 — *Theology and Political Society, The Hulsean Lectures in the University of Cambridge,* Cambridge: Cambridge University Press

Davis, Kortright 1987 — "Third World Theological Priorities," *Scottish Journal of Theology,* Vol. 40, pp. 85-105

Dena, Lal, — *Christian Missions and Colonialism:*

1988	*A Study of Missionary Movement in North East India With Particular Reference to Manipur and Lushai Hills 1894-1947,* Shillong: Vendrame Institute
Dermot, A. Lane, 1984	*Foundation of Social Theology for a Social Theology: Praxis, Process and Salvation,* London: Gill and Macmillan
Derr, Thomas S., 1973	*Ecology and Human Liberation: A Theological Critique of the Use and Abuse of our Birthright,* Geneva: WCC
Dewan, Vijay Kumar, 1985	*Assam Issue, The Beginning-the End and the Beginning,* Guwahati: Hemkosh Printers
Dominguez, Ben, 1980	*The Human and the Holy* Eds by Emerito P. Nacpil and Douglas J. Elwood, New York: Orbis
Dokhuma, James., 1975	*Zoram Kohhran Tualto Chanchin,* (History of Sectarian Groups in Mizoram) Aizawl: Tlangnuam Press
1994	"Impact of Christianity on the Status of Women Among the Hill Tribes of North East India" A lecture delivered in the Professor H.K. Barbujari Endowment Lectures, organised by the Department of History, North Eastern Hill University, 1994
Dube, S.C. (ed) 1977	*Tribal Heritage of India,* Vol. 1, Ethnicity, Identity and Interaction. New Delhi: Vikas Publishing House
Dubey, S.M. (ed), 1978	*North East India: A Sociological Study,* Delhi: Concept Publishing Company
1982	"Inter Ethnic Alliance, Tribal Movements and Integration in North East India," in *Tribal Movement in India,* K. Suresh Singh (ed), Vol. 1, New Delhi: Manohar
Durkheim, Emile, (1912) 1976	*The Elementary Forms of the Religous Life,* London: George Allen & Unwin

Edwards, Denis, 1992 — "The Integrity of Creation: Catholic Social Teaching for an Ecological Age," *Pacifica,* Vol. 5, No. 2, June, pp. 182-203

Engineer, Asghar Ali and Kocherry, Thomas, 1989 — "Religion and Social Change: Social Activists Speak," *Social Action,* Vol. 39, April-June, pp. 179-190

Encyclopaedia Britannica, Micropaedia, Vol. X, 1979

England, John C., 1981 — *Living Theology in Asia,* London: SCM

EATWOT, 1992 — "A Cry for Life: Thc Spirituality of the Third World, A Statement from the Third General Assembly of the Ecumenical Association of Third World Theologians, on 5-16, 1992, Nairobi, *Asian Journal of Theology,* Vol. 6, No. 2, pp. 333-347

Etzioni-Halvey, Eva and Etzioni A. (ed), 1968 — *Social Change: Source, Patterns and Consequences,* New York: Basic Books, INC Publishers

Fabela, Virginia, M.M and Torres, S. (ed), 1983 — *Irruption of the Third World: Challenges to Theology,* Papers from the Fifth International Conference of the Ecumenical Association of Third World Theologians, August 17-29, 1981, New Delhi, India, Maryknoll: Orbis Books

Farquhar, J.N., 1930 — *The Crown of Hinduism,* London: Oxford University Press

Fei, Hans, W., 1974 — *Eclips of Biblical Narrative: A Study in Eighteen and Nineteen Centuries Hermeneutics*, New Heaven: Yale University Press

Femandes, Walter, (ed), 1985 — *Development with People, Experiments with Participation and Non-Formal Education,* New Delhi: Indian Social Institute

1989 — *Forest, Environmental and Tribal Economy Deforestation, Improvement and Marginalisation in Orissa,* New Delhi: Indian Social Institute

1990 — "Forest Policy: A Solution to Tribal Deprivation," *The India Journal of Social Work,* Vol. 51, No. 1, Jan. pp. 35-55

Ferm, Dean William, (ed), 1987 — *Third World Liberation Theologies:* An Introductory Survey, Maryknoll: Orbis Books

Fisher, H.J., 1973 — "Conversion Reconsideration: Some Historical Aspects of Religious Conversion in Black Africa," *Arica* Vol. 43, pp. 27-40

Flannery, A.P. (ed), 1975 — *Documents of Vatican II,* Grand Rapids, Michigan: William B. Eerdmans

Gohrer, Georg, 1962 — "The Origin, Composition and Tradition of Isaiah I-XXXIX," *Annual of the Leeds University Oriental Society,* Vol. 3, pp. 3-38

Fohrer, Georg, 1970 — *Introduction to Old Testament* London: S.P.C.K

Foster, I.M., 1985 — *Reinventing Theology: as People's Work,* Madurai: Unemployed Young People's Association

Fraser, Peter, — *Slavery on British Territory: Assam and 1913 Burma,* Carnarvon: W. Gwenlyn Evans & Son

Frisch, Albert, 1982 — *Green Space: A Citizen's Guide to Proper Land Use,* Lexington, Ky: Appalachia-Science in the Public Interest

Freire, Paulo, 1970 — *Pedagogy of the Oppressed,* New York: Seabury Press

1970 — *Cultural Action for Freedom,* Cambridge, Mass : Harvard Educational Review

Gadamer, George, 1975 — *Truth and Method,* New York: Seabury Press

Godsey, J.D. ed., 1962 — *Karl Barth's Table Talk,* Richmond Virginia: John Nox Press

1977 — *Philosophical Hermeneutics,* Berkeley: University of California Press

Gellespie, G., 1977 — "Missionaries and Dictionaries: An Annotated Bibliography of Linguistic Works Prepared by the American Baptist Mission in North East India," *Indian Church History Review,* Vol. II, No. 1, June 1977, pp. 31-44

Ghosh, Arunabha, 1991 — "Probing the Jharkhand Questions," *Economic and Political Weekly,* Vol. XXVI, No. 18, May, pp. 1173-1181

Ghost, G.K., 1992 — *Tribal and Their Culture in Assam,* Meghalaya and Mizoram, Vol. I, II, III New Delhi: Ashish Publishing House

Gosh, S.K., 1987 — *Law Enforcement in Tribal Area,* New Delhi: Ashish Publishing House

Gibbs, Nancy, 1991 — "This Land is Their Land," *Time: The Weekly News Magazine* (Australia) Vol. 6, No. 1, Jan. 14, pp 34-35

Goldsmith, E. et al, (ed), 1972 — *A Blue Print of Survival,* The Ecologist 1/1972

Gorai, D.C., 1985 — "The Experiences of the Churches in Development" *Religion and Society,* Vol. 31, June, pp. 24-32

Government of India: — Fourth World Conference on Women: Beijing 1993: Country Report: Government of India, Department of Women and Child Development, Ministry of Human Resources Development

Gorrel, Donald, K., 1991 — "Social Gospel Movement," *Dictionary of the Ecumenical Movement,* edited by Nicholas Lossky, et al, Geneva, WCC

Goswami, B.B., 1979 — *Mizo Unrest: A Study in Politicalization of Culture,* Jaipur: Allekh Publishers

1980 — "Hill Tribes of North East India: The Impact of Christianity" in *Tribal World and Its Transformation* edited by Bhupinder Singh and J.S. Bhandari, New Delhi: Concept Publishing Company

Government of India 1899 — *Annual Report of the Government of Assam on the Administration of the Lushai Hills for the Year* 1898-99

1909 — *Linguistic Survey of India,* Vol. I, 1967 reprint of 1909, Tibeto-Burman Family, Himalayan Dialects, North Assam Group, Delhi

1948 — *Constituent Assembly Debates,* (Assam) 4th November, Vol. II, Appendix-C

1960 — *Report of the Committee on Special Multipurpose Tribal Blocks* (headed by Verrier Elwin), New Delhi: Manager of Publications

1960 — *Report of the Committee* (headed by R.B. Vaghaiwalla) *Appointed by the Governor of Assam to Examine the Financial Conditions, etc., of Each District Regional Council,* Shillong: Government Press

1963 — *Report on Development in Mizo District of Assam* by R.S. Krishnashwami, Programme Adviser, Planning Commission, New Delhi

1965 — *Report of the Study Team on Tribal Development Programme,* (headed by Shilu Ao), Committee on Plan Projects, Planning Commission, New Delhi

1976 — *Statistical Hand Book Mizoram,* (1976)

Aizawl : Department of Economics and Statistics, Government of Mizoram

1981 *Report on Development of North Eastern Region* by A National Committee on the Development of Backward Areas, New Delhi: Planning Commission

1984 *Report of the Working Group on Administration of Justice in the North Eastern India* - Planning Commission, May, 1984

1984 *Report of the Working Group on Land System Among Tribals in the North Eastern India,* Planning Commission

1985 *Challenge of Education - A Policy Perspective,* New Delhi

1985 *Statistical Hand Book Mizoram,* (1985) Aizawl: Department of Economics and Statistics, Government of Mizoram
1986 *National Policy on Education* (1986)

1986 *Report of the National Commission for Scheduled Castes and Tribes for 1986-1987*

1987 *Statistical Hand Book Mizoram,* (1987) Aizawl: Department of Economics and Statistics, Government of Mizoram

1987 *Mizoram: Era of Peace and Progress,* Aizawl: Department of Information and Public Relations

1989 *Statistical Hand Book Mizoram,* (1989) Aizawl: Department of Economics and Statistics, Government of India

1990 *Basic Statistics of North Eastern Region 1990* Shillong: North Eastern Council

1992 *Annual Plan 1991-92,*

Government of Mizoram,
Aizawl: Planning & Programme Implimentation Department
Mizoram Hnam Thurochhiah Dan 1956, Inheritance of Property Act, 1956 of Mizoram

Govt. of Mizoram, 1960 — *Mizo Hnam Dan* (Mizo Curstomary Law), (Enforced with effect from 30th November 1956 fide Hnamdan Dan (Operation) Order, 1957) (As amended in 1960), Aizawl: Goernment of Mizoram Law, Judicial and Parliamentary Affairs Department (Customary Law Cell)

Gouldner, A., 1971 — *The Coming Crisis of Western Sociology,* London, Heinemann

Gregorios, Paulos Mar, 1990 — "New Testament Foundations for Understanding of the Creation, "*Liberating Life: Contemporary Approach to Ecological Theology,* edited by Chilrd Birch, William Easkin and Jay B. McDaniel, Maryknoll: Orbis Books

Groome, Thomas H., 1980 — *Christian Religious Education: Sharing Our Story and Vision,* San Francisco: Harper & Row

Gutierrez, Gustova, 1974 (1971) — *A Theology of Liberation,* London: SCM

1974 — "Liberation, Theology and Proclamation," The Mystical and Political Dimension of the Christian Faith, *Concillium: Religion in the Seventies.* Vol. 16, edited by Gutierrez and Clude Geggine, New York: Herder & Herder

1983 (1979) — *The Power of the Poor in History,* London: SCM

Habermas, Jürgen., 1973 — *Theory and Practice,* Boston, Beacon Press

Hanks, Peter, Keon-Cohen, Bryan, ed., 1984 — *Aborigines and the Law: Essay in Memory of Elizabeth Eggleston,* Sydney, London, Boston: George Allen & Unwin

Haralambos, M and Heald, R.M., 1980 — *Sociology: Themes and Perspective,* Slough: University Tutorial Press

Hartshorne, Charles, 1976 (1948) — *The Divine Relativity: A Social Concept of God,* New Heaven: Yale University Press

Hasker, N and Luitui, Luingam, 1984 — *Nagaland Files,* New Delhi: Lancar International

Haldipur, R.N., 1972 — "Policy Towards and Administration of the Tribes of North East India," in *Tribal Situation in India,* edited by K. Suresh Singh, Delhi: India Institute of Advanced Study

Heirich, Max., 1977 — "Change of Heart: A Test of Some Widely Held Theories about Religious Conversion," *American Journal of Sociology,* Vol. 83, No. 3, pp. 653-679

Henry, Carl, F.H. and Mooneyham, W.S. (ed), 1967 — *One Race, One Gospel, One Task: World Congress on Evangelism, Berlin, 1966, 2* Vols. Minneapolis: World Wide Publications

Hesselgrave, D.J., 1979 — *Communicating Christ Cross Culturally,* Grand Rapids: Zondervan, 1978

Hluna, J.V., 1985 — *Church and Political Upheaval in Mizoram. A Study of Impact of Christianity on Political Development in Mizoram,* Aizawl: Mizo Academy of Letters

Hick, John, 1973 — *Philosophy of Religion,* Englewood Cliff: Prentice Hall

Hminga, C.L., 1987 — *The Life and Witness of the Churches in Mizoram,* Serkawn: Baptist Church of Mizoam

Hnuni, R.L. 1966 — "Impact of Christianity on Hill Tribal Women" a paper 1996 presented in the Seminar on Christianity and Tribal Culture in North East India, Serampore, 1996

1997 — "Women in the Context of the Bible and North East India," a paper presented at a Faculty-Student Seminar at ETC, Jorhat on 13th March, 1997

Hobel, E. Adamson, 1958 — *Man in the Primitive World: An Introduction to Anthropology,* New York: McGraw Hill Book Company

Horam, M., 1975 — *Naga Polity,* New Delhi: B.R. Publishing Corporation

Houten, Christiana va, — *Aliens in Israel Law, JOST Supplement* 1991 *Series 107,* Sheffield: Sheffield Academic Press

Hrangkhuma, F., 1990 — "Transformational Change: A Study of the Process and Nature of Mizo Cultural Change and Factor that Contributed to the Change," Ph.D Thesis submitted the School of World Mission, Fuller Seminary, USA (unpublished thesis)

1991 — "Why are There Many Christian Groups in Mizoram?" *Indian Missiological Review,* Vol. 13, No. 3, Sept., pp. 24-29

Hudson, Winthro, S. (ed), 1984 — *Walter Rauschenbusch: Selected Writings,* New York: Paulist Press, 1984

Hutton, J.H., 1991 — *The Angami Nagas,* London: Oxford University Press

1922 — *The Sema Nagas* (Reprinted 1968)

Jacob, Donald R., 1978 — "Culture and the Phenomena of Conversion," *Gospel and Context*, Vol. 1, No. 3, July, pp. 4-13

James, William, — *Varieties of Religious Experience,*

1928 (1902) — London: Longmans, Green and Co.

1978 — "The Divided Self and Conversion," Section from *The Varieties of Religious Experience,* reprinted in *Conversion: Perspective on Personal and Social Transformation,* edited by Walter E. Conn. New York, Alba House

Julio de Santa, Ana, 1977 — *Good News to the Poor,* Geneva: WCC

1978 (ed)., — *Separation Without Hope: Essays on the Relationship Between the Church and the Poor During the Industrial Revolution and the Western Colonial Expansion,* Geneva: WCC

Jyrwa, Forties J., 1980 — *The Wondrous Works of God: A Study of the Growth and Development of the Khasi-Jaintia Presbyterian Church in 20th Century,* Shillong: Mrs. M.B. Jyrwa

Kanakaikil, Jose, 1985 — *Seventh Plan and Development of Weaker Section,* New Delhi: Indian Social Institute

Karotemprel, S. (ed), 1987 — *The Tribes of North East India,* Calcutta: Firma KLM Private Limited

Karna, M.N., 1982 — "Agrarian Studies in North East India: Some Reflections," *The Eastern Anthropologists,* Vol. 35, pp. 151-163

1990 — "Aspect of Tribal Development in North East India," in *Tribal Demography and Development In North East India,* edited by Ashis Bose, et al, Delhi: B.R. Publishing Corporation

Kappen, S., 1993 — "Towards and Indian Christian Theology of Liberation," *Reading in Indian Christian Theology,* Vol. 1, Edited by R.S. Sugirtharajah and Cecil Hargreaves

Kee, Alistair, — *The Scope of Political Theology,*

1978	London: SCM
Keer, Dhananjay, 1962	*Dr. Ambedkar: Life and Mission,* Bombay: Popular Prakhasan
Keitzar, Renthy, 1987	"The Indigenization of Naga Christian Theology," *ETC Journal,* Vol. No. 1, 1987, pp. 4-24
1995	*In Search of A Relevant Gospel Message,* Guwahati: Christian Literature Centre
Keitzar, Renthy (ed)., 1995	*Good News for North East India* Guwahati: Christian Literature Centre
Kellerman, D., 1975	"Ger" *Theological Dictionary of the Old Testament,* Vol. 2, trans: J.T. Willis, ed by G.J. Botterweck and H. Ringgren, New York: W.B. Eermans
Keon-Cohen, Bryan, 1984	"Indigenous Land Rights in Australia and Canada," *Aborigines and the Law,* edited by Peter Hanks and Bryan Keon Cohen, Sydney: George Allen & Unwin
Kipgen, Mangkhosat, 1997	*Christianity and Mizo Culture* Aizawl: Mizo Theological Conference
Khawlhring, Siamkima, 1986	*Zalenna Ram,* (A Land of Freedom), Aizawl: Mr & Mrs. M.C. Lalrinthanga
Kirpatrick, Frank, G., 1985	"Towards A Metaphysic of Community," *Scottish Journal of Theology,* Vol. 38, pp. 565-581
Kluchohn, Clyde, 1949	"The World View of Navaho," *Ideological Foundations of World Orders,* edited by F.S.C. Northrop, New Heaven: Yale University Press
Knitter, Paul, 1975	*No Other Name?* A Critical Survey of Christian Attitudes Towards the World Religions, Maryknoll: Orbis Books, London, SCM

Kootoom, Raj, Kr., 1988 — "Tribal Voice is Your Voice," *Tribal Voice: Voice of the Persecuted Tribals,* 15 Nov., 1988, Premier Issue, p. 1

Kothari, Rajini, 1984 — "The Non-Party Political Press," *Economic and Political Weekly,* Vol. XIX, No. 5, Feb. 4, pp. 216-224

Kuttupallil, George, 1991 — "Mass Movement Among the Adivasi Immigrant of Brahmaputra Velly Towards Catholic Church: A Case Study of Tezpur Mission 1932-1940," *Indian Missiological Review,* Vol. 13, No. 3, Sept., pp. 58-66

Kraft, Charles H., 1979 — *Christianity in Culture: A Study in Dynamic Biblical Theologies in Cross Cultural Perspective,* Maryknoll: Orbis Books

Kraemer, Hendrik, 1938 — *The Christian Message in a Non Christian World,* New York: Harper and Brothers

1960 — *World Culture and World Religions The Coming Dialogue,* Philadelphia: the Westminster Press, 1960

Kroling, Aloise, 1989 — "Christian Hope for Liberation and Popular Movement," (Brazilian CEBs, basic Communities), *Mission Studies,* Vol. 6, No. 1, pp. 35-40

Kaufmann, Gordon, 1965 — "Two Models of Transcendence," *The Heritage of Christian Thought. Essays in Honour of Robert L. Calhoun,* edited by R.E. Caushman and E. Grislis, New York: Harper & Row

Kuhn, Thomas S., 1970 (2nd edition) — *The Structure of Scientific Revolutions* Chicago: The University of Chicago Press

Kulkarni, Sharad, 1991 — "Distortion of Census Data on Scheduled Tribes," *Economic and Political Weekly,* Vol. XXVI, No. 5, Feb. 2, 1991

Küng, Hans, 1973 (1967) — *The Church,* London: Collins

Kummel, W.G. 1972 — *The New Testament: The History of the Investigation of Its Problem* (Trans S. Maclean and Howard Clark Kee) Nashville: Abingdon

Küng, H. and Tracy D., 1989 — *The Paradigm Change in Theology, A Symposium for the Future,* Edinburgh: T&T Clark

Kuppusawmy, B., 1989 — *Social Change in India,* New Delhi: Vikas Publishing House

Kurien C.T., 1966 — *Our Five Year Plan,* Bangalore: Christian Institute for the Study of Religion and Society

1978 — *Poverty, Planning and Social Transformation,* Bombay: Allied Publisher

Kwang sun Suh, David, 1981 — "Minjung Theology in Korea: A Biographical Sketch of an Asian Theological Calculation," *Minjung Theology,* Singapore: ACTC, CCA

Lacugne, Catharin M., 1982 — Theological Methodology of Hans, Küng, New York: Scholars' Press

Lacey, M.G., — *Census Report,* 1931

Lalbiaktluanga, 1989 — "Theological Trends in Mizoram," in *Towards A Tribal Theology: The Mizo Perspective,* Aizawl: Mizo Theological Conference

Lalsawma, 1975 — "The Shaking of Foundations in Mizo Society," *Mizoram Today,* Vol. 1, No. 2, January, pp. 20-25

1964 — *The Work of the Holy Spirit and Tribal Religious Emotionalism: An Interpretation on Christian Experience of the Work of the*

Holy Spirit in Relation to Some Theological Concepts and Practices Among the Tribal Christian Congregations in Assam from 1946 to 1958, (M.Th thesis submitted to Senate of Serampore)

Laltluangliana, B., 1989 — "Kristianna leh Mizo Sakhua" (Christianity and Mizo Religion) *Kristian Tlangau*, August, 1989

1993 — *Ka Lungkham Mizo Literature* Aizawl: M.C. Lalrinthanga

Lalbiaktluanga, (ed)., 1970 — *Uar Bik Nei Pawlte,* (Denominations with Special Emphasis), Aizawl: Synod Literature Committee, 1977

Lalhmuaka, 1981 — *Zoram Zirna Lam Chhinchhiahna,* (Records of Zoram Education), Aizawl: Tribal Research Institute

Liangkhaia, 1972 — *Mizorama Harhna Thu,* (The Revival Movement in Mizoram), Aizawl: V.L. Ringa & Sons.

Lalkhawliana, leh Laltluangliana, K, (ed)., 1989 — *Mizoram Politics & Economy Mizo Kristiante Thlir Dan* (Politics and Economy of Mizoram: The Mizo Christian Perspective), Aizawl: Young Men's Christian Association

Lewin, T.H., 1984 (1870) — *Wild Races of the Eastern Frontiers of India* Delhi: Mittal Publication

1977 (reprint of 1884) — *A Fly on a Wheel or How I Helped to Govern India,* Aizawl: Tribal Research Institute

Lindberg, Carter, 1993 — *Beyond Charity: Reformation Initiatives for the Poor,* Minneapolis: Fortress Press

Lianzuala, P.L., 1989 — "Towards A Theology of Tlawmngaihna," *Towards A Tribal Theology,* edited by K. Thanzauva, Aizawl:

Liburne, Geoffrey R., 1989	*A Sense of Place: A Christian Theology of the Land,* Nashville: Abingdon Press
Linqvist, Martti 1975	*The Economic Growth and the Quality of Life: An Analysis of Debate Within the World Council of Churches 1966-1974,* Helsinki: The Finish Society for Missiology and Ecumenics
Linyu, K.,	*The Angami Church Since 1950,* B.D Thesis, United Theological College, Bangalore: 1983
Lloyd, J. Meirion, 1957	*On Every High Hill,* Liverpool: Welsh Mission
1991	*History of the Church in Mizoram* Aizawl: Synod Publication Board
Lobo, George, V., 1991	*Human Rights in Indian Situation,* New Delhi: Commission for Justice, Peace and Development, Catholic Bishops' Conference of India.
Lonergan, Bernard, 1972	*Method in Theology* London: Darton, Longman & Todd
Longkumer, Akumla, 186	*Revival in Nagaland: Fact or Fallacy,* Dimapur: Nagaland Times Printing Press
Longchar, A. Wati., 1995	*The Traditional Tribal World View and Modernity*, Jorhat: Limala
Lorrain, Reginald A., 1912	*Five Years in Unknown Jungles,* London: Lakher Pioneer Mission
Lausanne II, 1989	*Proclaim Christ Until He Comes: International Congress on World Evangelization,* Minnesto: World Wide Publications
Luther, Martin,	"Secular Authority: To What Extend It Ought

1523 — to be Obeyed," WA II

Mabry, Hunter, P. (ed)., 1987 — *Christian Ethics: An Introductory Reader,* Kottayam: Indian Theological Library

Macquarrie, John, 1966 — *Principles of Christian Theology,* London: SCM

1988 (1963) — *20th Century Religious Thought,* London: SCM

1990 — *Jesus Christ in Modern Thought,* London: SCM

Majumdar, D.N., 1972 — "A Study of Tribe - Caste Continuum and the Process of Sanskritization among the Bodo Speaking Tribes of the Garo Hills," in *Tribal Situation in India,* edited by K. Suresh Singh, Delhi: Indian Institute of Advanced Study

1984 — "A Decaying Institution - What has Happened to the Nokpante?: A Study Among the Garos," *Tribes of North East India,* edited by S. Karotemprel, Calcutta: Firma KLM Private Limited

Maimela, Simon S., 1986 — "The Task of Theology in South Africa Today," *Dialog (Minnesota)*, Vol. 25, No. 4, pp. 281-283

Manuel, George and Posluns, Michael, 1974 — *The Fourth World: An Indian Reality,* Donald Mills, Ontario: Collier Macmillan Canada

Matthew, T. (ed), 1990 — *Tribal Economy of the North Eastern Region* Guwahati: Spectrum Publications

Marx, Karl and Engels, Friedrich, 1932 (1848) — *Manifesto of the Communist Party,* New York: International Publishers

Mathani, B.P., and Haloi, K., — "Implementation of IRDP: Nagaland Experience," *Journal of Rural Development,*

1988 — Vol. 7, No. 5, pp. 501-518

Mathani, B.P., 1988 — "Strategy for Rural Development in the North Eastern Region," *Journal of Rural Development,* Vol. 7, No. 2, pp. 194-212

Matthew, T. (ed), 1980 — *Tribal Economy of the North Eastern Region,* Gauhati: Spectrum Publication

Mathur, P.R.G., 1991 — "Tribal Medicine: A Study in Rural Science and Superstition," *Tribal Thought and Culture,* edited by Baidynath Saraswati, New Delhi: Concept Publishing House

Mathur, P.G. R.G., 1995 — *The Khasis of Meghalaya: A Study in Tribalism and Religion,* New Delhi: Cosmos Publications

May, John D'Arcy, — "Human Rights as Land Rights in the Pacific," *Pacifica,* Vol. 6, No. 1, Feb. pp. 61-80

Mbiti, John, 1972 — "African Indigenous Culture in Relation to Evangelism and Church Development," *The Gospel and Frontier Peoples,* edited by R. Pierce Beaver, Pasadena: William Carey Library

McCall, A.G., 1977 Reprinted — *Lushai Chrystalis* Aizawl: Tribal Research Institute

McCann, Dennis, P., 1981 — *Christian Realism and Liberation Theology, Practical Theologies in Creative Conflict,* Maryknoll, Orbis Books

McFague, Sallie, 1989 — "Imaging a Theology of Nature: The World as God's Body," *Liberating Life,* edited by Charles Birch, William Eakin and Jay B. McDaniel, Maryknoll: Orbis Books

McGovern, A.F., 1989 — *Liberation Theology and Its Crisis, Toward an Assessment,* Maryknoll: Orbis Books

Meier, Geral M., — *Leading Issues in Economic Development,*

1989 (5th edition)	London: Oxford University Press
Metz, John B., 1969	*Theology of the World,* New York: Herder and Herder
Milbank, John, 1990	*Theology and Social Theory: Beyond Secular Reason,* Oxford: Blackwell
Mill, J.P., 1926 (1973)	*The Ao Nagas,* Bombay: Oxford University Press
Milton, Sangma, (ed)., 1994	*Essay on North East India:* New Delhi Indus Publishing Company
Min, A.K., 1986	"Praxis and Theology in Recent Debates" *Scottish Journal of Theology,* Vol. 39, No. 3 pp. 529-549
Minz, Nirmal, 1991	"Primal Religion's Perspective on Ecology," *Ecology and Development: Theological Perspective,* edited by Daniel D. Chetti, Madras: Gurukul Theological College and Research Institute and BTESS
Miner, Horace M., 1968	"Community-Society Continua," in *Encyclopaedia of Social Sciences,* Vols. 3 & 4, David L. Sills (ed), New York: Macmillan and Free Press, pp. 175-180
Miri, Sujata (ed), 1980	*Religion and Society of North East India,* New Delhi, Vikas Publishing House
Miroslav Volf,	"Materiality of Salvation: An Investigation in the Soteriologies of Liberation and Penticostal Theologies," *Journal of Ecumenical Studies,* Vol. 26, No. 3, p. 455
Mishra, S.N.,	"Private Property Formation Among Highland Tribal Communities of North East India," in *Tribal Thought and Culture,* B. Saraswati (ed), New Delhi. Concept Publishing House
Mizoram Presbyterian	*Presbyterian Khawmpui Thurel Pawimawh*

	Kohhran, 1977 Lakkhawm (Collection of Important Resolutions of the Presbyterian Church of Mizoram), Aizawl: The Synod Press & Bookroom, 1977
Moltmann, Jürgen, 1967	*Theology of Hope: On the Ground and Implications of A Christian Eschatology,* New York: Evanston, ILL: Harper and Row; London: SCM
1974	"Liberation in the Light of Hope," *Ecumenical Review,* Vol. 26, pp. 413-429
1974	*The Crucified God,* New York: Harper and Row
1975	*The Experiment Hope,* London: SCM
1978	*The Church in the Power of the Spirit,* London: SCM
	"Meditation on Hope" *A Reader in Political Theology*
1992	"Reconciliation with Nature," *Pacifica*, Vol. 5
Moon, Cyris and Oracion, Levi V.,	"People," *Dictionary of the Ecumenical Movement,* Geneva: WCC, 1992
Moore, Wilbert E., 1960	"A Reconsideration of Theories of Social Change," *American Sociological Review,* Vol. XXV, 1960, pp. 818-824
Moberg, David O., 1992	*The Great Reversal: Evangelism Versus Social Concern,* London: Scripture Union
Morris, John Hughes, 1910	*The History of the Welsh Calvinistic Methodists' Foreign Mission to the End of the Year 1910,* Carnarvon: C.M. Book Room

1990 Reprint (1930), *The Story of Our Foreign Mission,* Aizawl: The Synod Publication Board

Murickan, Jose. (ed)., 1988 *Poverty in India: Challenges and Response* Bangalore: The Xavier Board of Higher Education in India

Morgan, L.H., 1877 (Rpt 1968) *Ancient Society,* edited by Lesli A. White

Murray, A.H. James (ed), "Convertion - Convert, 'A New English 1995 Dictionary of Historical Principles, (Vol. II), Oxford: Oxford University Press

Muthayya, B.C, et al., 1988 "Motivational Patterns of Beneficiaries of Special Rural Development Programme," *Journal of Rural Development,* Vol. 7, No. 5, pp. 467-500

Myrdal, Gunnar, 1972 *Asian Drama: An Inquiry into the Poverty of Nations,* (A bridged by Seth S. King) London: Allen, the Penguine Press

Nosangchilla, 1995 "The Place of Women in the Socio-Cultural Changes" *Feminism: A North East Indian Perspective,* edited by Kim Vaiphei, Imphal: Manipur Baptist Convention

Newbegin, Lesslie, 1954 *The Household of God,* London: Friendship Press

Niebuhr, R. Reinhold, 1941 *The Nature and Destiny of Man,* Vol. I, New York: Scribner

Niebuhr, H. Richard, 1951 *Christ and Culture,* New York: Harper & Row

1960 *Radical Monotheism and Western Culture,* New York: Harper & Row

Nirmal, A.P., 1989 "Towards A Christian Dalit Theology," A Paper presented in the Theological Teachers' Conference, Bangalore

Nisbet, Robert A., 1978 (1953) — *The Quest for Community,* London: Oxford University Press

Novak, M. (ed), 1979 — *Capitalism and Socialism: A Theological Inquiry,* Washington D.C: American Enterprise Institute for Public Policy Research

Nuh, V.K., 1986 — *Naga Church and Politics* Kohima, V. Nuh and Bro.

Nunthara, C., 1990 — "Social Aspects of Tribal Development," in *Tribal Demography and Development in North East India,* Ashis Bose, et al, (ed), New Delhi: B.R. Publishing Corporation

Nygren, Anders, 1972 — *Meaning and Method, Prolegomena to a Scientific Philosophy of Religion and a Scientific Theogy,* Philadelphia: Fortress Press

Nyamiti, Charles, 1973 — "African Theology: Its Nature, Problems and Method: The Scope of African Theology," in *Gaba Pastoral Papers Nos. 19 (1971) and 30 (1973)*

Oates, Wayne E., 1978 — "Conversion: Sacred and Secular," *Conversion: Perspectives on Personal and Social Transformation,* edited by Walter E. Conn, New York: Society of St. Paul

O'Brien, David J and Shannon, Thomas A., — *Catholic Social Thought, The Documentary Heritage,* Maryknoll: Orbis Books 1992

O'Gorman, Frances, 1992 — *Charity and Change: From Bandaid to Beacon,* Melbourne: World Vision

Omvedt, Gail, 1991 — "Gandhi and Ambedkar," A Review article of the book *The Moral and Political Writings of Mahatma Gandhi, Vol. 1, Civilisaiton, Politics and Religion; Vol. 2, Truth and Non-Violence* edited by Raghavan Iyer, Oxford: The Clarendon Press, in *Economic and Political Weekly,* May, pp. 1154-1155

Oommen, T.K., 1987 — "Mobilization for Social Development: The India Situation," in *Social Movement for Development,* edited by S.K. Srinva and A.L. Srinavas, Allahabad: Chugh Publications

Orr, J. Edwin, 1970 — *Evangelical Awakening in India,* New Delhi: Christian Literature Service

Padilla, C. Rene, 1995 — "Evangelism and Social Responsibility: From Wheaton '66' to Wheaton '83'", *Transformation,* Vol. 2, July/Sept., No. 2, pp. 27-32

Pannikar, R., 1978 — *The Intra-Religious Dialogue,* New York: Paulist Press

1981 — *The Unknown Christ of Hinduism,* London: Darton, Longman & Todd

Parker, David, 1991 — "Evangelical Spirituality Reviewed: *Evangelical Quarterly,* Vol. 63, No. 2, pp. 123-148

Parry, N.E., 1976 — *A Monograph on Lushai Customs and Ceremonies,* Aizawl: Tribal Research Institute

Patrick, D., 1985 — *Old Testament Law,* Atlanta, John Knox Press

Parsons, Talcott, 1951 — *Essay in Sociological Theory,* New York: Free Press

1961 — "Functional Theory of Change," *Rural Sociology,* Vol. XXVI, No. 3, pp. 219-230

Parvathamme, C., 1972 — *Schedule Caste and Tribes,* New Delhi: Ashish Publishing House

Peacocke, A.R., 1979 — *Creation and the World of Science,* Oxford: Clarendon Press

Peck, M. Scott, — *The Different Drum: The Creation of True*

1987	*Community - the First Step to World Peace,* London: Rider & Co.
Phillip, P.T., 1976	*The Growth of the Baptist Churches in Nagaland,* Guwahati: Christian Literature Centre
Pieris, Aloysious, S.J., 1979	"Towards an Asian Theology of Liberation: Some Religio-Cultural Guideline," *Zeitschrift für die neutestamentliche Wissenchaft und die Kundi der atteren Kirche,* Vol. 63, No. 3, pp. 161-182
1985	*An Asian Theology of Liberation,* Edinburgh: T & T Clark
Polsby, N.W., 1968	"Community: The Study of Community Power" in *International Encyclopaedia of the Social Science,* Vol. 3 & 4, David L. Sills, New York: Macmillan Company and Free Press
Prabhakar, M.E, (ed), 1988	*Towards a Dalit Theology,* Delhi: ISPCK
1988	"The Search for A Dalit Theology," *Towards a Dalit Theology,* Delhi: ISPCK
Prabhakar, M.E. (ed), 1990	"Focus on Backward Classes Mandal and Chinnappa Reddy Commission Reports," in *Samata: documentation by the caste class study programme of the Christian Institute for the Study of Religon and Society in Co-opeation with the William Carey Study and Research Centre,* Vol. 2/1990
Prasad, R.R., 1988	"Tribal Development in India: Strategies and Programmes," *Journal of Rural Development,* Vo. 7. No. 1, pp. 81-102
Prasad R.N., 1989	*Government and Politics in Mizoram,* New Delhi: North Book Centre

Premnath, D.N., "The Process of Latifundialization Mirrored in Isaiah 5:8-10: A Test Case for the Use of Comparative and Historical Sociology as a Methodological Component in the Old Testament Studies," a paper presented in the Faculty-Student Seminar at the United Theological College Bangalore on 30th Jan., 1985

Presbyterian Church of Welsh Foreign Mission *Printed Report of the Foreign Mission of the Calvinistic Methodist or Presbyterian Church* of Wales, 1894-1964, Liverpool

Presler, Henry., 1971 *Primitive Religions in India* Madras: The Christian Literature Society

Progoff, Ira, (trans), 1969 *The Cloud of Unknowing,* New York: Jullian Press

Puthenpurakal, Joseph, 1984 *Baptist Mission in Nagaland,* Shillong: Verdrame Missiological Institute

Rahner, Karl, 1974 *Theological Investigations,* Vol. II, London: Darton, Longman and Todd

"Universal Salvific," *Sacramentum Mundi,* Vol. 5, New York

Rajshekar, V.T., 1986 *Why Godse Killed Gandhi,* Bangalore: Dalit Sahitya Akademy

Rayan, Samuel, 1983 "Theological Priority in India Today," in *Irruption of Third World: Challenge to Theology,* Virginia Fabella, M.M. and Sergio Torres (ed) Maryknoll: Orbis Books

Ray, Animesh, 1982 *Mizoram Dynamics of Change,* Calcutta: Pearl Publishers

Ray, Niharranjan, 1972 "Introductory Address to the Seminar on the Tribal Situation in India held from July 6 to 19 at the Indian Institute of Advanced Study, Simla," in *The Tribal Situation in India,* Sureh Singh (ed)

Redfield, Robert, 1947 — "The Folk Society," *American Journal of Sociology,* Vol. 52, pp. 293-308

1953 — *The Primitive World and Its Transformation,* New York: Cornel University Press

Ricoeur, Paul, 1974 — *The Conflict of Interpretation: Essay on Hermeneutics,* North Western University Press

1979 — *Interpretation Theory,* Fort Worth, Tex: The Texas Christian University

Reddy, Subba N., 1988 — "Depriving Tribals of Land: Andra Move to Amend Land Transfer of Laws" *Economic and Political Weekly,* Vol. XXIII, June, p. 1457-59

Richards, Ghyn, 1987 — "Faith and Praxis in Liberation Theology, Bonhoffer and Gandhi," *Modern Theology,* Vol. 3,JL, pp. 353-373

Roberts, J. Deotis, 1976 — "Contextual Theology: Liberation and Indigenization," *Christian Century,* Vol. 93 pp. 64-68, June 28

Robinson, John A.T., 1963 — *Honest To God,* London: SCM

Rao, Venkata P., 1988 — *Institutional Framework for Tribal* Development, New Delhi: Inter Indian Publications (T-126)

Robins, Thomas, 1981 — *Civil Liberties, 'Brainwashing' and 'Cult': A Bibliography,* Berkeley: Centre of the Study of New Religious Movements

Ruivah, Khasim, 1984 — "Long Shim of the Tangkhuls," *Tribes of North East India,* Edited by Sebastian Karotemprel, Calcutta: Firma KLM Private Limited

Samuel, Vinay and Sugden, Christopher (ed), 1987 — *The Church in Response to Human Need,* Grand Rapids, Michigan: Eerdmans

Sanders, Irwin T., 1968
"Community: Community Development," in *International Encyclopaedia of Social Sciences,* Vol. 3 & 4, David L. Sills (ed), New York: Macmillan and Free Press, pp. 169-173

Sanders, Thomas G., 1973
"The Theology of Liberation: Christian Utopianism," *Christianity and Crisis,* Vol. 33, No. 15, Sept. 17, pp. 167-173

Sanjay, B., 1980
Assam, A Crisis of Identity, Guwahati: Spectrum Publications

Sank, T. Howland, 1980
"Liberation Theology and Social Gospel," *Theological Studies,* Vol. 41, pp. 668-682

Sarin, V.K. (ed), 1982
Indian North East in Flame, New Delhi: Vikas Publishing House

Saraswati, Baidaynath, 1991
Tribal Thought and Culture, Essay in Honour of Surjit Chandra Sinha, New Delhi: Concept Publishing House

Sargunam, E. Ezra (ed), 1992
Mission Mandate: A Compendium on the Perspective of Missions in India, Madras: Mission India 2000

Sastry, Kuruganty and Vithal, C.P.,
"Participatory Dimension in Rural Develpment," *Journal of Rural Development,* Vol. 7, No. 6, pp. 689-700

Scriven, Charles, 1988
The Transformation of Culture: Christian Social Ethics After H. Richard Niebuhr, Scottdale: Herald Press

Schwitzer, Albert, 1968
The Quest of the Historical Jesus: A Critical Study of Its Progress from Reimarus to Wrede, New York: Macmillan, 9th Printing

Seamands, John T., 1981
Tell It Well: Communicating the Gospel Across Cultures, Missouri: Beacon Hill Press

Sen, Shipra, 1987
Tribes of Nagaland, Delhi: Mittal Publications

Serril, Michael S., 1992 — "To be Themselves," *Times of Australia,* Vol. 7, No. 42, Oct. 19, pp. 21-25

Sethi, Harsh, 1984 — "Groups in a New Politics of "Transformation," *Economic and Political Weekly,* Vol. XIX, No. 8, Feb. 11, pp. 305-316

Setty, E. Desingu, 1988 — "Field Approach to Integrated Rural Development," *Journal of Rural Development,* Vol. 7, No. 6, pp. 675-688

Sheth, D.L., 1984 — "Grass-roots Initiatives in India," *Economic and Political Weekly,* Vol. XIX, No. 6, Feb. pp. 259-262

Shakespeare, J., Reprint 1988 — *The Lushai Kuki Clans,* Aizawl: Tribal Research Institute

Shorter, A., 1988 — *Towards A Theology of Inculturation,* Maryknoll: Orbis Books

Sider, Ronald K. (ed)., 1974 — *The Chicago Declaration,* Coral Stream, ILL: Creation House

Shideler, E.W., 1960 — "Darwin and the Doctrine of Man" *Journal of Religion,* XL, July 1960

Singh, G.R., — "The Local Congregation - Some New Testament Insights," *The Local Congregation Its Mission in India,* Delhi: ISPCK

Singh, K. Surresh, (ed)., 1972 — *The Tribal Situation in India,* Delhi: Indian Institute of Advanced Study

1982 — *Tribal Movement in India,* Vol. 1 & 2, New Delhi: Manohar

1984 — "Colonialism, Anthropology and Primitive Society, The Indian Scenario (1928-47)," *Man in India: A Quarterly Journal of Anthropology*, Vol. 64, No. 4, Dec., pp. 400-412

Singh, Paul G.K.(ed)., 1986 — *The Report of Hermeneutics Consultation in Central Tribal Belt of India* held at Ranchi, March 1-3, 1984, Ranchi: G.K. Paul Singh

Sinha, Surajit., 1981 — "Tribes and India Civilization: Transformation Process in Modern India," *Man in India: A Quarterly Journal of Anthropology,* Vol. 61, No. 2, June, pp. 105-142

Sinha, Raghuvir, 1977 — *Religion and Culture of North Eastern India,* New Delhi: Abhinau Publication

Singh, Shankar R., 1986 — *Changing Occupational Structure of Scheduled Tribe,* New Delhi: Inter-Indian Publications (T-121)

Sing, Yogendra, 1980 — *Social Stratification and Change,* New Delhi: Manohar

Smartha, Stanley J. (ed), 1974 — *Living Faith and Ultimate Goals: Salvation and World Religion,* Geneva: WCC

1974 — *The Hindu Respond to the Unbound Christ,* Madras: CLS

1981 — *Courage for Dialogue: Ecumenical Issues in Inter-religious Relationship,* Maryknoll: Orbis Books

1994 — "Dialogue in a Religiously Pluralistic" in *The Multi-Faith Context of India: Resources and Challenges for Christians,* Edited by Israel Selvanayagam, Banglore: The Board of Theological Text Books Programme of South Asia

Smith, W.C., 1925 — *The Ao Naga Tribes of Assam* London: McMillan Company

Smith, Timothy L., 1975 — *Revivalism and Social Reform: American Protestantism in Mid-Nineteenth Century America,* New York: Abingdon

Snaitang, O.L., 1991 — "A Study of the Role of Christianity in Social Change Among the Khasi and Jaintia Hill Tribes of Meghalaya 1941 to the present," A D.Th Thesis Submitted to the Senate of Serampore

Song, C.S., 1978 — "Liberation of People in History," *South East Asia Journal of Theology,* Vol. 19, No. 2, pp. 14-25

Souza, S.A., 1982 — *The Growth and the Activities of the Catholic Church in North East India (1757-1858),* Mangalore: Vitus Probhudas O.F.M. Cap

Spencer, Herbert, 1892 — *Sociology,* Vol. 1, New York: Appleton and Co.

Spina, F.A., 1983 — "Israel as Gerim. Sojourners in Social and Historical Context" *The World of the Lord Shall Go Forth, Essay in Honour of David Noel Freedman, in Celebration of his Sixth Birthday,* ed by C.L. Mayers and M. O'Connor, Winnona Lake IN: Alisenbrauns

Srinivas, M.N., 1972 — *Social Change in Modern India,* Bombay: Orient Longman

Steward, Julian H., 1956 — "Cultural Evolution," *Scientific American,* CXCIV, No. 5, pp. 70-80

Stachouse, M.L., — "Mission," *The Encyclopaedia of Religion,* Charles J. Adams, et al, (ed) London: Macmillan

Stanley, Brian, 1990 — "Evangelical Social and Political Ethics: A Historical Perspective,: *The Evangelical Quarterly Review,* Vol. 62, No. 1, pp. 19-36

Stone, James John, 1971 — *Manipur and the Naga Hills,* Delhi Vivek Publishing House

Stott, John R.W., 1975 — *The Lausanne Covenant: An Exposition and Commentary,* Minnesato: World Wide Publicaiton

1984 — *Issues Facing Christian Today,* Baskingstoke: Marshall Morgan & Scott

Strain, Charles R., 1982 — "Liberation Theology: North American Perspective," *Religious Studies Review,* Vol. 8, No. 3, pp. 239-244

Surin, Kenneth, (ed), — "Special Issue: Theology, Truth and Liberation," *Modern Theology,* Vol. 3, No.1, pp. 1-106

Swingewood, Alan, 1984 — *A Short History of Special Thought,* London: Macmillan

Syiemlieh, David, 1989 — British Administration in Meghalaya: Policy and Pattern: New Delhi: Heritage Publishers

1990 — *A Brief History of the Catholic Church in Nagaland,* Shillong: Vendrame Institute

Taylor, John B, (ed), 1976 — *Primal World Views,* Geneva: WCC

Thaosen, S.R., 1967 — "Why the Hills and Plain Do not Unite," *Common Perspective for North East India,* edited by Pannalal Dasgupta, Calcutta

Thanzauva, K. (ed)., 1992 — *Towards A Tribal Theology: The Mizo Perspective,* Aizawl: Mizo Theological Conference

1989 — "Christianity and Tribal Culture in North East India," a paper presented in the Consultation on Tribal Issues in North East India, Guwahati

1985 — "Mizo Tlawmngaihna and Nishkama Karma," *UTC Magazine 1984-1985,* Bangalore: United Theological College

1988	*I Ram Lo Thleng Rawh Se,* (Thy Kingdom Come), Lawngtlai: A.C. Press
1989	"Women in Society: Traditional, cultural and Anthropological Factors that Define and Influence Women in India" a paper presented in the North India Theological Students' Conference, Jorhat, 1989
1992	"Conversion as a Basic of Social Transformation," *Asian Journal of Theology,* Vol.6, August 25, 1992, pp. 73-82
1996 (compiled)	*Reports of the Foreign Mission of the Presbyterian Church of Wales on Mizoram 1894-1957,* Aizawl: Synod Literature and Publication Board
Thomas, M.M., 1969	*The Acknowledged Christ of the Indian Renaissance,* London: SCM
1970	*Salvatiopn and Humanization,* Madras, Christian Literature Centre
Thomas, M.M. and Thomas, P.T., 1989	*Towards Indian Christian Theology: Life and Thought of 1992 Some Pioneers,* Tiruvalla: New Day Publication of India
Thumra, J.H., 1989	"An Implications of Sanskritization," *The Assam Tribune,* December 11, 1989
Tillich, Paul, 1964	*Theology of Culture,* New York: Oxford University Press
1978 (1953)	*Systematic Theology,* Vol. 1, London: SCM
Tlanghmingthanga, 1993	"An Appraisal of the Eschatological Content of Selected Reference to the Significance for the Church in Mizoram" an M. Th Thesis submitted to the Seante of Serampore, 1993

Tracy, David, 1981 — *The Analogical Imagination: Christian Theology and the Culture of Pluralism*

Tracy, David and Nicholas Lash, 1983 — *Cosmology and Theology,* Edinburgh: T & T Clark

Tribal Research Institute 1983 — *Mizo Sakhua* (Mizo Religion) Aizawl: Tribal Research Institute

UNO — *Documents of the UN Conference on the 1972 Human 1990 Environment, Stockholm 5-16, 1972* United Nations Publications

1990 — *Global Outlook 2000: An Economic, Social, and Environmental Perspective:* United Nations Publications

Upadhyaya, K.K., 1986 — *Development Problems and Prospects of Mizoram,* New Delhi: Inter-India Publications

Vaiphei, Kim, Ed., 1995 — *Feminism: A North East Indian Perspective,* Imphal: Women Department of Manipur Baptist Convention

Vanengliana, 1992 — *Khawiahnge Mizo Mipate,* Aizawl: Synod Social Front

Vanthuama, 1989 — "Pianthar Harhna Hi," (Revival of Born Again), *Kristian Tlangau,* June, 1989

Verhelst, Thierry, S., (English trans 1990) — *No Life Without Roots: Culture and Development,* London: Zed Books Ltd.

Weber, Leonard, 1987 — "Land Use Ethics: The Social Responsibility of Ownership" in *Theology of the Land,* Bernar E. Evan and Gregory D. Cusak, Minnesota, Collegeville: The Liturgical Press

Weber, Leonard, 1987 — "Land Use Ethics: The Social Responsibility of Ownership" in *Theology of the Land,* Bernar F. Evan and Gregory D. Cusak, Minnesota, Collegeville:

Weber, Max., 1958 (1930)	*The Protestant Ethic and the Spirit of Capitalism* (translated by Talcott Parsons) New York: Charles Scribner's Sons
1947	*The Theory of Social and Economic Organisation,* New York: Oxford University Press
WCC 1926	*The Stockholm Conference 1925, Official Report,* edited by G.A.K. Bell, London: Oxford University Press
1968	*The Church for Others and the Church for the World: A Quest for Missionary Structures for Missionary Congregations. Final Report of the Western European Working Group and North American Working Group of the Department on Studies in Evangelism,* Geneva: WCC
1968	*The Uppsala Report 1968.Offical Report of the Fourth Assembly of the World Council of Churches, Uppsala July 4-20, 1968*, edited by Norman Goodall, Geneva: WCC
1968	*The Uppsala Report 1968: Report of the Fourth Assembly of the WCC,* Geneva: WCC
1972	*Ministry in Context: The Third Madate Programme of Theological Education Fund of WCC (1970-1977),* Bromley, Kent: New Life Press
1973	*Bangkok Assembly, 1973, Minutes and Reports of the Assembly of the Commission on World Mission and Evangelism of the World Council of Churches, December 31, 1972 and January 9-12, 1973,* Geneva: WCC

1974 *Science and Technology for Human Development. The Ambiguous Future and the Christian Hope. Report 1974 World Conference in Bucharest,* edited by Charles and John B. Cobb, Report 1974 World Conference in Bucharest, (June 24 - July 2, 1974), Geneva: WCC

1976 *Breaking Barrier: The Official Report of the Fifth Assembly of the WCC, Nairobi 23 No. - 10 Dec., 1975,* Edited by David M. Palton, London: SPCK

1980 *Thy Kingdom Come: Mission Perspective. Report of the World Conference on Mission and Evangelism, Melbourne, Australia, 12-25 May 1980*, Geneva: WCC

1983 *Mission and Evangelism - An Ecumenical Affirmation. A Study Guide.* Compiled by Jean Stromber, WCC, 1983

1990 *Now is the Time: Final Documents and Other Texts, World Convocation on Justice, Peace, Integration of Creation, Seoul 1990,* Geneva: WCC

1990 *Vancouver to Canberra 1983-1990: Report of the Central Committee of the World Council of Churches to the Seventh Assembly,* edited by Thomas F. Best, Geneva: WCC

1990 *Vancouver to Canberra 1983-1990: Report of the Central Committee of the World Council of Churches to the Seventh Assembly,* edited by Thomas F. Best, Geneva: WCC

1991 *Peace with Justice,* a document issued by the European Ecumenical Assembly, Basel 15-21, May

1991	*World Council of Churches: Sings of the Spirit: Official Report of Seventh Assembly, Canberra, Australia 7-20 Feb.,* Geneva: WCC
Whitehead, Alfred A., 1968	*Models of Thought* New York: Free Press
Weber, Leonard, Evans, Bernard F. and Cusack, Gregory D. (ed), 1987	*Theology of Land,* Minnesota: The Liturgical Press
Webb Paulien, 1991	"Women in Church and Society," *Dictionary of Ecumenical Movement:* Geneva: WCC
Wilson, Fredrick, R., Mission in 1990	*The Saint Antonio Report: Your Will Be Done Christ's Way,* Geneva: WCC
World Bank, 1989	*World Development Report 1988,* New York: Oxford University Press
Wright, Christopher J.H., 1990	*God's People in God's Land: Family, Land, and Property in the Old Testament,* Grand Rapid: Eerdmans and Paternoster
Wright Mills, C.W., 1959	*The Sociological Imagination,* New York: Oxford University Press
Xaxa, V., 1990	"Tribal Development in the North East: Trends and Perspective," in *Tribal Demography and Development in North East India,* Ashish Bose, et al, (ed), New Delhi: B.R. Publishing Corporation
1991	"Sociological Impact of Evangelization in North East India," *Indian Missiological Review,* Vol. 13, No. 3, pp. 15-25
Younger, J. Milton, 1965 (1857)	*Religion, Society and Individual: An Introduction to Sociology of Religion,* New York: Macmillan Company

Yunupingu, James G., 1976	"Letter from Black to White," *Land Rights News,* NLC, December
Zawla, K., 1976	*Mizo Pi Pute leh An Thlahte Chanchin,* (The History of Mizo Ancestors and Descendants), Aizawl: K. Zawla
Zairema, 1978	*God's Miracles in Mizoram: A Glimpse of Christian Work Among Head-Hunters,* Aizawl: Synod Publication Board
1989	"Mizo and Their Religion," in *Towards A Tribal Theology: The Mizo Perspective,* edited by K. Thanzauva, Aizawl: Mizo Theological Conference
1989	"Bible Translation in North East India" in *A Trainer of Leaders: Essay in Honour of Jonathan H. Thumra,* Edited by Renthy Keitzar, Jorhat: Eastern Theological College